JACKIE

&

CAMPY

JACKIE

&

CAMPY

The Untold Story of
Their Rocky Relationship and the
Breaking of Baseball's Color Line

William C. Kashatus

UNIVERSITY OF NEBRASKA PRESS

LINCOLN AND LONDON

Library of Congress Cataloging-in-Publication Data
Kashatus, William C.
Jackie and Campy: the untold story of their rocky relationship and the breaking of baseball's color line / William C. Kashatus.
pages cm
Includes bibliographical references and index.
ISBN 978-0-8032-4633-1 (cloth: alk. paper)—ISBN 978-0-8032-5447-3 (epub)—ISBN 978-0-8032-5448-0 (mobi)—ISBN 978-0-8032-5446-6 (pdf) 1. Robinson, Jackie, 1919–1972. 2. African American baseball players—Biography. 3. Campanella, Roy, 1921–1993. 4. Baseball players—United States—Biography. 5. Male friendship—United States. 6. Racism in sports—United States. 7. Discrimination in sports—United States. I. Title.

GV865.R6K37 2014   796.3570922—dc23   [B]   2013033133

Set in Minion Pro by Laura Wellington.
Designed by A. Shahan.

For Michael Zuckerman
and to the memory of
Peter Cline, gifted educators
who recognized and
cultivated my love of history

Contents

Illustrations

Acknowledgments

This book is dedicated to two educators who had a profound impact on my life. The late Peter Cline, a professor of history at Earlham College, was my undergraduate advisor and a dear friend. He read widely, thought deeply, and communicated his knowledge with gentle good humor and in a manner that was engaging and respectful of the young minds he taught. Peter encouraged me to pursue graduate school in history and secured a Mellon Fellowship for me after I left Earlham. But his greatest gift was cultivating in me a sense of intellectual self-esteem.

Michael Zuckerman, emeritus professor at the University of Pennsylvania, encouraged me to pursue a doctorate in history and served on my dissertation board. Though he would not allow me to settle for anything less than my best work, he did so in a manner that was respectful of me and the intellectual process itself. Mike also took a genuine interest in my dual career as a secondary school teacher and National Park Service Ranger by visiting my "classroom"—sometimes with his own students—and sharing ideas on pedagogy and curriculum. He continues to be a valued friend.

Both of these educators served as important role models because of their special ability to communicate with young adults from many different backgrounds. They understood that good teaching engages the student in life itself, challenging him to question the moral conventions and stereotypes of our society. In the process they showed me that teaching can be a challenging and personally rewarding profession because it demands intellectual rigor and high standards as well as compassion and faith in young people. For that, I am eternally grateful.

Special thanks are also due to all of the individuals who agreed to be interviewed for this book: Hank Aaron, Rich Ashburn, Gene Benson,

Ralph Caballero, Bill Cash, Mahlon Duckett, Carl Erskine, Stanley Glenn, Wilmer Harris, Gene Hermanski, Monte Irvin, Clyde King, James Mc-Gowan, Johnny Podres, Ken Raffensberger, Branch Rickey III, Robin Roberts, Ed Roebuck, Howie Schultz, Andy Seminick, Harry Walker, Marvin Williams, and Don Zimmer. The personal insight and candor of Carl Erskine and Monte Irvin are especially appreciated. They are among the few close friends of Roy Campanella and Jackie Robinson who are still with us and were willing to participate in this enterprise. I regret that the Robinson and Campanella families failed to return my phone calls and e-mails. Their insights would have contributed significantly to the substance and scope of the book.

The editorial staff at University of Nebraska Press was invaluable to improving the book, especially Rob Taylor and Courtney Ochsner. I am also grateful to Michael McGandy, Larry Hogan, and Larry Lester, all of whom provided helpful editorial advice and encouragement. John Horne at the National Baseball Hall of Fame Library and Carolyn McGoldrick of the Associated Press were extremely helpful in locating photographs and securing permission to reproduce them in this book.

Finally, I am grateful to my wife, Jackie, and our three sons, Tim, Peter, and Ben, who continue to tolerate my twin passions for writing and baseball and still offer their unconditional support and love.

JACKIE

&

CAMPY

Introduction

In 1956 Martin Luther King Jr., a young African American Baptist minister, achieved overnight fame when he led a black boycott of the Montgomery, Alabama, bus system. King's introduction of "massive resistance" as a legitimate form of racial protest inspired a Supreme Court decision declaring segregation in public transportation to be illegal and forced the City of Montgomery to abandon its discriminatory seating policies. It also marked the beginning of the modern civil rights movement.[1]

For the next twelve years King led various forms of nonviolent protest against racial discrimination. Though his life was threatened repeatedly and he was arrested many times for violating state segregation laws, he never wavered in his quest to win civil rights through nonviolent tactics and with the cooperation of like-minded whites. His efforts were admired worldwide and inspired the passage of the Civil Rights Act of 1964, which has been referred to as a Magna Charta for African Americans.[2]

King once confided to his closest aide, Wyatt Tee Walker, that Jackie Robinson's example in breaking baseball's color barrier inspired him to pursue racial integration on a national stage. "Jackie made it possible for me in the first place," he said. "Without him, I would never have been able to do what I did."[3] Surprised by the revelation, Walker asked him to explain. "Back in the days when integration wasn't fashionable," King said, "Jackie understood the trauma and the humiliation and the loneliness which comes with being a pilgrim walking in the lonesome byways toward the high road of freedom. He was a sit-inner before sit-ins and a freedom rider before freedom rides."[4]

When Roy Campanella, the first black catcher to break the color barrier and a teammate of Robinson's, learned of the remark, he was quick to point out that Jackie wasn't the only one who should be credited with the success. "Without the Brooklyn Dodgers you don't have *Brown v. Board of Education*," he insisted, referring to the 1954 landmark Supreme Court decision that declared racial segregation illegal in the United States. "We were the first ones on the trains. We were the first ones down South not to go around the back of the restaurants, the first ones in the hotels. We were the teachers of the whole integration thing."[5]

Campanella's defensiveness came from his belief that he, along with other African American teammates Don Newcombe, Joe Black, and Jim Gilliam, should also be credited with abolishing Jim Crow in American society. All of them endured racial abuse in the Negro Leagues longer than the single season Robinson apprenticed with the Kansas City Monarchs.[6] Unlike Robinson, who actively challenged Jim Crow, Campanella was more subdued in his protest because he knew white society wouldn't listen. Instead he played the game at an extraordinary level, believing that he could play just as well as if not better than any white Major Leaguer and that he could crack baseball's color line if an owner had the moral courage to give him the chance. Once given the opportunity, Campanella refused to jeopardize his Major League career by challenging directly the subtle forms of discrimination he faced or the state political and judicial systems that permitted it. He let his remarkable talent as a power hitter and catcher do the talking for him, believing that "ability," not "militancy," was the foundation upon which racial equality rested.

Jackie Robinson thought differently. He possessed a fierce pride, an unrelenting competitiveness, and a keen racial consciousness that had been cultivated on the streets and playing fields of Pasadena, California, a city that was hostile to blacks. Throughout his life Robinson fought against Jim Crow, beginning at age eight, when a white neighbor called him a "nigger," and continuing during his years as a stellar student-athlete at Pasadena Junior College and UCLA and, later, as a military officer and Negro Leaguer.[7] Although he did not provoke the racial discrimination he experienced, Robinson certainly didn't back down when he was made a victim of it. His defiance sometimes resulted in trouble with the law and a military court-martial.[8] Robinson's greatest challenge came in the mid-to-late 1940s, when he became the first African American to break Major League Baseball's whites-only policy. Starring for the Brooklyn Dodgers, he endured repeated death threats, racial slurs, and humiliating treatment from opposing players and fans. It was against his nature to suffer those indignities silently. But Robinson had promised Dodgers general manager Branch Rickey that he would not strike back for fear of setting the course of integration back a decade or more. The constant pressure and abuse he suffered resulted in pent-up anger. While he channeled the rage and hurt into a singular intensity that propelled him to greater feats on the playing field, those painful feelings also led to sleepless nights, graying hair, chronic stomach trouble, and perhaps a premature death at fifty-three in 1972.[9]

To be sure, Robinson and Campanella possessed different personalities that often clashed during their years with the Brooklyn Dodgers. Where Robinson was overtly aggressive and intense, Campanella was more passive and easygoing. Jackie's race consciousness and relentless drive were admired by teammates and eventually opponents, but those qualities certainly did not endear him to the white baseball establishment. Conversely, Campy's indefatigable enthusiasm and boyish charm made him one of the game's most popular players. The personality differences are best captured in the title and tone of each man's autobiography. In *I Never Had It Made*, Robinson reveals the sadness, pain, and bitterness he experienced as a black man in a white man's world, while Campanella, who spent the remainder of his life in a wheelchair after being paralyzed in a 1958 car accident, celebrates the enjoyable, sometimes amusing experiences of his baseball career in *It's Good to Be Alive*.

But personality issues were only part of the conflict between the two men. Some of the tension came from mutual jealousy. Both players were extraordinarily talented and would eventually be elected to the National Baseball Hall of Fame. Robinson won Rookie of the Year in 1947 as a first baseman when he hit .297 and led the National League in stolen bases with 29. Two years later, as a second baseman, he was named the league's Most Valuable Player, leading the circuit in hitting with a .342 average and steals with 37, while knocking in 124 runs. With Robinson as the catalyst, the Dodgers won six pennants and a world championship during his ten seasons in Brooklyn.[10] Campanella, a catcher, was also a mainstay of the Dodgers' pennant winners of 1949, '52, '53, '55, and '56. The seven-time All-Star was voted the National League's MVP in 1951, '53, and '55. In 1953, his best season, Campy batted .312 and scored 103 runs, while his 142 RBIS and 41 homers set Major League records for catchers.[11] Like other hugely successful teammates, Robinson and Campanella competed with each other for the spotlight. But they also treated the other's playing achievements with a silent resentment that rarely if ever revealed itself in public. The jealousy went further than the playing field too.

According to Sam Lacey, a sportswriter for the *Baltimore Afro-American*, "Campanella resented Jackie, who was a symbol for blacks because of his dark complexion." African American sportswriters and fans would "always circle around Jackie like he was theirs." Campy, the son of an Italian father and an African American mother, was "a hybrid, marginalized by blacks because of his [Italian] name and swarthy complexion."[12] Not even the three Most Valuable Player Awards the Dodgers' catcher captured could match Robinson's singular status among blacks as the trailblazer for integration. At the same time, Robinson resented Campanella's popularity among white sportswriters and fans and considered him an "Uncle Tom" because he was an agreeable black man in a white world.[13] Campanella's refusal to actively challenge Jim Crow irked Robinson, who near the end of his career admitted, "The more [I see] of Camp, the less I like him."[14] Not surprisingly the teammates became estranged in the mid-1950s, just when the Dodgers were experiencing their greatest success on the diamond.

It would be a mistake, however, to reduce the Robinson-Campanella rivalry to personality differences or petty jealousies. There was something much deeper to their feud, which one writer described as "combining the bitterness of the Hatfields and McCoys with the tragic comedy of Amos 'n' Andy."[15] That bitterness was caused by the inability of each man to understand and respect the approach of the other toward civil rights, and the tragedy was that both men shared the same goal: to secure equal opportunity for all African Americans. It was a conflict instigated by a fundamental dialectic in African American history itself, one that embodies a constant but inevitable tension between active defiance and passive resistance, aggression and docility, direct action and self-reliance. That dialectic emerged within the civil rights movement at the turn of the twentieth century and can be traced to the differing philosophies of Booker T. Washington and W. E. B. Du Bois.

1. Booker T. Washington, a former slave, became the founder of the Tuskegee Institute for industrial and vocational training. Considered by most whites to be the spokesman of the African American race at the turn of the nineteenth century, Washington's accommodationist philosophy was rejected by the majority of blacks during the post–World War II era. (Library of Congress)

Washington, a former slave, was recognized by most whites and blacks as "spokesman of his race" between 1895 and 1905. He believed that African Americans would progress only by winning support from the "better sort" of whites and by working hard, living frugal and moral lives, and developing and supporting black enterprises. For Washington, "employment" and "economic self-sufficiency" were the twin pillars upon which the foundation of racial equality rested.[16] It was a practical philosophy given the realities of race relations in the early twentieth century since it acknowledged segregation without accepting the inferior status it imposed on African Americans. "In all things that are purely social we can be as separate as the five fingers, yet one as the hand in all things essential to mutual progress," Washington said, giving comfort to white audiences. At the same time, he urged blacks to "make friends with the people of all races by entering the mechanics, commerce, domestic service and the professions."[17] Washington encouraged blacks to develop useful economic skills instead of protesting racial discrimination, and he founded the Tuskegee Institute to promote industrial and vocational education.

Although he worked behind the scenes against segregation, disenfranchisement, and lynching, Washington convinced white society that blacks would accept social segregation and disenfranchisement in exchange for educational and economic opportunities.[18] Whites hailed this "compromise" as the solution to the "race problem." Northern industrialist philanthropists such as Andrew Carnegie and John D. Rockefeller contributed millions of dollars to Tuskegee and other southern black schools. President Theodore Roosevelt, impressed by Washington's effort to blend practical education and political conciliation with whites, welcomed his counsel. But as Washington's influence grew, so did opposition to his accommodationist philosophy. Chief among his rivals was William Edward Burghardt Du Bois.

Du Bois, the first black to receive a PhD at Harvard, promoted integration of the races and full citizenship for blacks. Rejecting Washington's conciliatory stance toward white society as "silent submission to racial inequality," Du Bois accused him of "preaching a gospel of work and money" that "overshadows higher aims" for black people.[19] "If we make money the object of training we shall develop money-makers, but not necessarily men," he argued. "If we make technical skill the object of education, we may possess artisans, but not men. Men we shall have only as we make manhood the object of our schools." For Du Bois, the "object" of black education had to be "intelligence, broad sympathy, and knowledge of the world."[20] These are the same qualities that are necessary for full citizenship, and it is not coincidental that Du Bois equated them with "manhood." Unless blacks actively pursued and embraced these virtues, they would never be accorded the respect that comes with

2. William Edward Burghardt Du Bois, the first black to receive a PhD at Harvard, promoted integration of the races and full citizenship for blacks. In 1905 he organized the
Niagara movement to demand an end to racial discrimination in education, public accommodations, voting, and employment. Du Bois's philosophy of direct action placed
him at odds with Booker T. Washington but inspired the black activists who came of age
during World War II. (Library of Congress)

racial equality. Accordingly Du Bois believed that blacks were emasculated by Washington's accommodationist policies and, in 1905, organized the Niagara movement to demand an end to racial discrimination in education, public accommodations, voting, and employment. As a result, the African American community was split into two antagonistic camps: the "Bookerites" and the "Niagarites." Both groups maintained surveillance on the other and resorted to publishing essays critical of the other. While Washington's opposition resulted in the demise of the Niagara movement in 1909, Du Bois helped to establish its successor, the National Association of Colored People (NAACP), and became editor of its monthly journal, the *Crisis*.[21]

As the twentieth century unfolded, Washington became regarded by blacks as an Uncle Tom for his accommodationist philosophy. Du Bois, on the other hand, lost faith in integration and by the 1940s began to advocate a form of black self-segregation that led to his dismissal from the NAACP. Increasingly disillusioned with American society, he joined the Communist Party, renounced his U.S. citizenship, and joined the African nationalist leader Kwame Nkrumah in Ghana.[22] The two men's opposing philosophies inevitably created a permanent tension within the black community over the means of achieving full equality. The resulting dialectic embodied a contrast between self-reliance and direct action that was reflected in the movement to integrate Major League Baseball in the late 1940s and 1950s.

Although there is no documentary evidence to indicate that either Jackie Robinson or Roy Campanella was familiar with the specific philosophies of Du Bois or Washington, both ballplayers were acutely aware of the conflicting approaches to civil rights. That conflict was an inextricable part of the cultural currency of ideas that circulated within the African American community during the mid-twentieth century. Each man embraced a specific part of the dialectic in the movement to integrate Major League Baseball. Robinson thought that integration could be achieved only by challenging directly the segregated society in which he lived. Like Du Bois, he believed that racial discrimination attacked his manhood, and he protested, sometimes subtly, sometimes antagonistically. For Campanella, integration could be achieved only through a quiet self-reliance in which he could prove to whites that he was just as talented, just as able as they were. Like Washington, Campanella sought to better his economic circumstances in the hope of someday improving his social condition. In each case, the goal was the same, but the means were as different as fire and ice.

Many writers have explored Robinson's personal odyssey in breaking baseball's color barrier in the broader social and historical contexts of the civil rights movement. The most notable books are Jules Tygiel's *Baseball's Great Experiment* (1983), David Falkner's *Great Time Coming* (1995), and Arnold Rampersad's biography, *Jackie Robinson* (1997). While these accounts offer a more comprehensive understanding of Robinson's significance to the larger civil rights movement, none of the authors explores in depth the fundamental dialectic that emerged within the movement at the turn of the twentieth century and how it influenced modern baseball's first black player. Few authors, by comparison, have examined Campanella's role in integrating baseball or his personal conflict with Robinson. Those who have addressed the relationship either tend to marginalize the feud or deny it altogether.[23] Only by examining the dialectic, however, can historians gain a better understanding of the important roles Robinson and Campanella played in the integration of baseball.

Jackie and Campy goes beyond the existing accounts by examining the relationship of these black Dodgers stars in the broader context of the modern civil rights movement and the dialectic that defined their competing approaches to integrating the game. It is not an attempt to examine the storied history of the Brooklyn Dodgers of the 1950s or their rivalries with the New York Giants and Yankees. Nor does the book pretend to be a comprehensive biography of Robinson or Campanella. Readers interested in those topics can find many other books that are more suitable. Instead *Jackie and Campy* offers an important corrective to what has become a sanitized retelling of their relationship and its impact on baseball's integration process. I begin with the lackluster early history of the Dodgers and establish the social context of the story by describing the changing demographics of Brooklyn during the first half of the twentieth century. Ebbets Field became a melting pot for European immigrants, their children, and blacks. Brooklynites subordinated their social differences to root for the Dodgers. In the process they created an ideal setting for baseball's noble experiment with integration.

Dodgers president Branch Rickey, a visionary with a strong Christian ethic, tapped into the existing pool of talent in the Negro Leagues to break the so-called gentleman's agreement among club owners that prohibited signing black players. He was aided in his quest for integration by a perfect storm of forces: the popularity of Negro League Baseball among both black and white fans, suggesting that the integration of the Majors would be a lucrative enterprise; a younger generation of African American veterans who had served in World War II and desired greater political, social, and economic opportunities; and the receptiveness to integration of a new baseball commissioner.

Jackie Robinson and Roy Campanella were the first two black players selected by Rickey. No two individuals could have been more different in their background, personality, and approach to civil rights. Robinson was the son of a southern sharecropper who deserted his family. Raised by a God-fearing mother and his four older siblings in Pasadena, Jackie learned at an early age to strike back against the racial injustices he experienced. He channeled his frustration with Jim Crow into sports and became an outstanding college athlete. When the United States entered World War II, he served as a second lieutenant and challenged the segregated policies of the military. Threatened with a court-martial for refusing to sit in the back of an army bus, Robinson was honorably discharged. He joined the Kansas City Monarchs of the Negro Leagues, where Dodgers scouts discovered his talent. Rickey was immediately impressed by Jackie's outstanding athletic ability, competitive fire, and courage. These special qualities, along with Robinson's college and military experiences, convinced the Dodgers' president to select him for his experiment in integration rather than a more established Negro League star.

Campanella was also a product of the environment in which he was raised, but unlike Robinson, he enjoyed a stable home life as a youngster. He was the son of a black mother and an Italian father who sold fruits and vegetables on the streets of Philadelphia. The happy-go-lucky teenager quit high school to begin his professional career with the Baltimore Elite Giants. He soon challenged Josh Gibson as the dominant catcher of the Negro Leagues. During World War II, Campy, who as the married father of two children was exempt from military duty, completed his alternative service on an assembly line making steel plates for army tanks and managed to continue his playing career. After the war the Dodgers scouted the power-hitting catcher. Attracted by Campy's exceptional playing ability, leadership, and boyish enthusiasm for the game, Rickey seriously considered him as a candidate to break the color line but ultimately made him his second choice.

The year 1947 was pivotal for both players. Robinson broke Major League Baseball's color barrier and did so with a dignity and restraint never seen before or since in the sports world. While opposing players spiked him on the base paths and showered him with racial obscenities, opposing fans mailed him death threats. Through it all, Jackie persevered, channeling his anger into his on-field performance. In the process he brought the Negro Leagues' electrifying style of play to the Majors and quickly became baseball's top drawing card. Meanwhile Campanella distinguished himself as a catcher in the Dodgers farm system at Nashua, New Hampshire, where he proved that a black man did indeed possess the intelligence and physical ability to lead a professional baseball team. His leadership would become indispensable to the success of the Brooklyn Dodgers in the 1950s.

In the spring of 1948 Jackie and Campy were united in Brooklyn. As the only black Dodgers, they established a mutual support system on and off the field. But the following year their bond began to deteriorate, after Rickey removed the "no striking back" ban on his star second baseman. Jackie, now free to express himself, became increasingly combative. On the field he taunted opponents and antagonized umpires. Off the field he was an outspoken advocate of civil rights, voicing his sentiments to the House Un-American Activities Committee, which was holding hearings on the Communist infiltration of American minority groups.

After repeated attempts to discourage his friend's controversial behavior, Campanella began to distance himself from Robinson. The breaking point in their friendship came after the 1949 season, when the two teammates went on a barnstorming tour through the South. A disagreement over Campy's financial compensation and Robinson's unwillingness to rectify the situation irreparably damaged the relationship.

During the next seven years Robinson and Campanella struggled to keep their personal conflict in check so it would not interfere with the positive team chemistry that was essential to the Dodgers' success in the

1950s. Robinson was increasingly antagonistic toward baseball's white power structure and press and unapologetic about using his status as a star athlete to further the cause of civil rights whenever possible. His proactive approach against racial discrimination—both perceived and real—placed him on an inevitable collision course with Campanella, who refused to engage in racial politics; he led by example, believing that his on-field performance would do more for other black players than controversial ·remarks or protests.

Contrary to popular belief, Robinson and Campanella had very little in common aside from race and baseball. While both individuals mentored younger African American teammates, their different approaches to civil rights created tension among those same players. Fortunately for the Dodgers, Campanella and Robinson suppressed their differences on the playing field, allowing the team to capture their only World Series championship in 1955. But when Jackie retired after the 1956 season, he publicly criticized Campanella for his refusal to protest racial discrimination. Campy was quick to return the criticism, and the two men were estranged for nearly a decade.

Jackie and Campy is a very human as well as necessary account of the complicated relationship between Jackie Robinson and Roy Campanella. The book does not detract from either man's historic achievement as a pioneer in the struggle to integrate the national pastime as much as enhance the humanness of these baseball icons. More important, their examples reveal that public defiance is just as important as self-reliance in bearing witness against social injustice. While Robinson and Campanella may not have realized that essential truth, their conflict can serve as a meaningful lesson for others who hope to make a constructive contribution to race relations in our country. It is in that spirit that this book was written.

1

Brooklyn's Bums

On Saturday, April 5, 1913, Brooklyn was buzzing with excitement. Newspaper boys, tavern keepers, politicians, and ordinary people were all promoting or talking about the premiere that afternoon of the borough's brand-new ballpark, Ebbets Field. A preseason exhibition game was scheduled between the hometown Dodgers and the New York Yankees, cross-town rivals who would eventually become regulars in the annual fall classic known as the World Series. More than a thousand early birds had arrived by noon, crowding the main entrance behind home plate, though the pregame ceremonies were not scheduled to begin until three o'clock. As they waited patiently for the gates to open, the fans couldn't help but be impressed by the architectural grandeur that surrounded them.[1]

Located in Flatbush, just east of Prospect Park on a plot bounded by Montgomery Street, Bedford Avenue, Sullivan Place, and Cedar Place, Ebbets was, in accordance with the latest technology, a concrete-and-steel structure with a seating capacity of twenty-five thousand. The exterior façade of the ballpark was captivating. A row of fourteen small-pane, Federal-style windows separated by brick pilasters ran just above the main entrance to the top of the building's crown. Above these the words "Ebbets Field," in full caps, were mounted on the façade's setback. Below the windows was a galvanized-iron, glass-glazed marquis that ran fifty-six feet above the main entrance. Beyond were three curved doors that recessed into the wall on either side when the gates were opened. This majestic façade would come to define the ballpark in the national psyche for generations to come.

Inside the main entrance was a semicircular rotunda, the most ornate element of the ballpark. It contained a circular room, eighty feet in diam-

3. Brooklyn's Ebbets Field, opened on April 5, 1913, was among the first concrete-and-steel ballparks. The park eventually became famous for its circus-like atmosphere and the hapless play of the hometown Dodgers, more affectionately known as "dem Bums." (National Baseball Hall of Fame Library, Cooperstown, New York)

eter, with Italian marble columns and a marble mosaic tile floor patterned after the circular stitching on a baseball. Fourteen gilded-cage ticket windows were located along the circular walls. Each window had adjacent doors and a turnstile behind it to efficiently control the flow of fans into the ballpark's grandstands. The ceiling was elliptical and reached a height of twenty-seven feet at the center. The most charming element of the rotunda, however, was a magnificent chandelier with twelve facsimile bats suspending illuminated glass baseball globes.[2]

Anyone who entered the ballpark that day must have been awed not only by the impressive surroundings but by the fact that Dodgers owner Charles Ebbets, an infamous penny-pincher, had spent his money so extravagantly. At a cost of $750,000, the project was a huge financial risk, one that forced Ebbets to take his contractors, Stephen and Edward McKeever, as partners. He realized that the success of his franchise depended not only on building a winning team but on constructing a larger, more

permanent ballpark than the rickety old bandbox the Dodgers had called home for most of the past three decades. Ebbets risked his fortune on a hunch that the new ballpark would attract fans on a routine basis at a time when interest in baseball was growing across the nation. Besides, Flatbush was an ideal location, just a few miles from the Brooklyn Bridge and near more than a dozen transit lines. Ebbets predicted that those advantages would translate into a handsome return on his investment.[3]

If the pregame activity was any indication of the future, Ebbets had good reason to be optimistic. Eager fans jammed inside the Rotunda as game time neared. Designed to provide fans with shelter from the rain and a comfortable place to meet before the game or linger after it, the Rotunda on this day became a maelstrom of excitement, tension, and frustration. Incoming hordes pressed against those who had already purchased tickets, eliciting profane and colorful language. A few women were the victims of unsolicited pinches, and reports of pickpockets kept the police busy.

By 1:30 p.m., most of the seats in the grandstands and bleachers were occupied, and the bluff across Montgomery Street behind the left-center-field fence was packed with onlookers up to the corner at Bedford Avenue. While the fans settled in to the music of Shannon's 23rd Regimental Band, they were struck by the intimacy of the new ballpark.[4] Its covered double-deck grandstand, which began in right-field foul territory and wrapped around the diamond to just past third base, hugged the infield, allowing fans to interact with the players. On the third base side, the grandstand went only forty feet past the infield, and uncovered single-decked bleacher seats extended the rest of the way to the left-field foul pole. The fences were 9 feet high across the outfield, and the dimensions were 417 feet from home plate down the left-field foul line, 477 feet to dead center, and 301 feet down the right-field foul line. Unless you were a left-handed hitter, those were formidable distances. Predictably Ebbets Field would come to be known as a "pitcher's park."[5] Fans were also impressed by such innovations as a scoreboard that displayed not only line scores of out-of-town games but who was up in the batting order, and a microphone situated near home plate so balls and strikes could be heard throughout the ballpark.[6]

Shortly after three o'clock, Charley Ebbets accompanied Edward McKeever and his wife, Jennie, out to center field to begin the ceremonies. The players of both teams, dressed in their eight-button sweaters and with arms folded or hands behind their backs, stood behind the threesome as Jennie McKeever slowly hoisted Old Glory with an occasional pause for photographs. After the flag was raised, dignitaries, fans, and ballplayers removed their hats and the band played the national anthem. Ebbets assigned the honor of the ceremonial first pitch to his twenty-year-old daughter, Genevieve, who threw a perfect strike to umpire Bob Emslie. Then, to the roar of the crowd, the Brooklyn Dodgers took the field.

Dodgers ace Nap Rucker retired the Yankees in order in the first. In the bottom of the inning, Brooklyn second baseman George Cutshaw, batting second, singled up the middle for the first hit in Ebbets Field. Later that same inning, Zack Wheat provoked the first humorous blunder in the ballpark's long and storied comic tradition. Lofting a foul pop-up in third-base foul territory, Wheat stood and watched as Roy Hartzell, the Yankees' third baseman, took a headfirst dive into a group of band members, hitting his head on the bass drum. Fans laughed uproariously as the sound resonated throughout the ballpark and, true to form, unmercifully razzed the infielder for the remainder of the game.

Casey Stengel, the Dodgers' lead-off hitter, scored the first run in the fifth when he hit a long, hard line drive to left-center. Yankee center fielder Harry Wolter tried to cut it off, but as he reached for the ball he inadvertently kicked it. As the ball rolled to the wall, Casey scampered around the bases for an inside-the-park home run. The following inning, Jake Daubert replicated the feat, once again hitting a hard liner in Wolter's vicinity. Although the Yankees tied the game with a couple of runs in the top of the ninth, the Dodgers prevailed in the bottom of the inning when Red Smith singled in Wheat from third base, capping the 3–2 Brooklyn victory.[7]

"Rejoice, ye fans," urged the *Brooklyn Daily Eagle*, "and deliver thanks for Charles Hercules Ebbets' magnificent stadium, the greatest ballpark in these United States," dedicated in the presence of "25,000 wildly enthusiastic rooters and at least 7,000 others who witnessed the 3–2 trouncing of Frank Chance's Yankees from the bluffs that overlook the field."[8] The *Brooklyn Daily Standard Union* compared the new ballpark to the temples of ancient Rome and predicted that Ebbets Field would "last 200 years, or four times as long as the average structure." Pointing out that there was no apostrophe on the name "Ebbets Field" above the main entrance, the newspaper explained that while the "huge amphitheater is named after the man who built it," the ballpark is "really dedicated to the fans and the Brooklyn team."[9] Those last words were prophetic.

The history of Ebbets Field reflects the love affair between the Dodgers and their blue-collar fans. The losing tradition that unfolded there actually endeared the team to Brooklynites, who affectionately referred to the Dodgers as "dem Bums." Just as important was the comedic way the team lost: outfielders colliding in pursuit of a fly ball, wacky miscues on the base paths, and players forgetting the number of outs in an inning, leading to even more blunders. The comedy of errors made the team lovable because it reminded the fans of their own humanness. Essentially Brooklyn's fans embraced the Dodgers because cheering for the team was like rooting for themselves. In the process the fans discovered common ground with each other, especially after Jackie Robinson broke the color barrier in 1947. Baseball became the great equalizer, the one institution that allowed everyone to stand on equal footing, regardless of race or ethnicity. Ebbets Field became a melting pot for an ethnically diverse, racially mixed community. In fact Brooklyn was ready for the integration of baseball by the mid-1940s because the Dodgers and their ballpark were at the center of demographic trends and prevailing notions about ethnicity and race that allowed baseball to break its infamous color barrier. Ultimately Ebbets Field, the Dodgers, and their fans served as powerful catalysts for social change, playing a pivotal role in the integration of the national pastime.

Brooklyn's love affair with the Dodgers began on May 9, 1883, when a thousand or so fans turned out to watch their predecessors, the Brooklyn Polka Dots, defeat Harrisburg, 7–1, near Prospect Park. Known for their flashy, polka-dot hosiery, the team chalked up a second victory, 13–6, three days later against Trenton at their brand-new home, Washington Park. Situated in a hollowed-out basin some twenty-five feet below street level at Third Street and Fourth Avenue in the Red Hook section of the city, the ballpark sported a single-tier wooden grandstand along with bleachers to accommodate as many as two thousand spectators. The Polka Dots were owned and operated by real estate dealer Charles H. Byrne and his Manhattan gambling house partner, Joseph J. Doyle. Hoping to achieve greater respectability, Byrne arranged for his amateur club to join the American Association the following season. In 1887, when six of the players got married, the Polka Dots changed their name to the Brooklyn Bridegrooms, popularly called the "Grooms."[10]

After capturing the American Association pennant in 1889, the Grooms traveled across the East River to Manhattan to play the National League's Giants for bragging rights as the "best team in baseball." Although the Giants prevailed in the best-of-eleven-game series, six games to three, owner John Day proved to be a sore winner. "We will never play your team again," Day said to Byrne. "Your players are dirty. They constantly stall and complain. We've been deprived of three games by trickery," he complained, referring to Brooklyn's repeated attempts to stall and have the game called for darkness once they held a lead. "I don't mind losing games on their merits," Day added, "but I do mind being robbed of them."[11] Unfortunately for Day, Brooklyn jumped to the National League in 1890, and the acrimonious rivalry between the two New York teams was born. It was part of a larger competition with Manhattan that came to define Brooklyn's idiosyncratic culture.

Located on the southwestern tip of Long Island and situated on New York harbor across the East River from Manhattan, Brooklyn, Kings County, was once an independent municipality and, during the second half of the nineteenth century, the third largest city in the nation. The population of 396,099 in 1870 was exceeded only by the populations of New York City and Philadelphia. The other towns of Kings County were largely rural, with a combined population of less than 12,500. Gradually those nearest Brooklyn became annexed to it, including Flatlands, New Utrecht, Gravesend, Jamaica Bay, and Williamsburg. The steam railway and elevated train linked these towns to Brooklyn, making the downtown accessible to the growing population. As the 1880s unfolded, the working class and immigrants took up residence in the neighborhoods of the annexed area (called the Eastern District), most notably the German and Irish. Many of these residents formed the backbone of labor for the booming industries that dominated the waterfront of the Eastern District, including shipbuilding, grain storage, sugar refining, and glass manufacturing.[12]

The completion of the Brooklyn Bridge in 1883 established the first physical link between the nation's largest and third largest cities. It also symbolized the end of Brooklyn's independence as well as an impending political union with New York City. By 1898 unabated economic and demographic growth pushed Brooklyn to the limit of its allowable state debt and almost exhausted its ability to issue bonds. Republican reformers, realizing that Brooklyn's economic and political future was tied to New York City, defeated the Democratic machine, long in control of local government, and moved toward consolidation. On January 1, 1898, Brooklyn combined with Manhattan and the boroughs of Queens, Staten Island, and the Bronx to create modern-day New York City.[13] Brooklyn was now a borough and would eventually become the poor stepchild of the more refined Manhattan.

Brooklyn was known as the borough of well-attended churches, tree-lined neighborhoods, and trolleys, while Manhattan was "the city" of office buildings where professionals worked, women shopped, and anyone who had money spent their Saturday nights. Brooklyn had Coney Island, stickball in the streets, bargain racks, and doo-wop, but Manhattan had world-class museums, Sax Fifth Avenue, and Carnegie Hall.[14] Predictably Brooklynites developed an inferiority complex. Dominated by blue-collar, ethnic neighborhoods with names like Crown Heights, Bedford-Stuyvesant, Bay Ridge, Bensonhurst, and Flatbush, Brooklyn was home to a working-class people with a colorful, irreverent sense of humor and an eternal chip on their shoulder.[15] Boisterous and combative, they reveled in even the smallest victory over their cross-town rival and somehow managed to make a virtue out of any setback.[16] Baseball would prove to be the most popular ground for bragging rights.

In 1890 Brooklyn won the National League pennant, in spite of its roster being raided by the newly created Players League, established the year before. Flatbush businessman George Chauncey financed the renegade league's Brooklyn team and built a home ballpark in sparsely populated Brownsville, where he had extensive real estate holdings. When the Players' League folded, Chauncey arranged a merger of his team with the Bridegrooms, who left Washington Park for the more "modern" Eastern Park in Brownsville. It was a bad decision. Brownsville was not very accessible by public transportation and the town's residents were mostly new immigrants who didn't understand the sport.[17] In addition, most of the seats were too expensive, a fact that did not escape the writers of the *Brooklyn Eagle*. "Twenty-five cents" should be the price to see a game, they argued. "Not only does baseball cost more, but the ball game is held on the outskirts of town, the seats are hard, the grandstand is open to the wind, snow and rain, there are no reliefs of scenery or music—nothing but sandwiches and frankfurters—and no guarantee that a poor, spiritless show may not be given."[18] For eight forgettable years the team remained in Brownsville until it was rescued by Charles Ebbets, a ticket taker who had risen to president and stockholder of the club. Ebbets returned the team to Washington Park with the financial assistance of several transportation moguls who profited by having the ballpark reachable by their streetcar lines.[19]

When the Grooms' majority stockholder Charles Byrne died in 1898, the owners of the Baltimore Orioles, Ned Hanlon and Harry Von der Horst, saw the opportunity to invest in Brooklyn's more lucrative market. In 1899 they purchased a half interest in the Bridegrooms and changed the team's name to Superbas, after a popular vaudeville act, Hanlon's Superbas. While Hanlon retained the presidency of the Orioles, he took over as manager in Brooklyn. He also brought along with him the talented core of the Orioles, including Joe Kelley, a regular .300 hitter with a rifle arm; "Wee Willie" Keeler, a five-foot-four-inch outfielder and the game's most prominent place hitter; and Hughie Jennings, a fiery shortstop who hailed from the Pennsylvania coal mines. These future Hall of Famers were notoriously profane and brought a fierce, combative style to Brooklyn as well as such controversial tactics as "tipping the bat" and the "hidden ball play." The fans adored them and flocked to the ballpark to see them play. The Superbas' combination of ferocity, skill, and trickery enabled them to win National League pennants in 1899 and 1900.[20] But the good fortune didn't last long.

In 1902 Charles Ebbets purchased a majority interest in the Superbas and changed the team's name to Dodgers, a reference to the adept skill of Brooklynites to "dodge" the city's many street trolleys.[21] That same year the Dodgers' roster was raided by the upstart American League, and the team was left with few star players. What's worse, constant clashes between Ebbets and Hanlon, who continued to manage the team, hastened the club's decline, and the Dodgers slipped into the second division, where they remained for more than a decade. Hanlon was fired in 1905 after the club finished in last place, fifty-six and a half games out.[22] Perhaps the only thing that kept the Dodgers alive was their interborough rivalry with the New York Giants, who always attracted a sellout crowd.[23]

Perennial losers, the Dodgers attracted most fans to Washington Park by the sheer amusement of their incompetent play. Ebbets's penny-pinching ways forced the team to remain in their rickety old bandbox. To spite him, many fans shunned the admission price to watch games from the Ginney Flats apartment building, just beyond the center-field wall. Neighborhood saloonkeepers encouraged their rowdyism by selling discounted beer, adding to the circus-like atmosphere. Outfielder Casey Stengel, who began his playing career with Brooklyn in 1912, quickly learned to trade insults with the best of them and developed a quick wit that would see him through many a losing season, both as a player and a manager.[24]

Ebbets eventually realized that the only way to secure a sizable return on his investment was to build a larger, more permanent ballpark that would attract fans on a routine basis. To that end, he purchased a site in the underdeveloped section of Flatbush, just east of Prospect Park, for $100,000. Ground was broken in March 1912, and the new stadium opened the following year.[25]

The opening of the new ballpark marked the beginnings of a new, more promising era in Dodgers baseball, a fact that was underscored by the hiring of Wilbert Robinson as the team's new manager in 1914. Once an outstanding catcher for the Baltimore Orioles, Robinson would go on to become pitching coach and, in 1902, manager of the Orioles. Known for his jovial and easygoing disposition, the portly manager was nicknamed "Uncle Robbie" by the Brooklyn sportswriters. Together with ace pitcher Jack Pfeffer and aging stars Rube Marquard and Jake Daubert, Robinson led the team to National League pennants in 1916 and 1920 and was hailed as a genius by the fans, who called his teams the "Robins." Of course, the Robins were called less complimentary names after they dropped the World Series to the Boston Red Sox in 1916 and to the Cleveland Indians in 1920. Still, as long as Charles Ebbets ran the club, the Dodgers were successful. But when he died in 1925, club officials named Robinson as the new president, and the club returned to the second division. Despite featuring several future Hall of Famers like Max Carey, Zach Wheat, and Dazzy Vance, the team could never quite reach the top. Robinson's absentmindedness and casual approach to life became trademarks of his teams, which were appropriately named the "Daffiness Boys."[26]

The comedic highlight of these miserable years occurred on August 15, 1926, when the Dodgers, in a game against the Boston Braves, loaded the bases with one out in the bottom of the seventh of a tie game. Up to the plate stepped Babe Herman, a superb hitter, who promptly smacked a line drive off the fence in right-center field. Two runs should have scored, but only one crossed the plate. When the dust cleared there were three Dodgers base runners standing on third base. The umpire called out two of the runners to retire the side.[27] The wacky miscue became part of Dodgers folklore and gave rise to a popular joke about the cab driver who was cruising past Ebbets Field and asked a spectator how the game was going. When the fan replied, "The Dodgers have three men on base," the cabbie asked, "Which base?"[28]

While the Dodgers were floundering in the second division, Brooklyn's black teams were flourishing. Negro League Baseball had been popular in the borough since 1904, when John Connor, proprietor of the elite Royal Café in Bedford-Stuyvesant, established the Brooklyn Royal Giants. Conner believed that black baseball would be good for business and recruited such outstanding players as shortstop Grant "Home Run" Johnson and catcher Bruce Petway, a college student in Nashville. Initially the Royal Giants operated primarily as a traveling team because of the abundance of Negro League clubs within a hundred-mile radius, including the Philadelphia Giants, Cuban X-Giants, Genuine Cuban Giants, Quaker Giants of New York, Baltimore Giants, and Keystone Giants of Philadelphia.[29] In 1912 the Royal Giants began playing regularly at Washington Park, and the team's fortunes thrived under a new owner, Nat Strong, a white booking agent. Strong added future pitching ace "Cannonball" Dick Redding and catcher Louis Santop, the first great power hitter in Negro League history and a regular .400 hitter. As a result, the Royal Giants occasionally contended for the Eastern Colored League title during the 1920s.

Another great team was the Lincoln Giants, who regularly played in Brooklyn before establishing a regular home in Harlem. The club's ace was Smokey Joe Williams, an imposing six-foot-five-inch right-hander with a blazing fastball and pinpoint control. With Williams on the mound, the Lincoln Giants were arguably the very best team in black baseball.[30] A third Negro League team, the Brooklyn Eagles, played at Ebbets Field before relocating to Newark, New Jersey, in 1936. They would go on to become a first division club in the Negro National League.[31] With such teams as the Royal Giants, the Lincoln Giants, and the Eagles, as well as a dozen other Negro League teams that visited the borough, Brooklynites grew accustomed to watching exceptional black baseball. In the process the borough's Negro League teams served to gain a modicum of respect among white fans as well as lessen the social tensions that existed between the two races during the early decades of the twentieth century.

Contrary to popular belief, Brooklyn was not always a melting pot where different ethnic and racial groups lived happily together. Historically neighborhoods were divided along ethnic and racial lines. While rich in social diversity, the different groups did not really associate with each other. Hostilities were especially pronounced between the hundreds of thousands of immigrants who came to Brooklyn at the turn of the century from southern and eastern Europe and the German and Irish immigrants who had settled in the borough earlier.[32] Italians settled in Williamsburg, Sunset Park, and the South Brooklyn–Red Hook area, where the men could find work as laborers along the docks or in the warehouses, plants, and piers of the shipyard.[33] Jews, who fled from religious persecution in eastern Europe, settled in the old German neighborhoods of Williamsburg and Brownsville, located between Bedford-Stuyvesant and Canarsie. By 1930 Brownsville had become the largest Jewish community in the United States. But these were not the same kinds of Jews who had settled earlier in Williamsburg. Those were German, middle-class Jews, with a strong work ethic and an appreciation for education and Wagnerian opera. The new Jews, according to the *Hebrew Standard*, were "of a low class" and had "no religious, social or intellectual ties to their predecessors in Williamsburg."[34] The more established Jewish population distanced itself from these recent arrivals.

In 1924 the United States passed legislation restricting immigration from southern and eastern Europe, and for the next forty years the newcomers were mostly African Americans from the rural South. Lured by northern job recruiters and promises of a better life in the industrial North, thousands of southern blacks migrated to Brooklyn between World War I and the 1930s in what has become known as "the Great Migration."[35] Unlike the European immigrants who preceded them, however, blacks faced not only discrimination but de facto segregation in their efforts to seek

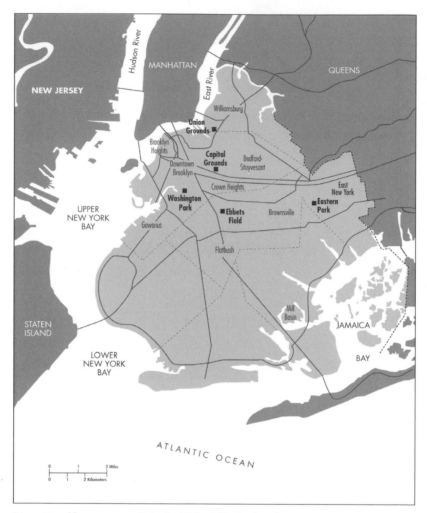

Map 1. Brooklyn, ca. 1940s. (Map by Michael Hockenbury)

employment and housing. Weeksville, the largest and best-known black neighborhood, was called "Blackville" by whites who lived on its periphery. Similarly whites dubbed a nearby elevation "Crow Hill" because of "all the darkies who lived there," according to a retired white policeman who once patrolled the area.[36] Brownville's Jews begrudgingly tolerated rather than accepted blacks on an equal footing in a neighborhood that became known as the home of the Socialist Labor Movement and the Murder, Inc. mob. Racial tensions between blacks and whites also existed in Bedford-Stuyvesant, where whites, encouraged by the Ku Klux Klan, established restrictive covenants to prevent blacks from purchasing property.[37] As outlying residential areas developed, black migrants flocked to the downtown neighborhoods, where they rented rooms and apartments in converted one-family houses. Decline and deterioration in these neighborhoods followed.[38]

Despite the racial tensions, Brooklyn's African American population enjoyed greater stability than blacks in other major American cities because of the existence of a prosperous middle class. Some came from the Fort Greene–Washington Park area, where they opened churches, clothing stores, restaurants, and nightclubs. Others were transplants from Manhattan drawn by Brooklyn's better educational facilities for blacks.[39] By 1930 Brooklyn had ninety-four black-owned businesses with combined net sales of $500,000.[40] The existence of such a prosperous middle-class disproved notions of African American inferiority among Brooklyn's whites, showing that the American Dream of social and economic mobility transcended racial boundaries.

Social acceptance of minorities by whites increased during the Great Depression. Brooklyn became home to a growing African American population drawn to the borough by less expensive, roomier housing than elsewhere in New York City. Joining blacks were an increasing number of Puerto Ricans who left their poverty-stricken homeland in search of jobs in the Navy Yard area and Greenpoint. White residents were increasingly forced to live in the same neighborhoods with these minorities as poverty became a social and economic equalizer among Brooklynites.[41] The Democratic Party strengthened the bonds between these different racial and ethnic groups through employment in its New Deal work programs. Hoping to displace the borough's Republican hegemony, Democratic politicians actively courted and won over African Americans, Puerto Ricans, and working-class whites, all of whom relied on the services of municipal government.[42]

Bill Reddy, a white who grew up in Borough Park in a predominantly Irish and Jewish neighborhood, recalled, "The great thing about being a kid in Brooklyn during the 1930s was that it didn't matter what your ethnic background was. . . . Everybody was the same. Nobody had anything."[43] Joe Flaherty, Reddy's neighbor, admits that white kids were naïve about race relations. "We didn't know we had a race problem," he said. "We liked to think that Negroes didn't need anything, that they were happy in their place. Sure, there were some tough black kids. But there wasn't this myopic focus on blacks that there is today."[44] Both Flaherty and Reddy suggest that color blindness prevailed during their childhoods, at least in Borough Park. But such a perspective is tainted by the fact that neither individual had much contact with blacks during their youth. Jim McGowan, an African American who was raised in Bedford-Stuyvesant, agrees that the "racial climate was entirely different than it is today" but bases the claim on his experience in an integrated neighborhood:

> Growing up in the 1940s, I was part of a multicultural society that included Jews, Italian and Irish Catholics, and blacks of many skin tones. I really never knew what racial discrimination was because of the exposure I had to all kinds of people. Blacks and whites lived together in the same neighborhoods, worked together, and went to school together.
>
> I also think that being the son of a white father and a black mother, which was pretty common in Brooklyn in those days, allowed me to be fairly open-minded about race relations.[45]

Regardless of the perspective, one thing is clear: Brooklyn's blacks and whites did not believe they had a "race problem" in the 1930s and 1940s. Most of the whites were immigrants or the sons and daughters of immigrants. Half of these were Jews who had escaped persecution, first by Russian czars and later by the Nazis. The rest were Irish and Italian Catholics who had fled Europe to escape economic hardship and political or religious persecution. There was also a growing African American population, whose history was inextricably tied to persecution, first through slavery and later through Jim Crow. Persecution, racial or religious, was the common denominator for all of these groups. In addition every social group that resided in the borough came as a minority. Everyone was poor, and everyone struggled to make a living. These common circumstances created a strong sense of identity in which race and ethnicity were much less important that one's character as a human being and how one treated one's neighbors. It's also what allowed Brooklyn to become the biggest melting pot in the nation and play a pivotal role in breaking baseball's color line.

But baseball's integration was still a decade away; in the mid-1930s the Dodgers were more concerned about winning ball games and improving attendance rates than social justice. A succession of managers followed Wilbert Robinson, none of them able to build a contender. But the local press managed to find some humor in an otherwise hopeless situation. Sportswriter Sid Mercer dubbed the Dodgers "Bums," inspired by a leather-lunged fan who regularly sat behind home plate and shouted "Ya bum, ya!" whenever the team committed an error. The name stuck, and soon the newspaper headlines featured "Bums" as often as "Dodgers." Cartoonist Willard Mullin underscored the label by creating the "Flatbush bum," which quickly became a nationally known symbol for the team as well as for Brooklyn itself. By 1938 Ebbets Field was in a state of disrepair and the team was in debt to the Brooklyn Trust Company for $500,000. George McLaughlin, president of the Trust, warned that the club's credit would be severely restricted unless it improved its leadership.[46]

When the Dodgers hired Larry MacPhail as general manager in 1938, their fortunes changed for the better. MacPhail rejuvenated the organization both on and off the field. He began immediately by repainting Ebbets Field, renovating its bathrooms, and installing electric lights for night games. Accordingly on June 15, 1938, the Dodgers hosted Cincinnati in baseball's first night game before a sellout crowd. Night baseball was only one of many promotions MacPhail introduced, though not all of them proved to be successful. On August 2, for example, Brooklyn experimented with yellow baseballs in a game against the St. Louis Cardinals. Although yellow was supposed to be easier to see than white, the players didn't like the innovation and the experiment was dropped. Similarly MacPhail hired former Yankee great Babe Ruth as a first-base coach for the second half of the season. Though Ruth believed that he was being given a trial as the team's next manager, MacPhail was simply exploiting the star's popularity, realizing that fans would turn out early to watch the Bambino knock balls out of the park. Of course, Ruth, still yearning for the spotlight, obliged.[47] As a result of the various promotions, attendance doubled to 660,000 for the season.[48] The Dodgers' new popularity was even memorialized in an irreverent poem by Dan Parker of the *Daily Mirror*, who wrote about

"Murgatroyd Darcy," a baseball groupie, who forsook the "juke joints" for Ebbets Field to root for her "gallant knights," the Dodgers.[49]

After the 1938 season, MacPhail replaced manager Burleigh Grimes with one of his players, shortstop Leo Durocher, and spent freely to acquire veteran stars who combined with talented prospects to turn the team into one of the best in the National League. Durocher, who was loud, obnoxious, and driven, distanced some of the players and was quickly dubbed "Leo the Lip." But he inspired more than he alienated. His fierce desire to win overcame complaints against him, and the Dodgers steadily rose in the standings. After a third-place finish in 1939 and second-place in 1940, the Dodgers clinched the pennant in 1941, winning one hundred games.[50] The team was led by veteran first baseman Dolph Camilli, who led the league in home runs (34) and RBIs (120); center fielder Pete Reiser, who led the league in batting (.343), slugging (.558), and runs scored (117); right fielder Dixie Walker, who was supposedly over the hill but somehow managed to hit .311; and pitchers Kirby Higbe and Whitlow Wyatt, both of whom were tied for the league lead with twenty-two wins apiece.[51]

The Dodgers faced the New York Yankees in the World Series that year. After three games the Yanks enjoyed a two-games-to-one lead. However, the Dodgers threatened to come back. With two outs in the ninth inning of Game Four, Brooklyn held a 4–3 lead and looked as if they'd tie the Series. Tommy Henrich came to bat for New York, facing Dodgers hurler Hugh Casey. Casey recorded two quick strikes on Henrich before throwing a rapidly sinking curve ball. Henrich swung and missed for strike three. But the ball got past Dodgers catcher Mickey Owens and rolled all the way to the backstop, allowing Henrich to reach first base easily. It was all the Yankees needed. New York went on to win the game, 7–4.[52] The following day the Bronx Bombers clinched the championship, and another painful tradition was born: losing to the Yankees in the World Series. After the '41 Fall Classic ended, the *Brooklyn Eagle* ran a headline that would become famous: "Wait till Next Year!"[53] It would become the rallying cry for Brooklynites, who became renowned for their fortitude and obstinate belief in "next year."

Although MacPhail never won a world championship in Brooklyn, he is credited with laying the foundations of the team's golden age. One of his greatest moves was luring a young, sweet-talking broadcaster by the name of Walter "Red" Barber from Cincinnati to New York during the winter of 1938–39. Prior to that time, none of New York's Major League teams allowed their games to be broadcast over the radio, fearing that it would lead to a decrease in attendance. MacPhail, on the other hand, believed that radio could serve to promote the game by advertising it. His instinct proved to be correct. With Barber at the microphone on Opening Day of 1939, New York City experienced its first radio coverage of big league baseball. By the end of the season, attendance at games rose to 955,000—up by 295,000 from the previous year—and the Dodgers outdrew the Yankees by 100,000 and the Giants by 250,000.[54]

Radio became an instant hit, and many fans began to build their lives around the Dodgers because of it. Radios were everywhere—in homes, cars, stores. During the summer months Brooklynites would pipe the Dodgers broadcast into the streets. In fact in some neighborhoods it was possible for pedestrians to hear the game uninterrupted because of the popularity of the practice. At first Barber's southern drawl and down-home expressions startled listeners. If the Dodgers were launching a rally, he'd say, "The boys are tearing up the pea patch." If Brooklyn appeared to clinch the game, it was "tied up in a crocus sack." A bench-clearing brawl was a "rhubarb." Base runners in scoring position were "ducks on the pond." Barber's distinctive voice and engaging personality soon won over the hearts of Brooklynites, especially women. Female interest in baseball increased, and MacPhail capitalized on it by promoting "Ladies Day," giving free admission to women.[55]

Barber was much more than a play-by-play announcer, though. He was a reporter who used his reportorial skills to educate listeners about the game. Using personal insight and amusing anecdotes, he was able to make a 10–1 rout interesting. He'd arrive three hours before game time and stand around the batting cage, where he'd pick up tidbits of information on a particular player's hitting mechanics or a pitcher's delivery. That information would be interspersed throughout his broadcast.[56] And while Barber was making Brooklynites the most knowledgeable fans in the game, he was also cultivating a personal connection with them. Brooklynites invited him into their living rooms each day, where they listened from their sofas and armchairs. Businessmen and secretaries made him part of the office. Kids mimicked his idiosyncratic expressions while doing their own play-by-play in neighborhood stickball games. Radio made Red Barber a household name in Brooklyn. But television made him a broadcasting legend on August 26, 1939, when NBC put him behind the microphone for the first televised baseball game, a Saturday afternoon double-header, pitting the Dodgers against the Cincinnati Reds.[57] Together—radio, television, and Barber—changed the nature of baseball forever.

Despite his success, MacPhail was not long for Brooklyn. For years he had struggled with alcoholism, and after one of his benders he allegedly traded the entire Dodgers team to the St. Louis Cardinals. But Sam Braden, the Cardinals' owner, was unable to raise the $3 million needed before the Dodgers' stockholders nixed the deal.[58] Furious at having lost the '41 World Series, MacPhail bore down harder on Durocher. The final straw came in July 1942, when center fielder Pete Reiser crashed into the concrete wall at Ebbets in pursuit of a fly ball. He lost consciousness and was taken to the hospital. Diagnosed with a fractured skull and a severe concussion, Reiser was told by the attending physician that he was through for the season. But MacPhail refused to accept the diagnosis. Believing that the star outfielder could prove to be the difference for the Dodgers in a hotly contested pennant race with St. Louis, he ordered Durocher to play the youngster. Reiser complied, despite suffering from double vision. Naturally he was ineffective both at the plate and in the field, and the Dodgers lost the pennant. MacPhail, already infuriated by the team's stockholders, who criticized him for his excessive spending, resigned on September 24, 1942, and accepted a commission as colonel in the U.S. Army.[59] Shortly afterward the Dodgers named Branch Rickey, recently dismissed as general manager of the Cardinals, as MacPhail's successor.

Rickey promised to make Brooklyn "the baseball capital of America."[60] Little did anyone realize at the time that he had plans to do much more than that. Rickey believed that Brooklyn, with its racial tolerance, growing African American population, die-hard working-class fans, and penchant for the underdog was the ideal place to launch a noble experiment to integrate baseball.[61] Within the next five years he would not only revolutionize the national pastime but would help to inspire the modern civil rights movement in the United States.

2

Rickey's Choice

At the center of Branch Rickey's plan to rebuild the Brooklyn Dodgers was scouting and signing African American players. It was a plot to break the "gentleman's agreement" that had banned black athletes from baseball since the late nineteenth century. Rickey recognized the enormous pool of talent that existed in the Negro Leagues and sought to capitalize on it, both on the field and at the turnstiles. But winning teams and big profits were not the only reasons for integrating the sport; there was also a nagging personal motive. Since 1912, when he entered baseball as a scout, Rickey harbored a deep sense of guilt over devoting his life to a child's game instead of a more altruistic profession.[1] Integration would allow him to unburden his conscience by redressing a long-held social injustice. It was nothing less than a religious obligation for him. To that end, the Dodgers' president carefully orchestrated the process of identifying and signing the ideal African American ballplayer to break the color line.

Wesley Branch Rickey, named after John Wesley, the founder of the Methodist faith, was hardly suited to the blue-collar sport of baseball, with its incorrigible athletes, rowdy fans, and deceitful style of play. Rickey's most defining trait was his fierce morality. Sportswriters dubbed him "the Deacon" and "the Mahatma" because he reminded them of a combination of "God and your father."[2] Raised in a devout Methodist family, Rickey as a youngster memorized Scripture and taught himself Latin, Greek, and algebra. His parents cultivated a strong work ethic by assigning him countless chores on their farm in southern Ohio. Promising his mother that he'd never drink, swear, or violate the Sabbath, the young Buckeye matured into a devout Methodist.[3] According to his grandson, Branch Rickey III, "his mother objected to the idea of her son playing baseball because the

4. Branch Rickey's commitment to integrating baseball began as a coach at Ohio Wesleyan University. After an unremarkable playing career, he became an administrator with the St. Louis Cardinals and later the Brooklyn Dodgers. (National Baseball Hall of Fame Library, Cooperstown, New York)

players, back at the turn of the century, often rode to the games on the back of a wagon drinking, and just as often, came home with women in the back of the same wagon. They were a loose crowd. There wasn't much morality around a baseball team back then."[4] Still, he could not shake his deep and abiding passion for the sport.

Rickey learned the game in the family's backyard by catching for his older brother. He quickly became a die-hard fan of the Cincinnati Reds and, by his late teens, proved good enough to catch for a local semipro team. In 1901 he enrolled in Ohio Wesleyan University, where he waited tables and helped coach the baseball team in order to pay his tuition. It was during this time that he allegedly made a personal commitment to integrating baseball. The pivotal events came in the spring of 1904, when the twenty-one-year-old witnessed the racist treatment of Charles "Tommy" Thomas, his black first baseman. In a game against Kentucky, the opposing players refused to take the field unless Thomas was removed, and began shouting, "Get that nigger off the field." Rickey, enraged by their belligerence, stormed the opposing manager, screaming, "You will play Tommy Thomas or you won't play OWU!" Kentucky reconsidered when the Wesleyan crowd began to chant, "We want Thomas! We want Thomas!" In the end, the game was played with Thomas at first base.[5]

A few weeks later Wesleyan traveled to South Bend, Indiana, to play Notre Dame. When Rickey tried to register his team at the Oliver Hotel, the clerk informed him that he and the rest of the team were welcome, but Thomas was not. Thomas, humiliated by the scene, suggested that he simply return to Ohio Wesleyan. Rickey flatly rejected the offer. Instead he threatened to remove his entire team from the hotel unless Thomas was allowed to stay. A stalemate ensued. Then Rickey proposed that Thomas could share his room if the hotel would place a cot in it. The hotel manager agreed to the compromise. That night Thomas couldn't sleep.[6] Rickey recalled that the black first baseman "just sat on the end of the cot, his huge shoulders hunched and his large hands clasped between his knees." "I sat and watched him, not knowing what to do," he confessed. "Tears welled, spilled down his black face and splashed to the floor. Then his shoulders heaved convulsively and he rubbed one great hand over the other with all the power of his body muttering, 'Black skin . . . black skin. If I could only make 'em white.' He kept rubbing and rubbing as though he would remove the blackness by sheer friction." Rickey insisted, "Whatever mark that incident left on Charley Thomas, it was no more indelible than the impressions made on me."[7]

After graduating from Ohio Wesleyan, Rickey signed as a catcher with Dallas of the North Texas League for $175 a month. He performed well enough to attract the interest of his boyhood team, the Reds, who purchased his Minor League contract. But once he was told that he'd have to play on Sunday—something he promised his mother he'd never do—Rickey refused and was let go. He caught on with the St. Louis Browns and later the New York Highlanders, both of whom agreed to honor his promise not to play on the Sabbath. An overstrained arm put an end to his undistinguished playing career after just two seasons. In 1906 Rickey married Jane Moulton, his childhood sweetheart and the daughter of a state senator. Enrolling in the University of Michigan, he earned a law degree in two years instead of the customary three.[8]

Despite his impressive education and domestic tranquility, the young lawyer was determined to succeed in baseball and joined the lowly St. Louis Browns as a scout. Promoted to manager in 1913, Rickey led the Browns up the American League standings until 1915, when the club was sold. The next year the cross-town rival St. Louis Cardinals, then an inept, debt-ridden team, hired Rickey as president. Though given little cash, the hardworking executive built a contender by obtaining Minor League clubs to develop Major League talent. It was the first modern farm system in baseball, transforming the way Major League teams built their rosters. Among other innovations, Rickey also introduced the idea of a permanent spring training camp, an organized system of scouts, sliding pits, and the use of a stopwatch to measure speed on the base paths. By 1940 the Cardinals owned thirty-two Minor League teams outright and enjoyed working agreements with eight others. Their success was reflected in the six National League pennants they captured between 1926 and 1942.[9]

But St. Louis was not the right place to implement integration. It had a southern temperament with conservative and racist traditions. "During my time in St. Louis," recalled Rickey, "a Negro had to sit in the bleachers. He couldn't buy his way into the stands. Mind you, this was more than a half century after Emancipation, after Negroes had been given the rights of citizenship under the constitution. It was unthinkable. So, when I went to Brooklyn, I wanted to do something about Negro participation in baseball."[10] By that time Rickey's commitment to integration had become both a personal and a professional quest. Nor did he care how the white baseball establishment or the white press viewed him, which wasn't very complimentary. According to Lester Rodney, sports editor of the *Daily Worker*, New York's Communist newspaper, Rickey was widely viewed as "pompous, arrogant and cheap." Even those who supported the integration of baseball on moral grounds believed that the Dodgers' president was "guilty of big-daddy patronizing behavior towards blacks." Despite the fact that Rickey was "no saint," Rodney acknowledges that he was "far shrewder and bolder than the other magnates" and credits him for "seizing the day by taking the giant step the others would not take."[11]

Shortly after he became president of the Dodgers, Rickey broached the controversial subject with George V. McLaughlin, president of the Brooklyn Trust Company, the bank that saved the franchise from bankruptcy during the Great Depression. McLaughlin was the trustee for the majority owners, and while he didn't sit on the club's board of directors, any important baseball decision would have to be approved by him. Rickey, careful to emphasize the on-field benefits of integration, downplayed his personal moral convictions. "The greatest untapped reservoir of raw material in the history of the game is the black race," he confided privately to McLaughlin. "The Negroes will make us winners for years to come, and for that I will happily bear being called a bleeding heart and a do-gooder and all that humanitarian rot." Although the banker gave his permission for Rickey to scout the Negro Leagues for qualified players, he cautioned him "not to try to solve any great sociological problem."[12] Accordingly in early 1943 the board of directors agreed to the search for a Negro Leaguer to break the color line and pledged themselves to secrecy.[13]

In the 1930s and early 1940s the Negro Leagues boasted some of the most exceptional talent in all of baseball. The Negro National and Negro American Leagues featured such outstanding players as Satchel Paige (Kansas City Monarchs), Josh Gibson (Homestead Grays), Ray Dandridge (Newark Eagles), Monte Irvin (Newark Eagles), Cool Papa Bell (Pittsburgh Crawfords), Judy Johnson (Hilldale), Biz Mackey (Baltimore Elite Giants), Luke Easter (Homestead Grays), Sam Jethroe (Cleveland Buckeyes), Buck Leonard (Homestead Grays), Martin Dihigo (New York Cubans), and Gene Benson (Philadelphia Stars). While these ballplayers never gained the fame of their white counterparts, they were every bit as talented. In fact white Major League stars played against Negro Leaguers more than four hundred times in the off-season and came to respect their abilities.[14]

Other owners had flirted with the idea of integration much earlier than Rickey, being attracted by both the talent of Negro Leaguers and the potential for significant financial profits. Clark Griffith, owner of the Washington Senators, reputedly considered signing Paige for $75,000 a year as early as 1938 but was discouraged by prominent Washingtonians. Four years later, in 1942, Griffith contacted Bell and Gibson and asked if they'd be interested in playing for the Senators, but nothing came of it.[15] That same year William Benswanger, the president of the Pittsburgh Pirates, invited Roy Campanella and Sammy Hughes of the Baltimore Elite Giants and Dave Barnhill, a pitcher for the New York Cubans, to a tryout, but he also reneged.[16]

Perhaps the closest attempt at integration came in 1943, when Bill Veeck tried to purchase the cellar-dwelling Phillies and stock them with Negro League stars. "With Satchel Paige, Roy Campanella, Luke Easter, Monte Irvin and countless others available, I had not the slightest doubt that the Phillies would have leaped from seventh place to the pennant," wrote Veeck in a 1962 autobiography. But Commissioner Kenesaw Mountain Landis and National League president Ford C. Frick scuttled the plan by arranging for another suitor to purchase the Phils at half the price Veeck was offering. Frick later boasted that he had "stopped Veeck from contaminating the league."[17]

Rickey followed these earlier efforts with great interest. Though each one was aborted, they seemed to indicate that the tide was turning against the "gentleman's agreement." Accordingly Rickey directed his chief scouts— Clyde Sukeforth, George Sisler, Wid Matthews, and Tom Greenwade—to search the Negro Leagues for the "best candidate" for his team.[18] In terms of talent there were two obvious choices.

Satchel Paige was unquestionably the premier pitcher and biggest draw in the Negro Leagues. A tall, lanky right-hander, Paige first achieved fame with the Pittsburgh Crawfords in the 1930s. He had an overpowering fastball that made hitters buckle at the knees. "Satchel might not have won every game he pitched, but he probably won more than any other pitcher in baseball," said Gene Benson of the Philadelphia Stars. "Satch was also exciting to watch for both black and white fans because he was such a showman. There'd be times he'd call in his outfield and then strike out the side. That kind of clowning was good for baseball. I don't think anybody,

5. Satchel Paige was the most entertaining player in the Negro Leagues and widely considered the best pitcher in the game. But his lack of a formal education and outspokenness prevented him from becoming Rickey's choice to break the color line. (National Baseball Hall of Fame Library, Cooperstown, New York)

maybe with the exception of Babe Ruth, dominated the game the way he did."[19] Stanley "Doc" Glenn, who caught Paige when he pitched briefly for the Stars, claimed that "as hard as he threw, his ball was like a feather, real light." "The greatest thing about him, though, was that he could locate his pitches," Glenn added. "You just put the glove up there where you wanted it and you didn't have to worry about him hitting the target."[20] By 1939, though, when he joined the Kansas City Monarchs, Paige's fastball had lost some of his bite. To compensate he developed several off-speed pitches and hesitation deliveries that baffled hitters.

For all of Paige's talent, however, Rickey did not consider him a suitable candidate to break the color barrier. The colorful pitcher was too outspoken, too self-absorbed, and his morals too loose for Rickey. Viewing himself as the centerpiece of black baseball, Paige cared more about himself than his teammates, routinely jumping from club to club. Nor did Rickey appreciate the image the star hurler projected. A consummate showman, Satchel gave the impression of a "Stepin Fetchit"—a happy-go-lucky character—playing to the fans as he ambled onto the diamond. Paige was also earning $37,000 a year with the Kansas City Monarchs, which made him too expensive for Rickey. Finally, Paige was thirty-nine in 1945 and clearly on the downside of his pitching career.[21]

The other outstanding Negro Leaguer was Josh Gibson, baseball's premier black slugger, who reportedly hit more than eight hundred home runs in a sixteen-year career. Gibson began his professional career at sixteen with the Homestead Grays in 1930. He jumped to the Pittsburgh Crawfords two years later and captured the first of nine home run titles. Some of his blasts are variously estimated at between 575 and 700 feet, including one he purportedly hit out of Yankee Stadium.[22] Gibson's fluid, compact swing also allowed him to hit for average as he compiled a .384 lifetime mark, the highest in Negro League history. An outstanding catcher, the black slugger had a strong arm and was a good handler of pitchers. Like Paige, however, Gibson was too unsophisticated for Rickey. His education was spotty and consisted primarily of vocational training. At six feet two and 230 pounds, Gibson, a fun-loving soul, gave to some observers the appearance of an ignorant man-child. Often the target of bench jockeys, he had a quick-temper, didn't take pressure well, and was known to explode at hecklers, something he would have to deal with as

6. Josh Gibson, a catcher for the Pittsburgh Crawfords, was the premier slugger of the Negro Leagues. Rickey ruled him out as a candidate to break the color barrier because of his lack of sophistication and struggle with alcohol. (National Baseball Hall of Fame Library, Cooperstown, New York)

the first African American in the Majors. Gibson also struggled with alcohol, sometimes going on extended benders. By the mid-1940s the thirty-three-year-old catcher was also grappling with his health. Suffering from recurring headaches and dizzy spells, he was hospitalized for ten days in January 1943 after doctors discovered a brain tumor. He refused to allow an operation and instead returned to baseball, while the headaches and blackouts continued.[23] None of these problems escaped the scrutiny of Rickey's scouts, who were instructed to keep careful records of the playing performances and personal lives of every candidate being considered.

To be sure, Paige and Gibson were extraordinarily talented athletes who easily met Rickey's criterion of playing ability. But their personal lives and examples did not meet the standard he envisioned for the first African American to integrate the game. For Rickey, that individual had to be taken seriously by the white baseball establishment as well as by the fans. It was imperative that the individual he chose had a strong moral character, the determination to succeed under extremely difficult circumstances, and a sense of loyalty to the American way of life. To that end, Rickey gave priority to those Negro Leaguers who had served their country during World War II. If anything, a black military veteran would at least be given the benefit of the doubt by whites because of his service to the country. In this respect, Rickey found common cause with a budding civil rights movement.

Civil rights leaders had already begun to focus on the military contributions made by blacks in order to secure greater respect in the armed forces and better employment opportunities at home. Nearly one million African Americans served in the military during World War II. Initially U.S. military leadership struggled to keep them out of combat, but NAACP president Walter White and A. Philip Randolph, president of the Brotherhood of Sleeping Car Porters and Maids, pressured President Franklin D. Roosevelt not only to ensure the enlistment of blacks but also to create African American fighting units.[24] Randolph believed that the war could also create an opportunity to achieve equality in the labor force, but only if blacks demanded it. Accordingly in 1941 the labor leader called on African Americans to march on Washington to demand an end to job discrimination. Not wanting to risk the embarrassment of such a spectacle, Roosevelt, using the leverage of federal defense contracts, acceded to their wishes. The organizers agreed to cancel the march in return for a presidential directive, Executive Order 8802, that established the Fair Employment Practices Committee to assure fairness in hiring. As the war years unfolded, the FEPC put pressure on the U.S. Employment Service to give preference in job referrals to employers who did not discriminate against minority groups and cited those industries that violated the president's order. As a result, an increasing number of blacks found jobs in government service and in defense industries.[25]

Despite their contributions to the war effort, black veterans and defense workers continued to face racial discrimination at home. Segregation was still the most distinguishing characteristic of race relations in the American South, where a rigid system of state and local ordinances enforced strict separation of the races in schools, restaurants, movie theaters, and even restrooms. Jim Crow laws relegated blacks to inferior public schools, health care, and public lodging, as well as discriminatory voter registration procedures that kept many of them disenfranchised. Veterans, having fought for their country, were no longer willing to buckle under to Jim Crow. They represented a young generation of blacks who expected justice and were determined to secure full political and social equality.[26]

Prior to 1945 their demands would have fallen on deaf ears among the white baseball establishment. Commissioner Landis was a staunch defender of the "gentleman's agreement." This unwritten rule had barred minorities from the game ever since 1896, when segregation was established by the Supreme Court ruling *Plessy v. Ferguson*.[27] Racist attitudes were reinforced by the significant numbers of white southerners who played in the Majors, as well as by the extensive Minor League system that existed in the South. But when Landis died on November 25, 1944, his successor proved to be more receptive to the idea of integration. Albert "Happy" Chandler, former U.S. senator from Kentucky, might have hailed from a segregationist state, but he had a strong sense of social justice. Shortly after Landis's death, Wendell Smith and Rick Roberts, black journalists from the *Pittsburgh Courier*, came calling to find out where the new commissioner stood. "I am for the Four Freedoms," he told them. "If a black boy can make it at Okinawa and go to Guadalcanal, he can make it in baseball."[28]

These circumstances created a perfect storm for Rickey, who, in the spring of 1945, accelerated his search to find a Negro League star who was also a military veteran. Initially his efforts focused on Monte Irvin, an outfielder for the Newark Eagles. Irvin was widely acknowledged as the best hitter in the Negro Leagues in 1940 and 1941. "Most of the black ballplayers thought Monte should have been the first black in the major leagues," said Cool Papa Bell, a star with several Negro League teams and still considered the fastest man in baseball history. "Monte was our best young ballplayer at the time. He could hit that long ball, he had a great arm, he could field, he could run. He could do everything."[29] Irvin possessed many of the attributes Rickey sought. He was one of the finest all-around athletes to hail from New Jersey, winning All-State honors in four sports in high school. After graduation he attended Lincoln University while playing in the Negro Leagues under the name "Jimmy Nelson" to protect his amateur status. An intelligent, articulate gentleman, Irvin had a calm demeanor that allowed him to endure the racial abuse he experienced as a player without letting it affect his self-esteem. What's more, he had served in the armed forces during World War II, earning the admiration of both white and black ballplayers.[30] Indeed Monte Irvin appeared to be the ideal candidate to break the color line. But he had just gotten out of the army and felt that he wasn't in the best playing shape:

> When Mr. Rickey was scouting the Negro Leagues, I was one of the leading candidates. In fact, Mrs. [Effa] Manley [owner of the Newark Eagles] once told me that I was supposed to be the guy to break the color barrier. She said that I had been selected by her and the other Negro League owners for that role. If it hadn't been for World War II, I might have been the one to break the color line, too.
>
> Before the war, I was playing my best baseball. I had a good arm. I could hit, and was doing some great fielding, too. Mr. Rickey contacted me after I got out of the service in 1945. But I was never told that I was being asked to break the color line. I was given the impression that Mr. Rickey was going to start another Negro League team in Brooklyn called the "Brown Dodgers." He told me that the team would include myself, Jackie Robinson, and Roy Campanella. But I wasn't in playing shape. I had three years of athletic rust and a bad case of war nerves. I needed to get back to my prewar playing condition. So I told him I wasn't ready and I'd let him know.[31]

At the same time, Rickey had developed a keen interest in Roy Campanella, the catcher for the Baltimore Elite Giants. Although Campanella was not a military veteran, he did meet Rickey's standards of playing talent and determination.[32] Unbeknown to the black catcher, Rickey had

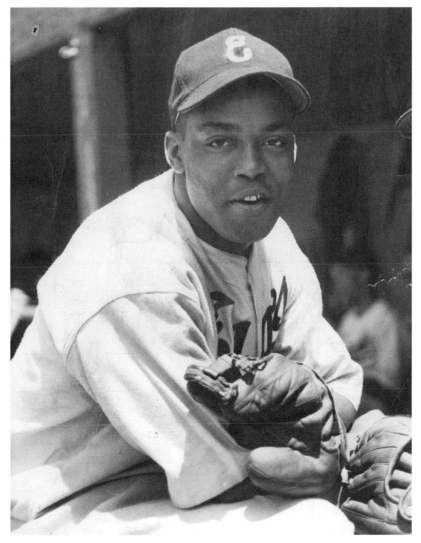

7. Monte Irvin, a star infielder with the Newark Giants, was the ideal candidate to integrate baseball. An army veteran who attended Lincoln University, the soft-spoken Negro
Leaguer refused the opportunity, telling Rickey that his playing skills had diminished
during his time in the military. (National Baseball Hall of Fame Library, Cooperstown,
New York)

hired Oscar Charleston, a former star and manager in the black leagues, to scout prospective candidates because he was able to slip in and out of Negro League dugouts and hotels without arousing suspicion. Rickey ordered Charleston to keep careful notes on the strengths and weaknesses, both personal and professional, of Campanella. When he finally met with the Brooklyn president in October 1945, Roy was surprised to learn that Rickey "had a book of notes on me three inches thick." "I didn't even realize that the Dodgers had been watching me," he added. Like Irvin, Campanella was told that he was being considered for the Brooklyn Brown Dodgers, another black club. He dismissed the inquiry outright because he was already making more money playing ball in Latin America.[33]

Ultimately Rickey decided that Campanella wasn't the best candidate to break the color line. He was concerned about Campy's ability to develop a working relationship with white pitchers and that the demands of catching would only serve to increase the already considerable pressures the first black ballplayer would face.[34] In addition Rickey had concerns about Campanella's personal background. He was a high school dropout who had a reputation for womanizing, which was not the image Rickey wanted to project for the first black ballplayer in professional baseball.[35] What's more, Campanella was of mixed ancestry, the son of an Italian father and an African American mother. According to Arnold Rampersad, a black scholar, Campy didn't match Rickey's idea of "what the first Negro player should look like—and what he thought black Americans would want the first to look like."[36] As a result, Rickey continued his search until he discovered Jackie Robinson of the Kansas City Monarchs.

Robinson was an intelligent, articulate young man who starred in four sports at UCLA and served as a second lieutenant in the army during World War II. He was proud of his African American heritage and his jet-black complexion, something he was quick to defend when confronted by the ugly specter of racial discrimination. Indeed Jackie Robinson possessed all the qualities Rickey was looking for. He was brought to Rickey's attention in the spring of 1945 by Wendell Smith of the *Pittsburgh Courier*.

Smith, the sports editor for the largest black newspaper in circulation, was at the forefront of the black press's campaign to integrate Major League Baseball as the key to creating equal opportunities in other sectors of American life.[37] Smith had been promoting Robinson along with two other talented Negro Leaguers, Marvin Williams of the Philadelphia Stars and Sam Jethroe of the Cleveland Buckeyes. Smith's influence as a journalist allowed all three players to secure big league tryouts. He had already wrangled tryouts from the Boston Red Sox that April, but despite the impressive performance of all three players Manager Joe Cronin passed on the opportunity to sign a single one.[38] Williams later revealed that the tryout was "more of a publicity stunt to promote Robinson" and that he, realizing the importance of integration, had "cooperated fully in the effort." Before the trio traveled to Boston, Smith informed them that he was "going to give Jackie more publicity because he had a degree from UCLA and he was a second lieutenant in the army." "If Jackie can fight alongside white soldiers," said Smith," he certainly should be able to play with them."[39]

At the April 16 tryout Robinson, Williams, and Jethroe joined a dozen white prospects at Boston's Fenway Park. After shagging flies in the outfield and taking infield, they were called in to bat and immediately demonstrated their ability to hit at the big league level. "We hit that Green Monster real hard—all of us," recalled Williams, referring to Fenway's legendary left-field wall. "We tried to tear it down. Jackie said, 'If we can't go over it, let's just knock it down.'"[40] Robinson confirmed the impressive performance. "In my view, nobody put on an exhibition like we did," he wrote in his 1972 autobiography. "Everything we did, it looked like the Lord was guiding us. Every ball the pitcher threw up became a line drive someplace. We tattooed that left field wall, that is, Marv and I did—and Jethroe was doing extremely well from the left side, too."[41]

The three players were not naïve, though. "Not for one minute," Robinson later admitted, "did we believe that the tryout was sincere." While Cronin and Coach Hugh Duffy praised their performances and had them fill out applications, the players were "certain that they wouldn't call us."[42] According to Williams, President Roosevelt's "unexpected death and the national mourning that followed resulted in the cancellation of another tryout with the Boston Braves." Soon afterward, Smith "launched a big publicity campaign to get Jackie into the majors."[43]

It isn't clear if Smith asked Rickey for a tryout or if he simply requested that a scout be assigned to look at Robinson. What is certain is that until Smith approached him, Rickey had not entertained Robinson as a serious candidate to break the color line. What's more, Rickey did not initially trust Smith. He believed that the black sports editor was allied with the American Communist press, which also promoted baseball's integration as part of a much larger campaign to end segregation in all phases of American life and to attract support from the working class and African Americans.[44] The Dodgers' president, who considered himself a "patriotic American," had good reason to be concerned.

During the 1940s there was a growing partnership between the civil rights movement and the American Communist Party, focusing on the issue of black trade unionism. Approximately 1.5 million blacks migrated from the South to northern cities, where they found better jobs. Related to this development was the significant increase in black membership in labor unions, a trend inspired by such New Deal institutions as the National Labor Relations Board and the Fair Employment Practices Commission as well as the inclusion of blacks in the Congress of Industrial Organization (CIO). Some of the labor leaders were Communist sympathizers, if not active members in the Party. They recruited working-class blacks by emphasizing the common goals of economic justice and racial equality, and CIO unions often worked with such civil rights organizations as the National Negro Congress and local branches of the NAACP in order to advance these goals. In New York, for example, labor unions with large black memberships addressed housing discrimination, police brutality, and racial discrimination in hiring practices.[45]

Labor civil rights were embraced by several left-oriented black leaders, including labor leader A. Philip Randolph; Paul Robeson, a former All-American football player who turned to opera singing and acting; and Benjamin J. Davis, a Harvard Law School graduate who sat on the New York City Council. These leaders viewed the integration of baseball as a major test case of civil rights in the labor sector and actively pursued that goal in the early to mid-1940s.[46] Davis, a member of the American Communist Party, was especially active on the issue. In 1945 he sought reelection to the New York City Council by making the integration of baseball the central theme of his campaign. Introducing a resolution to integrate the city's three Major League teams, Davis secured the Council's unanimous endorsement and sent copies of the resolution to the owners of the Yankees, Dodgers, and Giants.[47] Mayor Fiorello LaGuardia followed up the resolution by appointing a committee to investigate the reasons for the absence of black players on the teams. Among those to serve on the committee were Davis, Branch Rickey, and Larry MacPhail, president of the New York Yankees, who constantly ran interference for the owners. When committee members contended that "there is racial prejudice in the majors" and that professional baseball "should assume the development of black players" rather than "leaving the responsibility to the Negro Leagues," MacPhail countered that Negro Leaguers were "under contract" and that "the owners were unwilling to disregard those contracts" because it would result in "costly court action." Committee Chairman John H. Johnson disagreed, stating that Negro League contracts were "loose" and that many of the players "jumped their contracts in mid-season and no action was taken."

Changing course, MacPhail argued that "many who are familiar with Negro baseball feel that the teams meet a need among the local Negro community that would not be met even if their players were integrated into the white leagues." Other committee members rejected the Yankee president's premise, accusing him of "placing the onus of present Jim Crow practices on the Negroes themselves." "Organized Negro baseball would not have been necessary had Negroes been integrated into the system in the first place," they argued. "Thus, the Negro leagues, which arose from an evil, would become the reason for their perpetuation. Most people admit that the Negro leagues, under present arrangements, can never produce players qualified for big league competition. The leagues are powerless to bring themselves into Organized Baseball and no one from within the profession has seen fit to organize them into leagues capable of participating in such competition."[48]

Rickey, fed up with MacPhail's rhetoric, resigned from the committee. The episode also reinforced his distrust of politicians and journalists who were exploiting the integration issue to advance their careers, especially those who were Communist. Rickey actively avoided any association with left-oriented writers like Lester Rodney of the *New York Daily Worker* and Joe Bostic of Harlem's *Peoples' Voice*, who tended to filter integration through a radical lens that championed equality for all social and economic classes. Rodney in particular was more interested in social justice than baseball and sought to further labor civil rights by attacking segregation in the game on political grounds. Beginning in 1939 he organized petitions of New York baseball fans to end segregation and routinely sent those petitions to Commissioner Landis, National League president Ford Frick, and American League president Will Harridge.[49] He also promoted Negro League stars to Major League owners and cultivated a working relationship with the black press.[50] To that end, the *Daily Worker* often followed up on stories in the black newspapers that supported desegregation in baseball and sometimes reprinted, in their entirety, stories written by Smith in the *Pittsburgh Courier*.[51] Such activities served as proof, in Rickey's mind, of an alliance between the black and Communist presses.

Rickey didn't care for Bostic either. On April 6, 1945, the Dodgers' president became infuriated with the Communist writer when Bostic approached him at the club's Bear Mountain, New York, training camp to request a tryout for Terris McDuffie, a pitcher for the Newark Eagles, and Dave "Showboat" Thomas, a first baseman with the New York Cubans. Later Rickey publicly attacked the Communist press as well as the Negro Leagues, which he accused of being "dominated by gamblers" and rife with "shoddy business practices." Instead the Dodgers' president praised the recently established all-black United States League, founded that January by Gus Greenlee, former president of the Negro National League. Rickey also announced that he would establish his own team, the Brooklyn Brown Dodgers, to play in the new league.[52] While he was severely criticized by Negro League owners for his remarks, Rickey's assertion that he intended to create his own black team may have been a ruse to detract from his own covert activities in scouting their teams for a player to break the color barrier.

To be sure, Rickey purposely distanced himself from any organization or individual who he felt threatened his plan to integrate the Dodgers. Most likely he questioned Wendell Smith's motives until he was convinced that the sportswriter was genuinely committed to his cause and, just as important, "wanted to be completely divorced from any communist influence."[53] Only then did Rickey act on Smith's suggestion to scout Jackie Robinson and assigned two of his assistants, Wid Matthews and George Sisler, to the task.

Once they established mutual trust, Rickey and Smith were in constant contact throughout the 1945 season. Smith later admitted that he was "tempted to write about the Dodgers' interest in Robinson," but Rickey had "sworn him to secrecy." Besides, Robinson did not always present himself as the best candidate. Angered by the poor conditions and pay in the Negro Leagues, he threatened to quit the Monarchs on two occasions that summer. Worse, Robinson threatened to punch an umpire who he believed was baiting him. At one point Rickey expressed his concern to Smith over whether "Jackie was a belligerent type of individual." While the journalist didn't want to admit that Jackie was "tough to get along with," he did concede that the shortstop "had a sizeable temper when he was aroused." "But to survive in the Negro leagues," Smith added, "he couldn't be a Mickey Mouse."[54] Whatever personality problems may have existed, Robinson's exceptional athletic ability overshadowed Rickey's concerns about them. When favorable reports came back from Matthews and Sisler, the Dodgers' president followed up with Clyde Sukeforth, his chief scout.

Sukeforth, a native New Englander, had been a catcher for the Cincinnati Reds in his playing days. Like many backstops who went on to become managers and coaches, he had an encyclopedic knowledge of the game and a keen eye for Major League potential. Predictably he enjoyed Rickey's utmost trust and respect. In late August he was sent to Chicago to scout Robinson, who was there for a game against the Negro League's American Giants. "Mr. Rickey told me, 'I want you to pay particular attention to a shortstop named Robinson,'" Sukeforth recalled in a 1997 *New York Times interview*. "He told me: 'I want you to identify yourself and tell him I sent you. If you like this fellow's arm, bring him in.' Mr. Rickey didn't tell me what he wanted Jack for, but I thought I knew."[55]

When Robinson came out of the dugout to take the infield, Sukeforth called him over and introduced himself.

"Why is Mr. Rickey interested in me?" asked Robinson.

"I have no authority to answer that question," replied Sukeforth, deflecting the inquiry. "I just work for him. But I can assure you that there's a lot of interest in you in Brooklyn."

After Robinson informed the Dodgers' scout that a sore throwing arm prevented him from playing that night, Sukeforth asked that they meet at the team's hotel after the game. At that meeting, the two men "talked for about an hour and a half." "The more I talked with him, the more I was impressed with his determination, intelligence and aggressiveness," recalled Sukeforth. "I asked him to meet me in Toledo where I had to see a double header the next day."[56] Robinson agreed and, after the double-header, the two men traveled by train back to New York.

By the time the legendary meeting between Branch Rickey and Jackie Robinson took place, Rickey had maneuvered himself into a position of control within the Dodgers' organization. Just two weeks earlier, on August 13, 1945, he and his associates purchased 50 percent of the franchise, and Rickey, who was already team president, began acting as general manager as well.[57] He now had the administrative and financial authority to integrate the club, and he was prepared to partner with Robinson in order to realize that longtime ambition.

On Monday morning, August 28, 1945, Sukeforth accompanied Robinson to the Dodgers' executive offices at 215 Montague Street in Brooklyn, where he introduced him to Branch Rickey.[58] Like Irvin and Campanella, Robinson was under the impression that he was being considered for another Negro League team, but Rickey quickly dismissed that notion.[59] Greeting the shortstop with a vigorous handshake, he confessed that he was interested in him "as a candidate for the Brooklyn Dodgers." "Jack, all my life I've been looking for a great Negro ballplayer and I have reason to believe you might be that man," confessed the stocky, beetle-browed executive.[60]

Robinson was speechless. He was cynical toward all baseball club owners, especially white ones. It was a natural defense to protect him from any personal disillusionment.

"Have you got a girl?" Rickey asked, wanting to make sure that Robinson had the personal support necessary to succeed in such a risky venture.

"Yes," replied the Negro Leaguer, referring to Rachel Isum, whom he'd met when they were students at UCLA. "She's a nurse and we're engaged to be married."

Satisfied with the response, Rickey continued his examination. "So, what about it? You think you can play for Montreal?" he asked, referring to the Dodgers' top farm club.[61]

Awestruck, Robinson managed to say yes. He realized that if he made good at Montreal, he had an excellent chance to make the Major Leagues. "I just want to be treated fairly," he added.

"You will *not* be treated fairly!" Rickey snapped. "'Nigger' will be a compliment!"

For the next three hours, Rickey interrogated the star shortstop. With great dramatic flair, he role-played every conceivable scenario that would confront the first black player to break baseball's color barrier: first he was a bigoted sportswriter who wrote lies about Robinson's performance; next he was a southern hotel manager refusing room and board, then a racist Major Leaguer looking for a fight, and after that a waiter throwing Robinson out of a whites-only diner. In every scenario Rickey cursed Robinson and threatened him, verbally degrading him in every way imaginable.[62] The executive's performance was so convincing that Robinson later said, "I found myself chain-gripping my fingers behind my back." When he was through, Rickey told Robinson that he knew he was a "fine ballplayer." "But what I need," he added, "is more than a great player. I need a man who will take abuse and insults for his race. And what I don't know is whether you have the guts!"

Robinson struggled to keep his temper. Insulted by the implication that he was a coward, he could "feel the heat coming up into [his] cheeks." "Mr. Rickey," he retorted, "do you want a Negro who's afraid to fight back?"

"No!" Rickey barked. "I want a ballplayer with guts enough *not* to fight back. We can't *fight* our way through this. There's virtually nobody on our side. No owners, no umpires, virtually no newspapermen. And I'm afraid that many fans will be hostile too. They'll taunt you and goad you. They'll do anything to make you react. They'll try to provoke a race riot in the ball park."[63]

As he listened, Robinson became transfixed by the Dodgers' president. He felt his sincerity, his deep, quiet strength, and his sense of moral justice. "We can only win," concluded Rickey, "if we can convince the world that I'm doing this because you're a great ballplayer and a fine gentleman. You will symbolize a crucial cause. One incident, just one incident, can set it back twenty years."

To reinforce his point, Rickey produced an English translation of Giovanni Papini's *Life of Christ*. Flipping through the pages, he landed on a quote from Jesus, who admonished his followers, "Whosoever shall smite thee on thy right cheek, turn to him the other also." Rickey, who collected a thick file of information on the Monarch shortstop, knew he

8. On August 28, 1945, Jackie Robinson and Branch Rickey agreed to a noble experiment: breaking baseball's color barrier. (National Baseball Hall of Fame Library, Cooperstown, New York)

too was a devout Methodist. Now he was adding religion to his performance to convince Robinson of the necessity of breaking the color barrier without resorting to physical violence.

Robinson was a proud man who had actively fought back in the face of racial discrimination. "Could I turn the other cheek?" he asked himself as he listened to Rickey's speech. "I didn't know how I would do it. Yet I knew I must. I had to do it for many reasons . . . for black youth, for my mother, for Rae [his fiancée] and for myself. I had even begun to feel as if I had to do it for Branch Rickey."

"Mr. Rickey," he finally said, "I think I can play ball in Montreal. I think I can play ball in Brooklyn. If you want to take this gamble, I will promise you there will be no incident."

The agreement was sealed by a handshake. Until Rickey gave the word, Robinson would have to keep the arrangement secret.[64]

Over the years the Rickey-Robinson meeting has taken on a mythology of its own. Since all the principal actors at the meeting are deceased there is no way of confirming the details. Questions remain over what exactly transpired and whether there was more than one meeting before they reached an agreement.[65] Some believe that Rickey couldn't have been as intrusive as the legend maintains. Was it necessary, for example, to ask whether or not Robinson had "a girl"? At least one sportswriter, Sam Lacey of the *Baltimore Afro-American*, believes that Robinson's marital status was important for Rickey to ascertain and probably did inquire about it. "The fact that he was engaged to be married meant that Jackie wouldn't go after white women," said Lacey. "Rickey needed to be sure about that because it could destroy the entire enterprise."[66]

Similarly Monte Irvin wonders how necessary it was for Rickey to repeatedly provoke Robinson with name-calling and racial epithets. "He had one hell of a lot of nerve to do that," said Irvin in a recent interview. "It wasn't necessary to call Jackie a nigger to provoke him. Jackie had been called a nigger before. I'm sure he understood that he couldn't fight back even though it went against human nature to restrain yourself when attacked like that. He knew if he did, he'd be setting the process of integration back for some time."[67] But Branch Rickey III believes that it was necessary for his grandfather to provoke Robinson in order to ascertain "his capacity for confrontation." "It wasn't just the vocabulary he used, either," added Rickey. "My grandfather provoked him with the look of an eye, by the tightening of muscles in his face. Jackie's response to those confrontational scenarios allowed him to understand how successful the experiment would be."[68]

In addition there is a common belief among Negro Leaguers in particular that Rickey was motivated primarily by financial considerations, believing that breaking the color barrier would result in opening a new pool of talent to the Majors that would attract both black and white fans by the tens of thousands. In other words, integration was a matter of "dollars and cents."[69] Although Robinson himself does not discount the financial motive, he insists that there was "more than just making money at stake." According to Robinson, Rickey was taking "a big gamble." His health was "undermined by the pressures placed upon him by peers and fellow baseball owners" who wanted him "to change his mind," as well as by the press, who "condemned him as a fool and a demagogue." Some told Robinson that those "pressures" were simply a part of the price Rickey had to pay if he wanted to be successful at the gate and that the Dodgers' president was exploiting him for financial gain. But near the end of his life Robinson flatly rejected the notion, stating that Rickey was like "the father I had lost as a child" and that he had nothing but "admiration and respect for him."[70]

Like Robinson, Branch Rickey III insists that the financial considerations were secondary to his grandfather's fierce desire to do what was "morally right":

There was an invisible thread that ran through my grandfather's entire life. You need to understand that that thread started in 1904 with the Charley Thomas incident and continued through his tenure with the Dodgers. If you put yourself in my grandfather's shoes, what did he have to gain? He was going up against the owners of all the other teams, who were adamantly opposed to integration.

Why would a man in his sixties risk his reputation on a twenty-five-year-old black man who'd nearly been court-martialed by the U.S. Army for refusing to back down? Why would he risk his own reputation for some vague financial advantage that might come from attracting more black fans? What was it about my grandfather that Jackie trusted enough to turn the other cheek if not for that invisible thread that went back to 1904?[71]

To be sure, that "invisible thread" went back further than even his grandson acknowledges. It can be traced to Rickey's Methodist upbringing and the fierce resolve he possessed for doing what was morally right. That moral necessity not only inspired the Dodgers' president's quest to integrate baseball but convinced him to choose Jackie Robinson for the difficult task. Together Rickey and Robinson would improve the Brooklyn Dodgers' fortunes at the gate and on the playing field. In the process they would also correct a long-standing social injustice that plagued the national pastime.

3

Jackie and Campy

Jackie Robinson was assuming the burden of responsibility for the hopes and dreams of black America. He might have been an athlete by profession, but he would quickly become the most recognizable civil rights leader in the nation, a pioneer for social justice in an industry that had discriminated against blacks for nearly three-quarters of a century. His success or failure would have the most profound implications in the black struggle for full U.S. citizenship. But he was not alone.

Roy Campanella became Robinson's partner in the quest to integrate baseball, though he would not gain the same recognition for his efforts. While the two men did not know each other personally, they were well acquainted with the other's talent, having played against each other in the Negro League's East-West All-Star Game in 1945. Their relationship began in late October, when the two men crossed paths at Harlem's Woodside Hotel as they prepared to travel to Venezuela to barnstorm on the same Negro League All-Star squad. Engaging in a friendly game of gin rummy, the men began to shoot the breeze, and eventually the subject turned to Branch Rickey. Only then did Campanella learn that Jackie had signed with Montreal, the Dodgers' top farm club.

When Robinson confided that he was "going to be the first Negro in organized ball," Campy was flabbergasted. He had met with Rickey himself just a week before and was led to believe that the Dodgers' president wanted him for a Negro League team he was starting. "I'm really happy for you," he told Jackie. "I know you'll make it and I wish you all the luck in the world." Privately, Campy "could have given [himself] a good, swift kick." "Here, Mr. Rickey might have been trying to sign me for the big leagues," he later admitted, "and I thought he just wanted me for another colored team." He worried that his lack of enthusiasm during the interview might have cost him the very same chance that Jackie had been given. Before parting ways, Robinson swore the black catcher to secrecy.[1]

It's unclear whether Rickey seriously considered choosing Campanella over Robinson. Both Negro Leaguers possessed certain attributes as well as liabilities in terms of playing experience, temperament, and background. In fact no two men could have been more different. Jackie Robinson was defined by a fire that burned deep inside of him. It burned white-hot in the heat of athletic competition, where winning was the sole motivation that drove him. But racial discrimination fueled the flames of that deep-seated fire. Like W. E. B. Du Bois, Jackie believed that equality for the black man could only be achieved by challenging directly the segregated society in which he lived. Unless blacks actively pursued social, political, and economic equality, they would never be accorded the respect that comes with full citizenship. For Robinson, no less than for Du Bois, racial discrimination was emasculating. It attacked his manhood by demeaning his intelligence and fundamental worth as a human being. In the past Jackie had protested, sometimes subtly, sometimes with verbal or physical violence. He was not one to turn the other cheek.

Unlike Robinson, Campanella let racial abuse roll off his back. He refused to dignify racism by allowing it to affect him personally or professionally. Instead he dismissed the name-calling, racial epithets, and overly aggressive play as simply "part of a game where tension is sometimes at fever pitch."[2] Like Booker T. Washington, Campanella believed that protesting against discrimination was a futile exercise. Self-reliance was the key to securing social and economic advancement in baseball or any other walk of life. He also realized that upward mobility depended on winning the support of the white baseball establishment by working hard and leading a clean moral life. Campanella was no different from an earlier generation of blacks who supported Washington's accommodationist philosophy and conducted themselves accordingly.

If Jackie was defined by the fire that burned inside him whenever he was confronted with social injustice, Campy's most distinguishing trait was his coolness under the very same pressure. He was the original "ice man" who could survey a potentially volatile situation and defuse it with a quip and a smile. There was a softness to his personality that allowed him to cushion himself from the blows of racism without appearing cowardly. In fact he could take a racial slight and turn it to his advantage by revealing the offender for the bigot he was. That kind of poise made Campanella a leader by example, something that carried over to the baseball diamond. To be sure, both men were products of the environment in which they were raised. That simple fact would influence their approach to baseball as well as to civil rights.

Robinson learned at an early age that the world was not a very kind or forgiving place. Growing up in poverty, he came to realize that he would have to compete for anything he hoped to achieve and to fight back when provoked. These were matters of self-respect. But his early life had also taught him perseverance and discipline, virtues that tempered a natural instinct for retribution when provoked.

Born on January 31, 1919, in Cairo, Georgia, Jack Roosevelt Robinson was the grandson of a slave and the fifth child of a sharecropper. His father, Jerry Robinson, worked on a plantation for $12 a month. Just six months after Jackie was born, Jerry deserted his wife, Mallie, and their five children. Relocating her family to Pasadena, California, Mallie worked as a domestic to support the household. Her salary was so meager that she begrudgingly accepted welfare and even then was barely able to make ends meet.[3] But she still managed to teach her children the importance of family unity, religion, and sympathy for others, though the last was not always easy to learn.

Raised in a predominantly white neighborhood, Jackie and his siblings were verbally ridiculed as "niggers" and frequently pelted with rocks by neighbors. White residents signed several petitions to have the family evicted from their home on Pepper Street. Instead of enduring the humiliation, the boys formed a gang and began to return the fire. Known as the Pepper Street Gang, the group was composed of poor black, Japanese, and Mexican kids who indulged in petty theft, pranks, and occasional fisticuffs with the white kids who abhorred their presence in the neighborhood. Their activities did not go unnoticed by the Pasadena Police, whose sheriff once arrested Jackie for taking a swim in the city reservoir because the local public pool prohibited blacks from swimming there.[4]

During his adolescence Jackie struggled with a fragile self-esteem, which was aggravated by the racial abuse and lack of a father to mentor him. He once admitted that he would probably have become "a full-fledged juvenile delinquent had it not been for Carl Anderson and the Reverend Karl Downs." Anderson, a neighborhood auto mechanic, and Downs, the pastor of the local Methodist church, were "interested and concerned enough to offer me the best advice they could."[5] With their encouragement Jackie distanced himself from the Pepper Street Gang and focused on sports; it saved him from more serious trouble.

At John Muir Technical High School, Robinson distinguished himself as a quarterback on the football team and a shortstop and catcher on the baseball team, though he also enjoyed remarkable success in basketball and track. One teammate, Ray Bartlett, admitted that Robinson "was a hard loser." "He liked being the best," said Bartlett. "The rest of us might shrug off a loss, but Jackie couldn't let go of it."[6] Robinson's versatility earned him an athletic scholarship to Pasadena Junior College, where he led the football team to a perfect 11-0 record and became a standout in basketball, track, and baseball as well. With a student body of just four thousand, PJC was a small college with no more than seventy black students. Jackie mostly circulated among a small group of blacks and continued to feel the sting of racism.

When some of the white football players attempted to freeze out their black teammates, Robinson threatened to transfer to a rival school. After the head coach ended the rebellion, Jackie realized the value of protesting social injustice as well as how to exploit his value as a star athlete. At the same time, he emerged as a leader among his teammates, both black and white. As quarterback he made sure to spread the scoring to include the very same players who had discriminated against him. "It was smart to share the glory," he admitted. "In the final analysis, white people were no worse than Negroes, for we are all afflicted by the same pride, jealousy, envy and ambition."[7]

Robinson continued to apply these lessons when he transferred to the University of California at Los Angeles in 1939. There he became the school's very first four-letter man, earning varsity letters in football, basketball, baseball, and track as well as All-American honors on the gridiron. What distinguished him was a genuine desire to place the welfare of the team above personal glory. He treated his white teammates with the

9. At UCLA Robinson earned varsity letters in football, basketball, baseball, and track as well as All-American honors on the gridiron. (National Baseball Hall of Fame Library, Cooperstown, New York)

same respect as those who were black. But he also grew more intolerant of racial abuse, which led to occasional clashes with the law.

On September 5, 1939, for example, Robinson confronted a white motorist who had called him a "nigger." A crowd of some forty to fifty young blacks gathered at the scene, but when a Pasadena police officer arrived

they quickly dispersed. Jackie stood his ground and was arrested. Refused the right to make a phone call, he spent the night in jail. The next morning he pleaded not guilty to charges of hindering traffic and resisting arrest, paid the $25 bond, and was set free. For this and a similar incident, Robinson was acquitted, most likely because he was a talented, well-known college athlete.

These were defining experiences for him. Not only did they strengthen already existing personality traits—competitiveness, combativeness, impatience, and irascibility—but they also resulted in the myth that during his college years he was "frequently tossed into jail on a Friday night only to be released for Saturday's game."[8] However, Arnold Rampersad, Robinson's most recent biographer, has shown that the Pasadena Police did not consider Jackie a troublemaker but understood that he wouldn't allow a racist remark to go unnoticed. "Despite Robinson's quick temper in the face of racial discrimination," contends Rampersad, "he lived, on the whole, a life of discipline, restraint and self-denial. He thought of himself and his future in terms of moral and social obligation, rather than privilege and entitlement."[9]

Convinced that "no amount of education would help a black man get a good job," Robinson left UCLA in March 1941 without completing his degree.[10] But he also left with something much more valuable, a soul mate who would help him survive the difficult demands he would face in the future. Rachel Isum, a freshman nursing student, met Robinson during his senior year. "What I liked about him was his smile and the confident air he had about him without being cocky in person," she recalled. "He also wore his color with such dignity, pride and confidence. He was never, ever, ashamed of his [black] skin color."[11] Rachel complemented Jackie. Where he was introverted and impulsive, she was more open, organized, and practical. Where Jackie's identity was already fixed, hers was still evolving. Rachel quickly became a trusted confidant.

While Rachel continued her college education, Jackie looked for ways to channel his love of sports into a job. During the next year he would play football for the semipro and racially integrated Honolulu Bears and work construction at Pearl Harbor. Drafted by the army in the spring of 1942, he was assigned to a segregated unit at Ft. Riley, Kansas. He then applied to be admitted to Officers' Candidate School but was denied admis-

sion because of his race. His application was eventually approved, however, thanks to the help of boxing legend Joe Louis, who was stationed with Jackie at Ft. Riley.

Commissioned a second lieutenant on January 28, 1943, Robinson continued to defy discriminatory practices within the military. In an interesting case of double standards, he was barred from the Ft. Riley baseball team because of his color but asked to join the football team because of his All-American college status. He declined the invitation after learning that he would not be permitted to play against the University of Missouri, which refused to take the field against an opponent with a black player. Robinson was quickly labeled a troublemaker and transferred to Camp Hood, Texas, which was notorious for its Jim Crow regulations. In July 1944, when Jackie refused to move to the rear of a military bus, he was charged with insubordination and court-martialed. But the case against him was weak—the army had recently issued orders against such segregation—and a good lawyer won his acquittal.[12] Although he received an honorable discharge in November 1944, Robinson's time in the military had left him feeling vulnerable and uncertain about the future.

Shortly after his discharge, the Kansas City Monarchs, one of the most talented Negro League teams, offered Jackie a contract for $400 a month. While with the Monarchs, Robinson established himself as a solid defensive shortstop with impressive base-stealing abilities. He completed the season with a .345 batting average in forty-two league games with ten doubles, four triples, and five home runs.[13] But he hated the lack of discipline in the Negro Leagues. As one of the very few college-educated players, he did not fit in with his teammates, who spent their free time drinking, smoking, and partying. "This behavior and the lack of rules, or the failure to enforce rules," he said, "hurts the caliber of baseball and certainly cuts down fan interest. All the time I was playing in the Negro Leagues I was looking around for something else."[14] Nor was he fond of barnstorming through the South, with its Jim Crow restaurants and hotels, and frequently let his temper get the best of him.

Once, when the Monarchs were traveling through Alabama, the team bus stopped to get some gas. Jackie asked the attendant where he could find a restroom.

10. Second Lieutenant Jackie Robinson felt the sting of racial discrimination in the military. (National Baseball Hall of Fame Library, Cooperstown, New York)

"Yours is over there," the man replied, pointing to the woods behind the station.

Incredulous, Robinson snapped, "What the hell are you talkin' about?"

Not waiting for a response, the Monarchs' shortstop marched over to the filling station's bathroom and opened the door. No sooner had he turned the door knob that a white man lunged at him, cursing and screaming. Jackie let his instincts take over and punched him in the mouth. Fearing for their lives, four teammates pulled him into the bus. The traveling secretary left the money right on the gas pump and the Monarchs took off.[15]

Some teammates thought Jackie too impatient with the discriminatory treatment of blacks. Others admired him for his determination to take a stand against racism. But at that point in his life Robinson did not see himself as a crusader for civil rights as much as an athlete who had grown disillusioned with his chosen career.[16] His self-perception changed dramatically when Rickey asked him to break the color barrier. Robinson realized that signing a professional baseball contract placed him front and center in the struggle for black civil rights and that if he failed to make the grade he could set the course of integration back a decade or more. That possibility weighed heavily on his mind. Deep down, Robinson realized that he was not the most talented Negro Leaguer and worried that he could not succeed in the white Minors.

Roy Campanella was much more confident in his abilities. With nine years of playing experience behind him, Campy was a more refined player than Robinson. He might not have had a college education or have been in military service—both of which were extremely important to Rickey— but in terms of temperament and playing ability, Campanella would have been a better choice to break the color barrier. "If I had to make the decision, Campy would have been my first choice," said Monte Irvin in a recent interview. "He'd been in the Negro Leagues for a decade by 1947 and was already a proven star. Campy was humorous, talented, and had a good mind for baseball. What's more, he grew up in an integrated situation, playing sports in grade school and high school with white teammates, and had the kind of personality that could handle any situation without letting it affect him personally. Jackie had problems doing that."[17]

Campanella's ability to adapt to racial hostility and not let it affect his psyche was learned at a very young age. Born in 1921 in Homestead, Penn-

11. Robinson played shortstop for the Kansas City Monarchs during his single season in the Negro Leagues, 1945. (Library of Congress)

sylvania, near Pittsburgh, Roy Campanella was the product of a mixed marriage and the youngest of John and Ida Campanella's four children. His father was an Italian fruit and vegetable peddler, and his mother an African American housewife. When Roy was seven, the family relocated to an ethnically diverse neighborhood in Philadelphia called Nicetown.[18] But the youngster quickly discovered that the name was misleading, much like the misnomer "City of Brotherly Love."

In the mid-1920s Philadelphia, with a population of 1.9 million, was the third largest metropolis in the nation. Approximately 7.4 percent of the residents were African American, which was fairly significant for the urban North. Concentrated in the South Street area and in parts of North and West Philadelphia—the poorest sections of the city—most African Americans were forced to compete for cheap, unskilled labor with their white, eastern European immigrant neighbors. Those who secured employment were mostly stevedores, street and sewer cleaners, trash collectors, porters, and waiters. Employed or not, Philadelphia's black population was generally the object of violent prejudice, rioting, and continuous political attack.[19]

Race relations in Nicetown, however, were not as divisive. Located in North Philadelphia, Nicetown was an ethnically diverse community of blacks, newly arrived Italian immigrants, Irish and Polish Catholics, and Russian Jews. It was a working-class neighborhood where most of the residents were employed by Midvale Steel, Tastykake Bakery, the Budd Company, and the Pennsylvania Railroad. Here poverty was the great equalizer among blacks and whites.[20] While racial prejudice existed, it was not as explosive as in the other wards where blacks lived. In Nicetown black kids teamed up with Polish, Italian, and Irish kids to play stickball in the streets and baseball at the local Hunting Park, and they "seldom had any real run-ins." The Campanellas lived in a corner row house at 1538 Kerbaugh Street, where the adults sat on their front steps on summer evenings and traded stories while they watched the youngsters play in the streets.[21] As in all of Philadelphia's row-house communities, the residents, regardless of color, wanted the same thing for their children—social and economic mobility—and the way to achieve it was with a stable home life, a high school education, and a good job.

John and Ida Campanella were no different from their neighbors. They raised their children to respect themselves and others and to work hard so that they could achieve their objectives. Sometimes those were hard lessons to learn. "One day I was coming home from grade school," recalled Roy, "and another boy called me 'half-breed,' and I hit him. I just couldn't get it out of my head, though. Was it good or bad that I had a white father and Negro mother? Was it something to be ashamed of?" When Roy finally asked his mother, she told him that his father was a devoted husband and father and a good provider for their family. "And, above all," she added, "he gives us what many folks, white or black, can't buy with all the money in the world. He gives us love, Roy. What more can anyone want?"[22] It was a compassionate explanation, but it did not address the realities of race relations in the 1920s or the sensitive issue of identity formation among children of mixed marriages.

Roy may have been considered black because of his mother's race, but by the social and legal conventions of the 1920s he was a "mulatto."[23] He would learn to use that fact to his advantage in forging amicable relations with both blacks and whites. The other major character trait that enabled Campanella to succeed in both the Negro Leagues and in the white baseball establishment was his self-reliance. That too was cultivated by his parents at an early age.

The Campanellas provided their children with a stable, loving home in order to cultivate a strong sense of independence and self-respect. Ida imbued each of her children with the lessons of her Baptist faith and carted them off to church every Sunday morning. Once, when Roy stole a catcher's mitt from the Hunting Park baseball field, she reprimanded him so severely he took it back. "That's the onliest glove I ever had," he said. "I had to borrow a mitt from the other boys when I played." John Campanella was a hard worker who expected his children to follow the example he set. Accordingly from the age of nine, Roy contributed to the family's income by shining shoes, cutting grass, and helping his older brother, Lawrence, on his milk route. He was permitted to keep a quarter a day and promptly spent the money at Shibe Park, home of the Philadelphia Athletics.[24]

Shibe was just a few blocks away from the Campanellas' house, and with bleacher seats being just 25 cents, the temptation was too great for Roy. Besides, Connie Mack's A's were among the very best teams in baseball during his childhood. Mack was in the process of building a championship dynasty in the 1920s, one that would capture three straight pennants and two World Series titles between 1929 and 1930. Mickey Cochrane, the A's catcher and one of the leading hitters on the team, was Roy's hero.[25]

Campanella's passion for baseball as well as his natural talent for the game quickly brought him to the attention of local coaches. As a result, he moved rapidly from the crude sandlots of North Philadelphia to professional Negro League baseball. At age twelve he joined the Nicetown

Giants, a sandlot team that competed in Philadelphia's Industrial League. Most of the players were two to three years older, but Campy held his own. He continued to play with the Nicetown club as a student at Gillespie Junior High School, where he gravitated to catcher.[26] When he matriculated to Simon Gratz High School in 1936, he volunteered to catch because no one else wanted to play the position. Impressed by his talent, Sam Roy, coach of Loudenslager, American Legion Post 366, persuaded Campanella to catch for his team that summer, and he became the first black ballplayer on the Legion squad.[27] Just fifteen years old, Campanella became the regular catcher of the Legion team. Playing at Shibe Park and Baker Bowl, where the Phillies played their home games, he homered into the left-field stands at both parks.[28]

Campanella played for Loudenslager again during the summer of 1937, attracting the attention of Tom Dixon, manager of the Bacharach Giants, a semiprofessional Negro League team. Based in Atlantic City, New Jersey, and named for the popular mayor of the seashore resort, the Bacharach Giants were, like most Negro League teams, dirt poor.[29] As a result, they played most of their games in the Philadelphia area, where their players resided and could stay during home stands to save money on room and board. To limit salary the Giants scouted local talent, hoping to find outstanding prospects before the higher paying and more successful Negro League teams nabbed them.[30] Campy was a perfect candidate. But Dixon first had to ask Ida Campanella's permission for her son to accompany the Giants on a weeklong trip through New Jersey, New York, and Connecticut. She agreed as long as he promised that her son would eat well, stay in a good hotel, and go to church on Sundays. "We have an honest, God-fearing bunch of boys, and we play an honest game of ball," Dixon assured her. "No cussing, no swearing, no gambling." The Giants' manager also explained that Roy would receive $35 for his services and the money would be paid directly to her.[31] Ida Campanella gave her permission.

That Saturday night the Bacharach Giants played at Beach Haven, New Jersey, and Roy caught the game. The Giants won 3–1, and though Campanella didn't get a hit, he impressed his manager by the way he called the game and threw out the only runner who tried to steal on him.[32] After a game at Mount Vernon, New York, the Bacharachs headed to Hartford, Connecticut. On the way, the team stopped in Harlem, where they stayed

12. Roy Campanella as an Elite Giant, 1942. (National Baseball Hall of Fame Library, Cooperstown, New York)

at the Woodside Hotel at 141st Street and Broadway, one of the few hotels that accommodated Negro League teams. There Dixon introduced Campanella to Biz Mackey, one of the most respected catchers and managers in black baseball. Mackey's Elite Giants were returning to Washington after a two-week road trip. Mackey, who had heard about the promising young catcher, was curious to see him play and offered him a tryout. It's uncertain when and where the tryout took place, but the next Monday, June 14, Mackey, en route to Washington, stopped off in Philadelphia and asked Roy to join his Elite Giants.

Roy had mixed feelings about accepting the offer. On one hand, he felt a sense of loyalty to Tom Dixon and the Bacharachs for giving him a shot at Negro League ball. On the other hand, he realized that Mackey was giving him the chance of a lifetime.[33] "To me, and to any Negro kid," he recalled, "the Elite Giants were like the New York Yankees. If a colored boy had dreams of making it to the big leagues, the Elite Giants, the Pittsburgh Crawfords and the Newark Eagles were the big time. Those teams packed 'em in wherever they played. So I almost swallowed my guts when Biz Mackey asked me to join his team."[34]

Dixon didn't stand in the youngster's way. In fact he encouraged Roy to "aim for the big time." "Remember," he said, "success ain't gonna chase you. You got to go after it. You're still a kid, but you got a good head on your shoulders and you got a way with you behind the plate. You can make it if you keep your nose clean, a sharp eye out, and keep your tongue in your mouth."[35] Self-reliance, hard work, and self-discipline were the keys to success for Negro Leaguers like Dixon, who did not challenge the discriminatory behavior of white society. He belonged to an earlier generation of blacks who adjusted to the realities of white racism without allowing the abuse to affect their self-esteem. They led by example, personally and professionally.[36] Accordingly Dixon's advice to "keep your nose clean" meant staying out of trouble with the law. His admonition to "keep a sharp eye out" was synonymous with recognizing and staying clear of white racism wherever and whenever it surfaced. The encouragement to "keep your tongue in your mouth" was code for "Don't provoke racial injustice by speaking out against it."

By contemporary standards, Dixon's advice seems to promote cowardice, but not in the first part of the twentieth century, when blacks were struggling to secure a position of respect in American society. Such an accommodationist philosophy was based on the belief that African Americans could achieve their professional goals on their own merit by proving to the white establishment that they had the talent, the work ethic, and the ambition to be as successful as any white person. Actions spoke louder than words for this generation of blacks. Congress and the courts would have to take care of larger civil rights issues; it wasn't their responsibility. What's more, Dixon's advice resonated with the young Campanella. It was the same message his parents had delivered.

Campanella caught for the Elite Giants in an exhibition against a local team at Norristown, Pennsylvania, the following day and again that night against the Philadelphia Stars. Baltimore won both games, and Roy collected his first hit in the Negro Leagues. But he returned home to Kerbaugh Street so late that night that his mother gave him a good spanking with a leather strap. Campanella finished out the last two months of the season with the Elite Giants. He received $60 per month, which was paid directly to his mother. But he didn't mind. Playing for one of the top teams in the Negro League was a dream come true. "I loved the life," he admitted. "Rarely were we ever in the same city two days in a row. Mostly we played by day and traveled by night; sometimes we played both day and night and usually in two different cities. We'd pile into the bus after a game, break open boxes of sandwiches and finish the meal with some hot coffee as we headed for our next game. The bus was our home, dressing room, dining room and hotel."[37]

When Campy returned to school in the fall, he couldn't concentrate on his studies. His two months with the Elite Giants convinced him that his future lay in baseball. He pleaded with his parents to let him quit school to play full time. Tom Wilson, the owner of the Elite Giants, made it difficult for the Campanellas to refuse by offering to pay $90 per month for their son's services. But the offer was contingent on Roy's being able to start training with the team in early spring. John Campanella didn't like the idea, not so much because his son would have to quit high school as because the color of his skin would prevent him from being as successful as his ability merited. Ida listened quietly as her husband expressed his concern. When he was finished, she replied, "Roy is a smart boy. Maybe the Negro league isn't the best there is, but it sure isn't the worst there is either. They pay our boy good, real good. In time, he can earn more money than he could in any other line of work. And to love what you're doing, that's important, too." John relented.

At the end of the fall term, fifteen-year-old Roy Campanella left Simon Gratz High School for good. Four months later, on March 17, 1938, he left home to join the Baltimore Elite Giants for spring training. Handing her son a Bible, Ida encouraged him to "turn to any page and start reading whenever your heart is troubled and pretty quick you'll feel much better." Roy thanked his mother, gave her a kiss, and said good-bye to his father and siblings.[38] He would spend the next decade in the Negro Leagues refining his skills with one of the premier black clubs.

Established in 1918 as a semiprofessional team in Nashville, the Elite Giants quickly became one of the strongest black baseball clubs in the South. Owner Thomas T. Wilson, a real estate agent who was one of the wealthiest black men in America, made several attempts to gain entry into the Negro National League but did not succeed until the early 1930s. Because of the declining economy, Wilson was forced to relocate the team first to Columbus, Ohio (1935), then to Washington DC (1936–37), and finally to Baltimore.[39]

Campanella joined the team in 1938, their first season in Baltimore. He shared catching duties with Manager Biz Mackey. Under Mackey's tutelage, Campy learned how to handle the spitball, how to block pitches in the dirt, and how to release the ball quickly on a throw to second base. He also learned to cut down on his swing in order to make contact more frequently instead of trying to smash the ball over the fence with each and every cut.[40] Just as important, Mackey reinforced the very same lessons that the youngster's parents and Tom Dixon of the Bacharach Giants emphasized: "Don't get involved in politics, just go out and play and everything else will take care of itself."[41]

At the end of the season, Wilson traded Mackey to the Newark Eagles and made Campanella the full-time catcher. After placing third in the first half of the 1939 campaign, the Elite Giants compiled the best second-half record. An elimination tournament was held between the top four teams to determine the Negro National League Champion. In the first round the Elites beat the Newark Eagles and the Homestead Grays defeated the Philadelphia Stars. When Baltimore prevailed over the Grays in the final round they were declared the champions. In the four-game series Campy collected five hits and seven RBIS.[42] Wilson rewarded him by raising his salary to $120 per month. It provided Roy with the financial security to marry Bernice Ray, his high school girlfriend. Within the next two years the couple would have two children, Joyce and Beverly.[43]

With a family to support, Campanella needed to make as much money as possible. "The trick," he explained, "was to stay in the line-up at any cost. So when I didn't catch, I played the outfield and even pitched sometimes. I kept playing as long as I could stand up. I had to. I got paid only if I played."[44] He not only made sure he played every day during the season, but he also played year-round. From March through October he played for the Elite Giants, and when the Negro League season ended he played winter ball in the Caribbean. Between the two seasons, Campy made almost double the white Major League salary of $5,000 a year.[45]

Campanella helped the Elite Giants to a second-place finish in 1940. The next two seasons were interrupted by World War II. In March 1941, while training in Hot Springs, Arkansas, with the Elite Giants, Campanella was contacted by the U.S. Draft Board to report for a physical examination. The United States was mobilizing for war and needed to increase the size of its armed forces. Although he passed the physical, Campy was not drafted. Instead he was assigned a job in the war industry. He returned home to Philadelphia, where he was hired as a janitor at the Bendix Aviation plant. The monotony of the $40-per-week job left him feeling not only frustrated that he couldn't make a more meaningful contribution to the war effort but restless for baseball. After two weeks he returned to the Draft Board to plead his case. They agreed to let him return to the Elite Giants on the condition that he stay in constant contact with them in the event that the country went to war.[46] By the end of April Campy was back in uniform with the Elite Giants and enjoyed one of his finest seasons. Named the starting catcher for the Negro National League in the annual East-West All-Star Game played at Chicago's Comiskey Park, he collected his first All-Star Game hit, threw out three base runners, and picked off a third. His excellent fielding earned him the Most Valuable Player Award in the East's 8–3 victory. Unfortunately the Elite Giants finished in third place that season.[47]

In the spring of 1942, shortly after Campanella returned from winter ball in Puerto Rico, the Draft Board contacted him again. This time they classified him 3A but gave him a deferment because he was the married father of two children. He took a legitimate defense job at North Philadelphia's Disston Steel Mill, which was producing armor plating for tanks. He worked on an assembly line for one month before the Draft Board allowed him to return to baseball.[48] That summer Campanella asked the Elites' owner, Tom Wilson, if he could play in an All-Negro League exhibition game in Cleveland to benefit the war effort. To be sure, Campy was also interested in the $200 he was being offered to supplement his income. Angered, Wilson not only denied the request but fined his All-Star catcher $250 for making the request. Feeling exploited, Campanella mulled over his future. A few days later he jumped to the Mexican League when Lazaro Salazar, the owner, manager, and star pitcher for the Monterrey Sultans, offered to double his salary.[49] Monte Irvin, who also jumped the Newark Eagles to play in the Mexican League that season, recalls that both he and Campanella "were worth four times what the Negro Leagues were paying us." "In the Mexican League there was always money to be made," he added.[50]

During the winter months Campanella played in Puerto Rico, where he was revered by the fans. Once, after he hit a pair of home runs, they expressed their appreciation for him by passing the hat. He returned their kindness by using some of the money to purchase a hundred-pound sack of potatoes, which he distributed in the slums.[51]

Campanella returned to Monterrey the following summer. He enjoyed playing there so much that he seriously considered playing year-round in Latin America. There wasn't much reason to return to the United States; his marriage had ended in divorce because of the long periods he spent away from home, and he could make considerably more money playing south of the border. But in the spring of 1944 Wilson lured him back to the Elites with an offer of $3,000 for a six-month season.[52]

Campanella played the next two seasons for Baltimore, posting batting averages of .366 and .349.[53] Once he caught a "double-double," or two double-headers in one day. Two of the games were played at Cincinnati's Crosley Field in the afternoon, and the other two were played that night in Middletown, Ohio. When later asked about the demands of playing four games in one day, Campy, true to his easygoing nature, replied, "It wasn't so bad. I grabbed a few sandwiches on the bus after the first double-header and I was ready for the next one."[54]

On April 30, 1945, Campanella remarried. His new bride was Ruthe Willis, a secretary and divorcee with a young son, David. Campy met the young woman a few years earlier during a night out in Harlem. Unlike his first family, Ruthe and David traveled to the Caribbean with him during the winter months so the family could be together. The couple would eventually have three of their own children.[55] Campanella was happier than he'd been in years, though the dream of playing in the white Major Leagues was never far from his mind.

On a rare day when the Elites weren't playing, he attended a Phillies game at Shibe Park. Afterward he approached the Phils' manager, Hans Lobert, and asked for a tryout. Lobert admitted he could use a good catcher and hitter like Campy and suggested that he contact the club's owner, Gerry Nugent. Wasting no time, Campanella went to the nearest pay phone and called the Phillies' owner, who told him that there was an "unwritten rule about Negroes in organized ball and that he was powerless to do anything about it."[56] Mahlon Duckett, who grew up with Campanella and later played in the Negro Leagues with the Philadelphia Stars, remembers how disappointed his friend was after the conversation: "The *Tribune* [Philadelphia's black newspaper] had been trying to talk the Phillies into giving Campy a tryout for some months. Supposedly they sent a scout to take a look at him and he said that Campy wasn't even good enough to play in the minor leagues. Of course, that was a lot of trash. He was a heckuva player and we all knew it. When Campy heard that, he went to the Phillies and asked for a tryout himself, but they refused to take a look at him. He just kind of laughed it off, saying, 'They didn't give me much of a tryout.' But I knew that he felt real bad. He wanted to play in the majors in the worst way."[57] John Campanella's biggest fear had come true: despite the fact that his son's talent warranted a shot at the big leagues, he was deprived of the opportunity because of the color of his skin.

In October 1945 Effa Manley, owner of the Newark Eagles, offered Campanella the opportunity to earn some more money by playing in an exhibition series against a squad of barnstorming Major Leaguers. Campy had a few weeks before he was to leave for Venezuela, where he would barnstorm with a Negro League All-Star team, so he agreed to play. Manley's Negro Leaguers lost the series, but Campanella played so well that he was approached by Charlie Dressen, a Dodgers coach who managed the Major League barnstormers. Unbeknown to the black catcher, Dressen and another Brooklyn coach, Clyde Sukeforth, had been scouting him for most of the season. Dressen informed Campanella that Branch Rickey wanted to see him the following morning at the Dodgers' executive offices in New York.[58]

A few days later, when Campanella entered Rickey's office, he was surprised to see the Dodgers' president puffing on a cigar and poring through a thick loose-leaf binder filled with information about his personal and professional life. Looking up from his desk, Rickey greeted Campanella and then began his inquisition.

"What do you weigh?" he demanded.

"About 215," replied Campy.

"Judas Priest!" roared Rickey. "You can't weigh that much and play ball."

Startled, Campanella paused to regroup. "All I know is that I've been doing it every day for years and it's worked out fine." Rickey, a brilliant actor, was trying to plant doubt in his visitor's mind, hoping the tactic would make him more willing to sign.

"The one thing that puzzles me is your age," he said, redirecting his remarks. "I have your age as 23. You sure this is your right age?"

Campanella had dropped out of high school at fifteen to begin his Negro League career, but his demeanor was that of a more seasoned veteran.

"Sure it's my right age," Campy insisted. "I'm 23. I was born November 19, 1921. I'll be 24 next month."

"You look older," the Dodgers' president retorted.

Campanella was noticeably annoyed. What right did Rickey have to question him about such personal matters? If he was interested in his ball playing, why didn't he limit his investigation to his catching and hitting? "Mr. Rickey, I've been playing ball a long time," he said in an abrupt way that indicated his patience had been exhausted.

Realizing the discomfort, Rickey came clean. "I've investigated dozens of players in the Negro Leagues," he confessed. "I've tried to learn as much as I could about their personal habits, their family life, their early education, their social activities, practically everything there is to know about them. I know that you are a hard worker, and that you get along well with

13. Negro League American All-Stars, Caracas, Venezuela, 1945. Standing (*left to right*): Blanco Chataing, Roy Campanella, Marvin Barker, Bill Anderson, Quincy Trouppe, George Jefferson, Parnell Woods, Roy Welmaker, Buck Leonard. Kneeling (*left to right*): Jackie Robinson, Gene Benson, manager Felton Snow, Verdell Mathis, team trainer Sam Jethroe. (National Baseball Hall of Fame Library, Cooperstown, New York)

coaches and teammates. That's why I brought you here." Flattered by the compliment, the black catcher became less defensive.

"You like to play with me?" asked Rickey, taking a puff on his cigar.

Campanella had heard that the Dodgers' executive was planning to start a Negro League team called the Brooklyn Brown Dodgers and assumed the offer applied to that club. "Mr. Rickey," he said, "I'm one of the highest paid players in the colored leagues. I earn around three thousand a year, and I make around two thousand playing winter ball in Puerto Rico, Venezuela, and Cuba. I've worked for the same man for nine years. I like the man. I'm doing all right." Indeed Campanella would have been foolish to abandon his current situation. He earned more money than most Negro Leaguers, and it didn't make any sense to risk it all on another black team that might easily fold. Still, he promised to stay in touch and agreed not to sign a contract for the 1946 season until the two men spoke again.[59]

Once Campanella learned that Rickey had signed Jackie Robinson to a professional contract, however, he spent the entire barnstorming trip to Venezuela second-guessing himself. "Campanella was just living to get a chance with the Dodgers," said Quincy Trouppe, who shared catching duties with Campy in Venezuela that off-season. "It was all he thought about and talked about."[60]

For Robinson, the Negro League barnstorming trip to Latin America was more productive. To prepare him for the challenges he would face in organized baseball, Branch Rickey made arrangements to have him mentored by Gene Benson. At thirty-four, Benson, a flashy centerfielder with the Philadelphia Stars, was in the twilight of his career. He was well-respected in the black baseball world not only for his talent but for his strong sense of humility, an exceptional ability to turn the other cheek in the face of discrimination, and a soft-spoken manner that endeared him to younger Negro Leaguers. All of these qualities made Benson the perfect choice to become Robinson's mentor.[61]

Over the course of the winter, Benson advised, assured, and encouraged Robinson, preparing him for the challenges he would face as the first African American in Major League Baseball. Years later Benson recalled:

> We talked baseball all the time, sometimes staying up half the night. "A lot of it really had to do with confidence-building. Jackie would say, "You're a better ballplayer than me. Why didn't they choose you?" I'd tell him, "I'm too old. No one is going to give a thirty-four-year-old a chance."
>
> "But you're young and you've got ability. You'll make it." But I wouldn't tell him that I was better than he was. He didn't know how good he was because he hadn't proven himself. He hadn't had the opportunity.

Benson convinced Jackie that Negro League pitchers were more difficult to hit than those in the Majors because they were permitted to throw at the hitter and use the spitball. "Over our time together in Venezuela, I could see that Jackie had the determination and intelligence to make it in the Majors," said Benson. "I saw that you needed to tell him something only once. He never forgot anything. He also carried himself like an athlete. Not only did he have great natural ability, but he respected that ability by the clean way he lived. He didn't drink or smoke or hang out with the wrong crowd. If he got into a fight it was because of his strong sense of pride and it was provoked. Never did he start anything."[62]

While Benson was preparing Robinson for his historic role, their teammates debated Jackie's chances for success. None of them appeared to doubt his ability to perform on the field as much as his ability to tolerate Jim Crow:

> "I just don't know how it's gonna work," confessed Felton Snow, the manager of the team. "How's he gonna travel with white players? Who's he gonna room with? How about when they play exhibition games in the South?"
>
> First baseman Buck Leonard agreed: "I'm afraid Jackie's in for a lot of trouble."
>
> But Campanella believed otherwise. "You may be wrong, too," he remarked. "I say if Robinson handles himself right it'll work out fine. And I'm sure he's smart enough to do it. I've played with and against white guys most of my life, and I never got into any trouble."
>
> "But you didn't play against those Southern boys," countered outfielder Marvin Williams. "Jackie's gonna run up against a lot of them in organized ball. Did you read some of those stories? I read where a southern ballplayer said he'd quit before he plays on a team with a colored man."
>
> "Yeah, but did you read what Mr. Rickey said about that?" Quincy Trouppe interjected. "He said that even if they do quit they'll get tired of working in some cotton mill or lumber camp and be glad to come back into baseball after one year."
>
> Everyone laughed.[63]

While the Negro Leaguers won eighteen of the twenty games they played in Venezuela, not everyone was happy during the trip. Robinson was concerned about his ability to deal with the race-baiting he was sure to face in the Majors. One mistake on his part could set the course of integration back a decade or more. How would he tolerate the racist barbs that would shower him from the stands, especially in cities like Cincinnati, St. Louis, and Philadelphia? Could he discipline himself to turn the other cheek when pitchers threw at his head or base runners spiked him with their cleats? On the other hand, Campanella spent the trip brooding over his missed opportunity, which affected his offensive performance; he batted just .211.[64]

In January 1946, when the team disbanded, Robinson returned to the United States, but Campanella remained in the Caribbean for the winter season. Not until March 1 did he receive a telegram from Rickey: "Please report to Brooklyn Office by March 10. Very important."[65]

Hours later, Campy was off for New York.

4

Breaking the Color Line

Jackie Robinson's first test with racial discrimination came on February 28, 1946, when he and his wife, Rachel, boarded an American Airlines flight in Los Angeles for Daytona Beach, Florida, where the Dodgers held their spring training. The couple, married just eighteen days earlier, were bumped from the flight in New Orleans and their seats given to white passengers. Bumped from another flight in Pensacola, Florida, they chose to take a Greyhound bus to Daytona. When Jackie boarded the Greyhound, the driver called him "boy" and ordered the couple to the back of the bus. Robinson had no choice but to obey because of Rickey's directive. "It would have been much easier to take a beating than to remain passive," he recalled. "But I swallowed my pride and choked back my anger because I knew the result would mean newspaper headlines about an ugly racial incident and possible arrest for not only me but also for Rae. By giving in to my feelings I could have blown the whole major league bit."[1]

Thirty-six hours after they left Los Angeles, the newlyweds finally arrived at spring training, exhausted, frustrated, and angry. Robinson seriously considered quitting until Wendell Smith and Billy Rowe of the *Pittsburgh Courier* talked him out of it. "We calmed Jackie down," recalled Rowe years later. "We tried to explain how important it was for him to shoulder the humiliation so that other black athletes could follow."[2] Unbeknown to Jackie, Branch Rickey had arranged for the two black journalists to help cushion the discrimination he would face that first season with the Montreal Royals, the Dodgers' farm team. The Dodgers' president also signed John Wright, a black pitcher, so Robinson would have a teammate in whom he could confide. Rickey himself appeared at the Dodgers' training site to meet with all the players. Insisting that Robinson and

14. Jackie Robinson played with the Montreal Royals, the Dodgers' top farm club, in 1946. The following year he was promoted to Brooklyn, where he broke Major League Baseball's color barrier. (Library of Congress)

Wright were "not signed because of political pressure," he emphasized his belief that the two black players could "bring a winning team to Brooklyn" and urged the white ballplayers to "comport themselves like young gentlemen" toward their new teammates.[3] He had a harder time selling Royals manager Clay Hopper on the idea.

Hopper, a Mississippi cotton broker in the off-season, believed that blacks were inferior to whites. Although he had worked for Rickey since 1929, he reportedly begged the Dodgers' president to reconsider giving him this assignment. During one of the early practice sessions, Rickey, standing alongside Hopper, watched as Robinson turned an extremely difficult double play, and observed that the action was "super human." Hopper turned, looked his boss straight in the eye, and asked, "Do you really think a nigger's a human being?" Rickey was stunned by the remark but chose to ignore it. "It reflected an inflexible attitude," he recalled years later. "To think that the Negro race is inferior is the root of all prejudice in this country. And racial prejudice can only be met on its blind side. You can't meet it with an argument. You only strengthen it if you do that. You must address prejudice in more subtle ways. Proximity was important. Once he got to know Jackie Robinson, Hopper would understand the illogic of his prejudice towards Negroes."[4] Rickey also believed that having a southerner at the helm of the Royals would head off some dissension among the players and that he could trust Hopper to handle any situation that might arise.[5] His instincts proved to be correct. By June the Royals manager had changed his opinion of Robinson, who admitted, "No one could outplay him at second base."[6] Still, Jackie felt that Hopper "never really accepted [him]" because "his prejudice against the Negro was so deeply ingrained."[7] At least Hopper gave him a chance. Robinson's presence was not appreciated in racially charged Florida, and he was reminded of that fact wherever he tried to play that spring.

Since the Dodgers did not own a spring training facility, scheduling was subject to the whim of local municipalities, several of which turned down any event involving Robinson and Wright. In Sanford, Florida, for example, the police chief threatened to cancel games if Robinson and Wright did not stop training there. In Jacksonville the ballpark was padlocked shut without warning on game day by order of the city's Parks and Public Property director. In DeLand a scheduled day game was called off, ostensibly because of faulty electrical lighting.[8] After much lobbying of local officials by Rickey himself, the Royals were allowed to host a game involving Robinson in Daytona Beach.[9] Jackie made his Royals debut at Daytona Beach's City Island Ballpark on March 17, 1946, in an exhibition game against the team's parent club, the Dodgers. Later in spring training, after some less than stellar performances, Robinson was shifted from shortstop to second base, allowing him to make shorter throws to first base.[10]

Robinson finally found some relief when the Royals broke camp and headed north for the regular season. Montreal was the most accepting of all the cities in the Dodgers' farm system. Undoubtedly racial prejudice existed, but it was not as virulent as it was in the American South. In addition Quebec had a history of blacks playing professional baseball dating to the 1920s. Some joined integrated teams in the Provincial League and other independent leagues, while others belonged to an all-black team in Montreal. Placing Robinson at the Triple-A level in Montreal was yet another part of Rickey's design to lessen the racial discrimination against him. Canadians quickly accepted him, seeming to cheer his every move on the playing field. They nicknamed him the "Dark Destroyer" for his hitting prowess and the "Colored Comet" for his extraordinary speed on the base paths.[11] "I owe more to Canadians than they'll ever know," said Robinson. "They were the first to make me feel my natural self and spared no effort in showing me that they were proud that I belonged to their home team."[12] Teammates also began to warm to him.

On April 18, 1946, when Robinson, making his professional debut against the Jersey City Giants, hit a three-run homer, teammate George Shuba greeted him at home plate with a handshake.[13] Up to that point, none of the Royals had made any real effort to be friendly to him, though the four hits, four runs, three RBIs, and two stolen bases he contributed to the Royals' 14–1 win that day certainly broke the ice.[14] A few weeks later, after pitcher John Wright was released by the Dodgers, Robinson was assigned a new roommate, Al Campanis. Campanis, a middle infielder, quickly endeared himself to Jackie by helping him make the transition from shortstop to second base.[15]

Naturally Robinson's success in the field improved his relationship with his teammates, who could not help but admire his talent. By June he was batting .340 with forty-three hits and seventeen stolen bases in thirty-six games.[16] Two months later he had improved his batting average to .371 due to a ten-game streak where he collected twenty-two hits in thirty-nine at-bats. Defensively he had committed just seven errors at second base. Mel Jones, Montreal's general manager, explained that 20 percent of Robinson's hits came off bunts from either side of the plate. "Because he gets such a fast jump, he beats out many of the bunts without a play even being made," said Jones. "Robinson can run faster than 75% of the players in the majors today. He can bunt better than 90% of them. He has good hands, a trigger-quick, instinctive baseball mind and an accurate arm. What makes him a big timer is that he never makes any play around second base look hard, not even the difficult ones."[17]

But Robinson's success on the diamond only served to provoke opponents. Throughout the 1946 season he endured racist remarks from opposing players and their fans and humiliating treatment in the South. Pitchers threw at his head. Runners spiked him and spit at him on the base paths. Never did he retaliate. By season's end the constant pressure and abuse had taken its toll; his hair began to turn gray, he suffered with chronic stomach trouble, and some thought he was on the verge of a nervous breakdown. Finding himself unable to sleep or eat, he went to a doctor, who concluded that he was suffering from stress. "You're not having a nervous breakdown," the physician told him. "You're under a lot of stress. Stay home and don't read any newspapers, and don't go to the ballpark for a week." Jackie, his wife remembered, stayed home for one day. The problem, she said, "came from his not being able to fight back." It was, as Rickey had warned him, "the cross that you must bear."[18]

Despite the tension and distractions, Robinson led the International League with a .349 batting average and .985 fielding percentage that season and was named the league's Most Valuable Player.[19] He also led the Montreal Royals to victory over the Louisville Colonels in the Little World Series, though seven of eight hits he collected in the best-of-seven-game series came in Montreal.[20] After the final game, Manager Clay Hopper, who once said that Robinson was "less than human" because he was a "nigger," approached Jackie, shook his hand and said, "You're a real ballplayer and a gentleman. It's been wonderful having you on the team."[21] Grateful Royals fans chased after Robinson, hoisted him on their shoulders, and carried him to the locker room. Moved by the scene, Sam Maltin of the *Pittsburgh Courier* wrote, "It was probably the only day in history that a black man ran from a white mob with love, instead of lynching on its mind."[22] The movement for integration was off to a successful beginning.

While Robinson was making converts in Montreal, Roy Campanella was proving his mettle in the low minors. Rickey planned to assign Campy and Don Newcombe, a pitcher for the Newark Eagles, to one of the Dodgers' lower level teams. Since three of the organization's five Class B teams operated in segregated states in the South, the only real possibilities were Danville, Illinois, and Nashua, New Hampshire. Initially Rickey hoped to start the two players at Danville, in the Three-I League, composed of Minor League teams in Illinois, Indiana, and Iowa. But the general manager there didn't want them. When Buzzie Bavasi, the young general manager at Nashua, was asked about the prospect of having two black players on his roster, he replied, "If they can play ball better than what we have, then we don't care what color they are."[23] Had Bavasi expressed any reservation, Rickey would have been forced to scrap his plans. The young general manager's willingness to accept the two black players not only endeared him to Rickey but enhanced his own position in the organization as a trusted advisor. Bavasi would play an instrumental role in the future of the franchise as it entered a critical phase in the integration process.

Campanella took a significant pay cut to join the Dodgers' farm system. Rickey signed him at $185 per month for the 1946 season. The contract amounted to a total of $1,017.50, about $400 less than what he earned the previous year playing in the Negro Leagues and the Caribbean. But Campy was on his way to realizing a lifetime dream, and he knew that if he "made good," the Dodgers "would make up some of the deficit in other ways."[24] "Making good" also meant more than achieving success on the playing field.

Though Rickey did not prepare Campanella and Newcombe as carefully as he did Robinson, he made clear to them that they would have to prove they "could be gentlemen off the field," "get along with teammates," and "handle [themselves] at team meetings and hotels." He also expected them to "avoid disputes" and ignore "taunts from opposing players and fans."[25] Shortly before they left for New Hampshire, Campanella and Newcombe met with Robinson in New York to discuss the upcoming season. "The three of us got together because we were embarking on this new idea and we had to have a sort of game plan to find out how we were going to operate as players," recalled Newcombe.[26] Throughout the season the three players stayed in touch, providing encouragement for each other, sharing advice, and comparing experiences.

According to Jules Tygiel, author of *Baseball's Great Experiment*, Rickey signed Campanella and Newcombe as a "second line of attack in his master plan for integration." While Robinson's performance with the Dodgers' top farm club in Montreal would capture national attention, the black battery-mates would begin a level lower, in Class B, "progress through the farm system in Robinson's wake," and eventually follow him to the Brooklyn club, the "dark heart of Rickey's envisioned dynasty."[27] This "second line of attack" was more than a matter of chronology, though. If Robinson's college and military credentials made him the ideal pioneer to break the color line, Campanella's talent, experience, and knowledge of the game made him the ideal ballplayer to prove that integration was no mistake. A catcher is the quarterback of a baseball team, the leader on the field. Not only does he call all the pitches, but as the only player who faces the entire field, he must be able to identify any vulnerability in the defense and realign it in a moment's time. To do that, a catcher must have an encyclopedic knowledge of the game, its strategy, and the opposing hitters' strengths and weaknesses. Campanella possessed all of these skills and more. As a veteran backstop in the Negro Leagues, he had already worked with some of the finest black pitchers in the game. It was no coincidence that Rickey paired him with Newcombe, a young power pitcher, who had the potential to be an outstanding hurler. If mentored properly, and away from the limelight, Newcombe might become the pitching ace of a future Brooklyn Dodgers dynasty.

Campanella and Newcombe had personalities as different as their physical appearances. Campy was a squat, five-foot-nine, two-hundred-pound catcher with the build of a fire plug, while Newcombe was a gangling six-foot-four-inch giant with the long arms and broad shoulders of a pitcher. Campy was boisterous, outgoing, and cheerful. At the age of twenty-five, with nine seasons in the Negro Leagues under his belt, he was a confident and seasoned veteran who could have gone directly into the Majors. Newcombe, at the tender age of nineteen, had pitched just two seasons in the black leagues. He suffered from control problems and was much less confident in his abilities. Predictably he also was reserved and sullen in his personal disposition. For all their differences, however, the two men quickly discovered that they complemented each other, and a strong rapport developed between them during their first season together at Nashua.

On Opening Day Campanella went three for four at the plate, including a mammoth 440-foot home run, as Nashua defeated the Lynn Red Sox, 4–3. After a strong start, however, Campy went into a prolonged slump, due in part to an ankle injury that kept him out of the lineup early on. He rebounded in mid-June and, after a twenty-one-game hitting streak, boosted his average from .235 to .300 and led the team in homers and RBIs. A local poultry farmer, noting the formidable distances of the outfield fences, offered Nashua players one hundred baby chicks for every home run they hit. By season's end Campanella had hit fourteen home runs' worth of chicks, which he sent home to Philadelphia for his father, who started a small poultry business.[28]

Manager Walter Alston was so impressed with his catcher that he asked Campanella to manage the team if he ever got thrown out of a game. The opportunity arose in mid-June in a game against the Lawrence Million-

15. Campy and pitcher Don Newcombe began their Dodgers careers together in Nashua, New Hampshire, in 1946. They became roommates and close friends over the next decade. (National Baseball Hall of Fame Library, Cooperstown, New York)

aires. Alston was ejected in the sixth inning for arguing a called strike. Taking his leave, he handed the lineup card to Campy. The very next inning Campy was forced to make a strategic decision; with a runner on base and Nashua behind by two runs, he called on Newcombe to pinch-hit. The black hurler, already the team's best pinch hitter, with a .311 batting average, smashed a home run to tie the game. Nashua went on to win the contest 7–5, giving Campanella his first victory as a professional manager.[29]

Both Campanella and Newcombe were quickly accepted by the town of Nashua, even though they were the only black residents. They didn't have any difficulty finding accommodations for themselves and their families or being served at local restaurants. The few cases of racial discrimination they did encounter came against opposing clubs. Once, in a game against Manchester, Campy was giving signals to his pitcher when the opposing hitter, Sal Yvars, bent over, scooped up a handful of dirt and threw it in his face. Incensed, Campanella stood up, took off his mask, and staring Yvars directly in the eye said, "Try that again and I'll beat you to a pulp."

Yvars pretended to ignore him but gave no further trouble. On another occasion, the general manager of the Lynn Red Sox, bitter over losing first place to Nashua in a closely contested pennant race, approached Bavasi and griped, "If it wasn't for them niggers, you wouldn't have beaten us." Bavasi charged the offending executive and had to be pulled away by his players.[30] "As long as people didn't put their hands on us physically," recalled Newcombe, "we knew we could control ourselves."[31]

With Campy behind the plate calling pitches, Newcombe elevated his game. He won his first four games before dropping a 1–0 decision on June 29. At season's end, the big right-hander had fourteen victories to his credit and a .349 batting average. He would return as Nashua's ace the following season and post a league-leading nineteen wins and 186 strikeouts. Campanella, on the other hand, was voted Most Valuable Player of the New England League for his .290 batting average, 13 home runs, 96 RBIs, and a league-leading 687 put-outs.[32]

The Minor League successes of Jackie Robinson and Roy Campanella cannot be overstated. Their campaign to integrate baseball took place at a time when Jim Crow defined the southern legal system and the early years of the cold war were stirring national hysteria over Communist infiltration of American society. Blacks had no choice but to tolerate racial abuse; those who fought back risked their lives. Lynching was still prevalent in America in the mid-1940s, and the campaign to end it, a major objective of the civil rights movement. Between 1882 and 1946 some 2,500 African Americans were lynched in the United States.[33] Since the turn of the century black intellectuals and journalists had been encouraging public education, actively protesting and lobbying against lynch mob violence and government complicity in it. The NAACP made the quest to secure federal antilynching legislation its primary goal in the 1920s. As a result, the number of lynchings dropped to about ten per year in southern states by 1930. But advocates were still far from securing a federal antilynching measure.

During the 1930s Communist organizations, including the International Labor Defense, joined the antilynching campaign, along with such prominent black advocates as Mary McLeod Bethune and Walter Francis White. Bethune and White campaigned for Franklin D. Roosevelt in 1932, hoping that the president would lend public support for their cause.

Other New Deal Democrats, like Senators Robert F. Wagner of New York and Edward P. Costigan of Colorado, introduced a bill to make lynching a federal crime and thus take it out of state hands. But the southern Democrats' hold on Congress and Roosevelt's fear of losing their support for his New Deal programs prevented passage of the Wagner-Costigan measure. Although FDR created the Civil Rights Section of the Justice Department in 1939 to initiate prosecutions of lynchings, the Department failed to win any convictions until 1946.[34] That year the lynching of four young sharecroppers in Walton County, Georgia, shocked the nation and motivated President Harry Truman's decision to make civil rights a priority of his administration.[35]

Instead of dealing with civil rights on a case-by-case basis, Truman sought to address the issue on a national level. He began by appointing an interracial committee to examine the condition of civil rights in the United States. In a report titled *To Secure These Rights*, the committee proposed a detailed ten-point agenda of reforms, including the creation of a federal antilynching law and "the elimination of segregation based on race, color, creed or national origin from American life," specifically in public education, employment, health care, housing, the military, public accommodations, and interstate transportation.[36] When, in February 1948, Truman submitted a civil rights agenda to Congress to address many of these issues, he provoked a storm of criticism from southern Democrats. Realizing that he didn't have the necessary support on Capitol Hill, Truman initiated three executive orders that would form the basis of future civil rights legislation, including the desegregation of the armed forces and equal employment opportunities for all persons applying for civil service positions.[37]

Truman's support of civil rights was greeted with open hostility and suspicion on Capitol Hill, in part because of the close affiliation of Communist organizations with that cause. Throughout his presidency Truman had to deal with accusations that the federal government was harboring Soviet spies at the highest level, especially after August 1948, when Whittaker Chambers, a former Soviet spy and a senior editor at *Time* magazine, testified before the House Un-American Activities Committee and presented a list of members of an alleged underground Communist network within the U.S. government. One of the accused was Alger Hiss, a senior State Department official. Though Hiss denied the accusations, he was convicted of perjury in a controversial trial.[38] The Chambers-Hiss incident opened the door for the demagoguery of Republican senator Joseph McCarthy, who accused Truman's State Department of having Communists on the payroll. Congressional testimony garnered nationwide attention and McCarthy quickly established himself as a national figure at the expense of thousands of people in government, broadcast and newspaper journalism, and entertainment who were wrongly accused of being Communists.[39]

Professional baseball was not immune from suspicions of Communist infiltration. The Federal Bureau of Investigation took an aggressive role in monitoring the activities of any American suspected of Communist ties. For FBI director J. Edgar Hoover, civil rights activism and American Communism were inextricably bound and represented a national security problem. Communist interest in baseball's integration, which continued to be heralded by leftist politicians and newspapers like New York's *Daily Worker*, confirmed his suspicions.[40]

Shortly after Robinson signed with the Dodgers, Hoover began what would become an extensive file monitoring his political activities.[41] Among the documents in the file were two feature articles on Robinson published in the *People's Voice*, a magazine that had been cited by the California Commission on Un-American Activities as "Communist initiated and controlled, or so strongly influenced as to be in the Stalin solar system." The FBI file also noted that Robinson served as New York's honorary state commander for the United Negro and Allied Veterans of America, which was cited as "a Communist front to provoke racial friction" by the Internal Security Subcommittee of the U.S. Senate Judiciary Committee.[42] Robinson might have suspected that he was under FBI surveillance, but entering the 1947 season he had much greater concerns on his mind.

At a meeting of the baseball owners in January, Rickey declared his intention to promote Robinson to the Dodgers. After discussing the issue, the owners voted fifteen to one against integration. Distressed by the opposition, Rickey met with Commissioner Happy Chandler who, to his surprise, agreed to "approve the transfer of Robinson's contract from Montreal to Brooklyn."[43] Rickey had dodged a bullet. Now he had to convince the players to buy in to his experiment. Because Robinson's success with Montreal had been so impressive, Rickey initially assumed that all the Dodgers would accept his promotion to the Majors for the 1947 campaign. "After all, Robinson could mean a pennant, and ball players are not averse to cashing World Series checks," he confided to an assistant.[44] To promote and protect his black star, Rickey made some additional moves. First, in order to avoid Jim Crow restrictions, he relocated the Dodgers' spring training camp from Florida to Havana, Cuba. Next, he shifted Robinson, an experienced shortstop and second baseman, to first base, where he would be spared physical contact with opposing players who might try to injure him deliberately. Finally, Rickey scheduled a seven-game series between the Dodgers and the Royals in order to showcase Robinson's talent.[45] "I want you to be a whirling demon against the Dodgers in this series," Rickey told Robinson. "You have to be so good that the Dodger players themselves are going to want you on their club. . . . I want you to hit that ball. I want you to get on base and run wild. Steal their pants off. Be the most conspicuous player on the field. The newspapermen from New York will send good stories back about you and help mold favorable public opinion."[46]

Robinson more than obliged, batting .625 and stealing seven bases in the series.[47] But instead of helping him, the performance only served to alienate him from his future teammates, many of whom were southerners. Alabaman Dixie Walker drafted a petition stating that the players who signed would prefer to be traded rather than play with a black teammate. The first signatures came from southerners Bobby Bragan, Dixie Howell, Hugh Casey, and Kirby Higbe. While the Dodgers were playing exhibition games in Panama, Walker proceeded to gather signatures from others, including Carl Furillo and Eddie Stanky.[48] Team captain Harold "Pee Wee" Reese, a Kentuckian, refused to sign. It was a tremendously courageous act on his part because, as the team's shortstop, he had more to lose than any other Dodger. "I didn't think of myself as being the Great White Father or anything like that," Reese recalled many years later. "I just wanted to play the game. If Jackie Robinson was good enough to take my job, he was entitled to it. It didn't matter to me if he was black or green."[49]

When Dodgers manager Leo Durocher learned of the petition, he was furious. He had asked Rickey to bring Robinson up to Brooklyn during the previous year's pennant drive. At a late-night team meeting, Durocher told Walker and the other petitioners that they could "wipe their asses" with the document. "Robinson is a real great ballplayer," he declared. "He's going to win pennants for us. He's going to put money in your pockets and money in mine." In case there was any uncertainty about Durocher's views on integration, the Dodgers' manager quickly dismissed them. "From what I hear," he added, "Robinson's only the first. *Only the first!* There's many more [black players] coming right behind him and they have the talent and they're gonna play. So, unless you fellows wake up, they're going to run you right out of the ball park."[50]

Durocher's unequivocal support for integration and the hard-line approach he took with the petitioners set the tone for the rest of spring training. Unfortunately the outspoken manager was suspended for one year by Commissioner Chandler for "conduct detrimental to baseball" prior to Opening Day. Rickey was forced to turn to Clyde Sukeforth as an interim manager until he secured the services of an old friend, Burt Shotton, a sixty-two-year-old former Phillies manager.[51] Unlike Durocher, Shotton was calm and level-headed but did not have as much respect from the players. Since he wore civilian clothes on the bench—which prohibited him from going out onto the playing field—he relied on his assistant coaches to argue with umpires. This would be problematic for Robinson because he'd have to rely on coaches, not the manager, to defend him. Ultimately, however, it really didn't matter who ran the team on the field. Rickey was determined to make his experiment succeed.

The very next morning after Durocher's team meeting, the Dodgers' president arrived in Panama and met with the ringleaders of the petition drive. Confronting each one, he laid down the law: "Robinson was going to play for the Brooklyn Dodgers and if any of them didn't like it, he'd make other arrangements for them." "I wasn't elated at all," admitted Bobby Bragan. "I told Mr. Rickey if I had my druthers, I'd rather be traded somewhere else."[52] Other players who signed the petition—Walker, Howell, and Higbe—made the same request.

Higbe, a pitcher who posted seventeen wins in forty-two appearances for the Dodgers in 1946, was the first to go. After the fourth game of the regular season, Rickey sent him to the Pittsburgh Pirates along with Dixie Howell, Gene Mauch, and Cal McLish for outfielder Al Gionfriddo and a cash payment of $200,000.[53] Higbe's departure was a significant loss for the Dodgers' rotation, but it underscored Rickey's determination to ensure the success of integration. Higbe had no regrets, though. "I still think I would have done what I did," he insisted long after his Major League career had ended. "I was brought up a southerner and I was brought up to stand by what you believed, even if you were the last one standing."[54] Walker was traded to Pittsburgh before spring's end. Bragan remained only because Rickey couldn't arrange a deal.[55] The rebellion squelched, Rickey announced on April 10, 1947, that Jackie Robinson had officially been signed to play first base for the Brooklyn Dodgers. The noble experiment was in full swing.

Robinson's first official appearance as a Brooklyn Dodger came against the Boston Braves on April 15, 1947. Despite the cold and rainy afternoon, more than twenty-six thousand fans packed Ebbets Field, and reportedly some fourteen thousand of those were African Americans. To ensure that the crowd would be orderly, Rickey had met with local black doctors, lawyers, and other professionals prior to Opening Day and told them how he expected the black community to behave when Robinson took the playing field. "The biggest threat to Robinson's success is the Negro people themselves," he told his African American audience. "We don't want Negroes to form gala welcoming committees. We don't want Negroes to strut, to wear badges. Nor do we want Negroes in the stands gambling, drunk, fighting, being arrested. If you do those things, you'll turn Robinson's importance into a national comedy and I'll curse the day I signed him to a contract."[56] The black professionals shared his concern and had their own preconceptions about the behavior of a growing black urban working class. Rickey was also aware of Robinson's feelings about being patronized by other blacks. "It upsets me," Jackie admitted during spring training, "when members of my own race make a big demonstration for me in the stands over some perfectly ordinary play I made. It could cause trouble, so I wish they wouldn't do it." A proud but humble man, the twenty-eight-year-old rookie wanted "to be judged solely on [his] merits as a ballplayer."[57]

Both Robinson and Rickey called on these African American leaders to police the black community, and they complied by mapping out a course of restraint. There were no exaggerated shows of emotion, no unruly behavior, nothing that would detract from the historic occasion. Although Robinson went hitless, he provided the crowd with a memorable moment in the seventh inning when he laid down a bunt and his blazing speed resulted in a Boston error. Having reached base safely, Robinson was later batted in by Pete Reiser with the go-ahead run in the Dodgers' 5–3 victory. Had he done nothing at all that day, it wouldn't have mattered. Just the sight of a black man on a Major League diamond during a regular season game proved that baseball had finally become deserving of the title "national pastime."[58]

When the Philadelphia Phillies arrived in Brooklyn a week later, however, all hopes that integration would come peaceably were shattered. The Phillies, led by Manager Ben Chapman, an Alabaman, launched a verbal assault on Robinson the likes of which had seldom if ever been heard in baseball. The abuse began during batting practice: "Nigger, go back to the cotton fields where you belong," Chapman yelled. By game time, many of the Phillies' players had joined their manager in the insulting chorus:

"They're waiting for you in the jungles, black boy."

"Hey, coon, did you always smell so bad?"

"Hey, snowflake, which one of you white boys' wives are you shackin' up with tonight?"[59]

The fusillade of bigotry continued throughout the game. Harold Parrott, the Dodgers' traveling secretary, claimed it was the worst racial attack he had ever heard: "Chapman mentioned everything from thick lips to the supposedly extra-thick Negro skull, which he said restricted brain growth to almost animal level when compared with white folk. He listed the repulsive sores and diseases he said Robbie's teammates would be infected with if they touched the towels or combs he used."[60]

Robinson, standing at first base, was initially stunned by the abuse. But as it continued he became enraged, like a time bomb waiting to explode. Nothing, not even Rickey's role-playing, laced as it was with the anticipated racial epithets, had prepared him for the treatment he was experiencing. Years later, Robinson recalled:

For one wild and rage-crazed minute I thought:

To hell with Mr. Rickey's noble experiment. It's clear that it won't succeed. My best is not good enough for them. I thought, "What a glorious, cleansing thing it would be to let go. To hell with the image of the patient black freak I was supposed to create. I could throw down my bat, stride over to the Phillies dugout, grab one of those white sons of bitches and smash his teeth in with my despised black fist. Then I could walk away from it, and I'd never become a sports star. But my son could tell his son someday what his daddy could have been if he hadn't been too much of a man."[61]

Once again Jackie's desire to strike back was fueled by his notions of manhood. To ignore the abuse might have been the moral high ground that Rickey demanded, but it was a reflection of cowardice to him. Each racial epithet fanned the flames of the fire that burned inside, and yet he had promised to restrain himself. Indeed it would have been a "glorious, cleansing thing to let go" and "smash the teeth of one of those [Phillies]," but the experiment with integration would have ended then and there. No doubt the Phillies knew that just as much as Robinson did, so they continued to provoke him, pushing him closer to the breaking point.

Jackie got some measure of revenge in the eighth inning. With the teams deadlocked in a scoreless tie, he singled, stole second, advanced to third on a throwing error by the Phillies catcher, and scored the game's only run on Gene Hermanski's single. Going hitless in the final two games of the series, Robinson's slump only added to the Phillies' contention that he "didn't belong in the majors" and was "only there to draw those nigger bucks to the gate for Rickey."[62]

Bench-jockeying was a tradition in baseball, and no topic was sacred. Personal problems, appearance, ethnicity, and race were all considered fair game. But the Phillies' verbal abuse of Robinson exceeded even baseball's broadly defined sense of propriety. Fans seated near the team's dugout wrote letters of protest to Commissioner Chandler, who responded by contacting Phillies owner Bob Carpenter and demanding that the harassment cease immediately or he would be forced to invoke punitive measures against the organization.[63]

When he learned of Chandler's edict, Chapman defended his actions, insisting that the Phillies would "treat Robinson the same as we do any other man who is likely to step to the plate and beat us." He noted that Hank Greenberg of the Pirates and Joe Garagiola of the Cardinals had been the targets of ethnic slurs. "There is not a man who has come to the big leagues who has not been ridden," said Chapman. "Besides, Robinson did not want to be patronized." He had been given nothing more than the "same test experienced by all rookies."[64]

Chapman's defense elicited the support of many Philadelphia fans and sportswriters who "commended him for his fair stand toward Robinson."[65] Robinson himself publicly downplayed the abusive treatment, stating that the Phillies' bench jockeys were "trying to get me upset" but it "really didn't bother me."[66] Just as he promised Rickey, Robinson turned the other cheek. His Dodgers teammates, however, were not as forgiving.

Dixie Walker, who began the petition drive against Robinson, chastised Chapman, a fellow Alabaman, for his inappropriate behavior. Eddie Stanky, another petitioner, called Chapman a "coward" and challenged him to "pick on someone who can fight back."[67] Inadvertently Chapman had rallied the Dodgers around their black teammate. They admired Robinson for his tremendous restraint in the face of discrimination. According to Rickey, Chapman's "string of unconscionable abuse unified thirty men, not one of whom was willing to sit by and see someone kick around a man who had his hands tied behind his back."[68]

Two weeks later, on May 9, the day before the Dodgers were to take a train to Philadelphia for the first extended road trip of the season, Robinson received two anonymous letters, warning him to "get out of baseball." Instead of turning the letters over to the police, he gave them to Rickey, who investigated the matter and concluded there was no real danger to Robinson's life.[69] On the same day Rickey received a phone call from Herb Pennock, the Phillies general manager. "You just can't bring that nigger here with the rest of the team, Branch," Pennock allegedly said. "We're just not ready for that sort of thing yet. We won't be able to take the field if that Robinson boy is in uniform."

"Great!" Rickey exclaimed, calling the Phillies' executive's bluff. "That means we win all three games by default, and the way things are going, we sure can use those victories." Infuriated by the response, Pennock hung up.

Whether the conversation was fact or fiction remains a subject of controversy. Originally quoted by Harold Parrott, the Dodgers' traveling secretary, in his 1976 book *The Lords of Baseball*, the purported exchange was given greater legitimacy by Jules Tygiel's 1983 book, *Baseball's Great Experiment*, which historians widely consider to be the most accurate record of

Robinson's quest to break the color line.[70] Neither Rickey nor Pennock is still alive to confirm the conversation, and Parrott's claim that the Dodgers' president allowed him to eavesdrop on the exchange casts a shadow of doubt over its legitimacy.[71] Robinson himself attributed the telephone call to the Phillies owner, Bob Carpenter.[72] More recently his widow admitted that she hadn't even heard of Pennock's alleged racial epithet and that because the conversation "is not sufficiently documented" she would "not take a position on it."[73]

Regardless of the substance of the phone call or who made it, one thing is clear: the Phillies front office had no intention of welcoming Robinson to Shibe Park. Just as clear was the team's intention to boycott the series. Of the Phillies who saw regular playing time in 1947, seven were from the South, including shortstop Lamar "Skeeter" Newsome, center fielder Harry "The Hat" Walker, and third baseman Jim Tabor.[74] In spite of the strong southern sentiment on the club, level heads prevailed. According to catcher Andy Seminick, the Phillies had intended to boycott the Dodgers series until Newsome "called a meeting and convinced us not to do it." "Our manager, Ben Chapman, was adamant about not playing against Robinson," recalled Seminick. "Being from Alabama, he just couldn't understand why whites should have to play against blacks. So we were all set to boycott the Brooklyn series, until Newsome convinced us that a boycott would be morally wrong. He believed that Robinson, like any other man, should have the opportunity to play baseball. The fact that Newsome also came from Alabama, I think, carried a lot of weight with the other players."[75]

The Phillies relented, but Robinson still wasn't welcomed in the city. When the Dodgers tried to check in at the Benjamin Franklin Hotel, the bellhops stacked their luggage out on the sidewalk at Ninth and Chestnut streets. Harold Parrott was told that no rooms were available and not to return "while you have any nigras with you." Instead of forcing a confrontation, the Dodgers changed their accommodations to the more expensive Warwick Hotel, where the manager said he'd be delighted to have them.[76]

At Shibe Park the following day, a huge crowd came to see—and jeer—Robinson. Shortly before game time he made a much publicized walk to the Phillies dugout for a conciliatory photograph with Chapman. In light of all the negative publicity of the first series between the two teams, both club owners requested the photo of the two men shaking hands. While Chapman agreed to pose for the photographers, he refused to shake Robinson's hand. The most he would do was share a bat with the Dodgers' first baseman. Rumors abounded that the Phils skipper agreed to pose for the picture only to save his job. But Chapman insisted that he agreed only because his good friend and general manager, Herb Pennock, asked him to do it for "*The New York Times*, which had requested the picture."[77] For Robinson, the photo shoot was a painful necessity. He later confessed, "[I] could think of no occasion where I had more difficulty swallowing my pride than in agreeing to pose for a photograph with a man for whom I had the lowest regard."[78]

When the game started, the Phillies picked up where they had left off in Brooklyn, harassing Robinson unmercifully. Chapman continued with his personal racial attacks. "God Himself could have come down from heaven and Ben would have been on him," said Phillies outfielder Harry "The Hat" Walker. "Chapman just had a way of stirring up trouble, and when the color barrier was broken no one knew what to expect from him."[79] Ken Raffensberger, who pitched for the Phillies, admitted that Chapman issued "a standing order that whenever any pitcher had two strikes and no balls on Robinson he had to knock him down. If he didn't, the pitcher was fined $50." Raffensberger, who was a control pitcher, ignored the order, refusing to put himself in that situation. "I'd make sure to start Robinson off with a ball," he said, "then I might go to two strikes. But I wasn't going to bait Robinson, nor was I going to pay any $50 fine!"[80] Howie Schultz, the Phillies' regular first baseman, had similar feelings.

Ironically Schultz had been traded to the Phillies from the Dodgers before the opening of that series in order to make room at first base for Robinson. But he had no ill feelings toward his onetime teammate. In fact Schultz developed a great deal of admiration for Robinson, having spent the entire season with him at Montreal in 1946 and seeing firsthand the admirable way he handled all the adversity. Now Schultz was playing for a man who, in his view, was "still fighting the Civil War." "While I certainly wasn't proud of the Phillies' behavior, I realized that I was the property of their organization and kept my mouth shut." When Robinson reached first base, Schultz, embarrassed, asked, "How can you stand this crap?" Robinson looked up at his former teammate and replied, "I'll have my

16. Phillies manager Ben Chapman led his team in a racist verbal assault on Robinson when the two teams met in the spring of 1947. When ordered to pose for a conciliatory photograph prior to a May 19 night game, Chapman grudgingly agreed, but he refused to shake Robinson's hand. (Bettmann/Corbis/AP Images)

day."[81] The Dodgers' first baseman had another bad game, which only led to more verbal abuse.

At the same time, however, Philadelphia's African American baseball fans turned out in record numbers to cheer for Robinson. "Never before had so many blacks come out to a Phillies game," recalled Stanley Glenn, who played catcher for the Negro League's Philadelphia Stars. "Blacks from as far as Baltimore, Harrisburg, and Wilmington, Delaware, chartered buses called 'Jackie Robinson Specials' and traveled all the way to Philadelphia just to see him play. We probably had close to twenty thousand blacks at Shibe Park for that Dodger series, and before Jackie broke the color barrier the Phils would be lucky to draw ten thousand—white or black—for a doubleheader."[82] Complaints from the city's black fans also prompted the National League to order an immediate stop to the assault.[83] Silenced by the edict, the Phillies attempted to humiliate Robinson the following day by pointing their bats at him and making gunshot sounds in a mock display of the death threats that had been reported in the Philadelphia newspapers.[84]

When asked if he instructed his players to ride Robinson, Chapman said, "Yes, I did. We not only did it to Robinson, but to all the other Brooklyn players. We're not treating him any better or worse than the other players. We didn't ride him because he's a Negro. We did it because we are trying to win."[85] But Chapman also insisted that the verbal abuse did not last long and was stopped on his orders, not those of National League president Ford Frick. "We found that every time we knocked Robinson down, verbally or physically, he would just get up and beat us," he said. "It was better not to get him mad, so after about the third time we played him I told our players to let him alone."[86]

As the season unfolded, Dodgers support for Robinson strengthened in response to the admirable way he handled all the adversity. Opposing pitchers threw at his head and ribs, while infielders would spit in his face if he was involved in a close play on the base paths. "Once I remember Jackie sliding safely into second after doubling to left-center field," recalled teammate Clyde King. "When the second baseman got the ball in the web of his glove he turned around and hit Jackie with it in the side of his face. It was so hard we could hear the impact in the dugout. But Jackie didn't say a word. He got up, dusted himself off, and stole third base."[87] Through it all, Robinson persevered. He even managed to keep a sense of humor.

Before one game in Cincinnati, when the Dodgers learned that their first baseman's life had been threatened, outfielder Gene Hermanski suggested that all the players wear Robinson's uniform number "42" on their backs to confuse the assailant. "Okay with me," responded Jackie. "Paint your faces black and run pigeon-toed too!"[88] When the Dodgers took the field, Reds fans and some of the players began to spew racial epithets at Robinson and Pee Wee Reese, a native Kentuckian, for playing on the same team with an African American. "We heard a lot of insults from the opposing bench and the fans," recalled Reese. "They were calling Jackie 'nigger' and 'water melon eater,' trying to rile him."[89] The Dodgers' captain, disgusted by their behavior, walked from his shortstop position over to Robinson at first base. Placing an arm across his teammate's shoulders, he gave him a simple word of encouragement, bringing a deafening silence to the crowd.[90] "I don't even remember what he said," Robinson remarked years later. "But his words weren't important. It was the gesture of comradeship and support that counted. The jeering stopped and a close lasting friendship between us began."[91]

Duke Snider, a twenty-year-old rookie lockered next to Robinson, marveled at his teammate's self-restraint as well as his ability to perform so well under pressure. On the field Snider "heard the taunts and insults from opposing players": "Opposing fans threw things at him. Players went out of their way to spike him. Pitchers threw at his head. After a game I'd see the anguish on Jackie's face—the frustration and the anger—because he wasn't allowed to say anything that first year. So he kept it all inside, but you could tell it was eating him up."[92]

Rival players weren't his only tormentors. Once, Robinson was playing poker with Hugh Casey, Marvin Rackley, and Spider Jorgensen. When Casey began losing he stunned everyone with a remark directed at his black teammate. "Ya know what I ah used to do down in Georgia when ah ran into bad luck?" he asked. "Ah used to go out and find me the biggest, blackest nigger woman and rub her teats to change my luck." Then he reached out and rubbed Robinson's hair.

Humiliated, Jackie swallowed hard, turned to Jorgensen, and said, "Deal the cards."[93]

Hate mail arrived daily. Most of it was directed at Jackie. Rarely were the letters signed, and even when they were they bore fictitious names. Occasionally there were threats to assault his wife, Rachel, or to kidnap their newborn son, Jackie Jr.[94] "We tried very hard, the both of us, to make our home a haven," said Rachel. "It was a place to relax, to assess things and be ready for the next day. So, Jack was as quiet and gentle at home as he was tenacious on the field."[95]

Initially the couple and their son stayed in a room at the McAlpin Hotel in Midtown Manhattan. There was very little privacy because of the constant intrusion of newspapermen. It was especially difficult for Rachel, who was trying to adjust to life with a baby. A few months into the season they rented an apartment in a two-family house on Tilden Avenue in the East Flatbush section of Brooklyn, at East 53rd Street. There the pace of life was slower. Jackie could be found wheeling his son in a stroller through the neighborhood or playing stickball with kids in the local schoolyard.[96] Now able to find refuge away from the playing field, he began to channel his anger and frustration into his play. "Jack found that the most powerful form of retaliation against prejudice was to 'hurt' the opposition by performing well," said Rachel.[97]

Robinson was a workmanlike baseball player. His fielding, hitting, and base-running were almost mechanical, lacking the gracefulness of a Pee Wee Reese, but he got the most out of his athletic ability. He was heavy in the legs and ran pigeon-toed. It was his quickness and intelligence, not his natural physicality, that made him a remarkable base runner. Jackie made things happen on the base paths. If he got on first, he stole second. If he could not steal third, he'd distract the pitcher by dancing off second in order to advance. And then he'd steal home. Using a thick-handled, thirty-six-ounce bat with a small barrel, just the opposite of most bats of the time, he swung down and through the ball, producing vicious line drives. If he singled to right field, he'd make a wide turn toward second, challenging the right fielder to throw behind him in order to nail him at first. But just as the throw reached the first baseman, Robinson was sliding into second. Extra-base hits resembled artillery fire, ricocheting off the outfield fences. It wasn't unusual for Jackie to turn a double into a triple or a triple into a run because it was almost impossible to catch him in a rundown. This style of play was nothing new in the Negro Leagues.

But in the white Majors it was innovative and exciting. The name of the game was to score runs without a hit, something quite different from the power-hitting strategy that had characterized Major League Baseball. During the next decade this new style of play introduced by Robinson would become known as "Dodger Baseball."[98]

Slowly the white baseball establishment began to embrace Robinson. In May Stanley Woodward of the *New York Herald Tribune* revealed an alleged plot by the St. Louis Cardinals to instigate a league-wide strike against Robinson by walking off the field in a scheduled game against the Dodgers.[99] Though Cardinal officials denied the report and Woodward later retracted major segments of the allegation, it did elicit a response from National League president Ford Frick, who vowed to suspend the ringleaders if they carried out their plan. "I don't care if I wreck the National League for five years," declared Frick. "This is the United States of America, and one citizen has as much right to play as another. The National League will go down the line with Robinson whatever the consequence."[100] If such a conspiracy did exist, it died on the spot. The following month, in a game at Pittsburgh, Robinson, trying to beat out a bunt, collided with Pirates first baseman Hank Greenberg. Greenberg, the former Detroit Tigers star who was in the final year of his playing career, managed to remain standing. Tension settled over Forbes Field as he advanced toward Robinson, who lay prostrate on the ground. Some anticipated trouble. But then Greenberg reached out to help Jackie to his feet.[101] "He stood there beside me at first base," recalled Greenberg, a Jew who had been discriminated against when he entered the big leagues in 1933. "I had a feeling for him because of the way I had been treated when I came up. I remember saying to him, 'Don't let them get you down. You're doing fine. Keep it up.'"[102]

Greenberg, a future Hall of Famer whose actions wielded significant influence among both players and fans, had given Robinson's crusade a moral validity with that simple gesture. Jews in particular could identify with Robinson because of their history of persecution. Robert Mayer, an eight-year-old Jew who was raised in the Bronx, rejected the Yankees because of Robinson. "It was out of some unconscious desire to root for the underdog," he confessed in a recent book, *Notes of a Baseball Dreamer*. "With his dark skin and pigeon toes, Jackie Robinson quickly became the most exciting player in the game as well as the Dodgers' claim to moral superiority before all the world."[103]

When the season ended, the *Sporting News*, which had gone on record earlier as opposing the integration of baseball, named Robinson the National League Rookie of the Year for his impressive performance that season: twenty-nine stolen bases, twelve home runs, forty-two successful bunt hits, and a .297 batting average.[104] Those efforts helped the Dodgers to capture a pennant, and on September 23 jubilant Brooklyn fans cheered their first baseman with a "Jackie Robinson Day" at Ebbets Field. In addition to a new car and other gifts, Robinson received tributes for his contribution to racial equality. "Twenty-five whites and one black on our team," said Bobby Bragan, who had signed a petition against Robinson earlier that season, "and we win the National League. That means we all get $4,500 apiece. You can bet we were all real grateful to the one black guy. We couldn't have done it without him."[105]

The Dodgers forced the New York Yankees to a seventh and deciding game in the World Series. When it was all said and done, the Yanks had added yet another World Series title to their illustrious history.[106] But not even that could tarnish the success of Robinson's season.

Despite all the abuse he took from opposing teams and their fans, Jackie Robinson managed to restrain his fury, channeling the anger into his play. The fire inside still burned white-hot, but instead of striking back at the bigots who provoked him with racial epithets it drove him to excel not only for himself but for his race. He might even have learned that the measure of a man could be found just as much in personal discipline as in physical retribution for an injustice. In the process he had not only proven that he belonged in the Major Leagues but had opened the door for other black ballplayers.

5

Teammates

Before the 1947 season was over, four more Negro Leaguers appeared in the Majors. Larry Doby of the Newark Eagles joined the Cleveland Indians in early July, becoming the first to break the color barrier in the American League.[1] Later that month the St. Louis Browns signed Willard Brown, an outfielder, and Harry Thompson, an infielder, both of whom played for the Kansas City Monarchs. When St. Louis played the Boston Red Sox on July 20, it was the first time black players appeared in a Major League game together.[2] And on August 26 Dan Bankhead, formerly a pitcher with the Memphis Red Sox, appeared for the Brooklyn Dodgers and hit a home run against the Pittsburgh Pirates in his first Major League at-bat.[3] Throughout the remainder of the '47 campaign, these black ballplayers suffered the same indignities that Jackie Robinson experienced, but with little media attention and even less support from teammates and Major League Baseball. While their presence might have threatened the white baseball establishment, it was clear that Branch Rickey had made some valuable allies.

Bill Veeck, owner of the Cleveland Indians, broke the color line in the American League by signing Larry Doby and established himself as a genuine proponent of integration. His purported bid to purchase the Philadelphia Phillies and stock the team's roster with star Negro Leaguers five years earlier no longer appeared to be an idle bluff. Veeck had now confirmed the permanence of integration in Major League Baseball. Richard Muckerman, owner of the St. Louis Browns, was a recent convert to the cause, though his intentions were strictly financial. Muckerman, owner of a perennial cellar dweller, was attracted by the novelty of black players to draw increasing numbers of fans. Noting that National League atten-

17. Jackie welcomes Campy to the Brooklyn Dodgers during spring training at Vero Beach, Florida, in March 1948. (AP Photo)

dance was up by 15 percent, he couldn't help but consider the financial rewards of integration. Brown and Thompson were signed to increase the gate. But regardless of their intentions, Muckerman and Veeck integrated their teams with the support of the black leagues. Unlike most of Rickey's signings, Veeck acknowledged the validity of Negro League contracts by negotiating with Abe and Effa Manley, owners of the Newark Eagles, to secure Doby's services. Muckerman did the same with the Kansas City Monarchs. This was an important step at a time when Negro League owners felt that their businesses were being threatened by the white baseball establishment.[4]

Emboldened by Robinson's success both on the playing field and at the gate, Rickey signed an additional sixteen Negro Leaguers. His prize catch was Roy Campanella, who continued to excel in the Brooklyn farm system. In 1947 Campy was promoted to Montreal, where his .273 batting average, 13 home runs, 75 RBIs, and remarkable .998 fielding average earned him the International League's Most Valuable Player Award.[5] He also proved to be an outstanding catcher.

Campy's calm demeanor made him a natural catcher. Like all good backstops, he had soft hands and a relaxed upper body that allowed him to receive the ball instead of stabbing at it. Pitchers who relied on breaking balls loved to throw to him because his soft hands and stationary position behind the plate accentuated the movement of the ball, giving the hurler a better chance for a called strike. At five feet nine and a weight that ranged between 200 and 215 pounds, Campanella possessed the ideal body type for a catcher. He was built like a fireplug, stocky and durable, which enabled him to stay low in the strike zone to give a target, receive pitches, and block errant throws. He was also smart. He knew his pitchers' strengths and weaknesses, not just their repertoire of pitches but which ones would be most effective that day. He also knew the strengths and weaknesses of opposing batters and their idiosyncrasies, like whether they were first-pitch hitters or tended to work the count. Campy knew the umpires too: whether they had a high or low strike zone, how much bench-jockeying they were willing to tolerate, and how flexible they were in calling a game. Armed with this knowledge, he was adept at readjusting the infield or outfield when necessary to defend against a particular offensive situation. With all of the mental and physical demands, the catcher is the natural leader of a baseball team. Catching is also the most exhausting position on the field.[6] Yet Campanella was extremely durable and loved the position.

By the spring of 1948 Rickey knew that his prize backstop was ready for the Majors. Although Campy was promoted to Brooklyn on April 1, the only playing time he saw was in the outfield. Rickey had other plans for him. He knew Campanella couldn't make it as an outfielder, so he'd be forced to demote him to Triple-A St. Paul after a month. "I know you can make the Dodgers as a catcher," Rickey told him, "but I want you to help me do something bigger, something very important to me, to you, and to baseball. I want you to become the first colored ballplayer in the American Association. I am going to option you to our farm club at St. Paul, to pioneer the Negroes into the American Association."[7] As incentive, Rickey increased Campanella's salary to $1,500 over the $5,000 Major League minimum. Not that it mattered much to Campy; he had waited a lifetime to reach the Majors, and now that dream was "being interrupted by a seemingly unnecessary departure to play another season in the minors."[8]

"Mr. Rickey," Campanella replied with obvious disappointment, "I'm a ballplayer, not a pioneer."[9] Heeding the counsel of his parents and his Negro League managers, however, Campy refused to create controversy. Demoted to St. Paul on May 15, he was extremely discouraged and it affected his performance. In his first game, on May 22, he went hitless in four at-bats, striking out twice. In the field he made a throwing error on a pick-off attempt. But he rebounded the very next week against the Minneapolis Millers, smashing three homers and a triple and fielding his position flawlessly in the three-game series. By the end of June he was hitting .325 with eleven home runs and thirty-nine RBIs and had earned a trip back to Brooklyn.[10]

As Campanella was tearing up the pitching in the American Association, the Dodgers were floundering in last place, and Robinson was still far from the impressive play he had shown the previous season. He had reported to spring training twenty pounds overweight that season, thanks to a winter on the banquet circuit. Neither Leo Durocher, who returned to manage the team after a one-year suspension, nor Rickey was happy about the weight gain and let him know it. Having traded Eddie Stanky to the Boston Braves, they planned to move Robinson from first to second base, a more natural position for him.[11] But the additional weight made it difficult for him to make the transition to a middle infielder. Durocher put Robinson through "furious physical paces" in order to lose the extra weight. Often he ordered a coach to take a bucket of balls and hit endless grounders to the overweight infielder. "Jackie came to camp hog fat," recalled Durocher, "and I let him know I was unhappy. What really made me mad was that he kept insisting he wasn't overweight. When I finally was able to get him on the scales, the needle went up to 216 pounds. The previous year he had come in at 195."[12] Durocher's boot-camp approach only served to make Robinson resentful. He showed no sign of losing the weight and entered the season eighteen pounds heavier than in his rookie year.[13]

When Brooklyn lost their home opener to the Philadelphia Phillies 10–2, Jackie was severely criticized by the press. Noting that the additional weight had resulted in a strained back, making it difficult for him to throw, Herbert Goren of the *New York Times* wrote that Robinson "cost the Dodgers at least three runs in the opener." In the second inning, with two outs and runners on first and third, the Phillies executed a double steal. Catcher Gil Hodges threw to second on a decoy. Robinson "cut off the throw and tried to nail Richie Ashburn [the Phils' speedy center fielder] at home." It was "an accurate but weak throw," and Ashburn beat the tag, scoring the first run of the game. Next "two straight base hits found their way through the right side of the infield." Neither was "hit hard," but Robinson "couldn't come up with either one." After missing a third grounder, some of the Dodgers' fans stood up and yelled, "We want Stanky back!"[14]

Robinson struggled to play second base throughout the spring. The weight problem not only resulted in a sore back but made it almost impossible to get to hard-hit balls in the hole or run the bases as effectively as he had the previous year. Durocher, believing in the power of negative motivation, benched him and made Gene Mauch, a utility infielder, the Dodgers' second baseman. Rickey went a step further and vented his frustration to the press. On May 26 the *New York Daily Mirror* reported that the Dodgers' president, displeased by the weight problem, placed Robinson on waivers, giving the impression that he was on the trading block.[15] Rickey was bluffing. He had forty-eight hours to remove Robinson's name from the waiver list, which is exactly what he did. Jackie finally got the message and took off the weight.[16] But his patience with Rickey's "no striking back" ban was wearing thin.

Although the ban was still in effect in 1948, Robinson became increasingly confrontational whenever he perceived a racial snub. After all the bigotry he had suffered in his rookie year, he did not make much if any distinction between a brush-back pitch or a take-out slide—which were accepted tactics among Major Leaguers—and racial abuse. He tended to treat any aggressive play directed at him as a racial affront. "At the beginning of the season, Jackie was still a reasonably quiet young man," recalled Durocher. "I wanted him to stay that way. But as the season progressed, he became more combative. My advice to him was when pitchers knock you down, take it as a compliment. Just get back up and keep your mouth shut."[17] It was sound advice. The Dodgers couldn't afford to have Robinson ejected from the game; his bat was too valuable. To appease him, Durocher, taking a gentler approach, promised to support Robinson if he was knocked down by an opposing hurler. He proved to be good to his word.

Shortly after their talk, the Dodgers played the St. Louis Cardinals in a four-game series at Ebbets Field. In the first game, a Redbirds pitcher threw at Robinson, sending him to the ground. Robinson jumped to his feet ready to explode, but Durocher interceded and convinced him to return to the batter's box and hit. The next time Stan Musial, the Cards' star hitter, stepped to the plate, Durocher ordered his pitcher to throw at him. Not only did the Brooklyn hurler level Musial with his first delivery, but the second one sent him sprawling as well. Musial, realizing that the payback was in order, didn't complain. But in the next inning he stopped Durocher, who was coaching third base, on the field and complained, "Hey Leo, I don't have the ball out there. I didn't throw at Robinson."

"Stan, old boy," replied Durocher, "you better tell your manager to let Robinson alone. As far as I know, I've got twenty-five players, too. Robinson is one of my best. You're the best player I know on the Cardinals. For every time he gets a knockdown pitch, it looks to me like you're going to get two." Apparently Musial delivered the message to his manager since Robinson was left alone for the remainder of the series. It also helped that Jackie paced the Dodgers in a come-from-behind win, going four for four with a grand slam in the ninth inning of that first game.[18]

To be sure, Robinson continued to experience knockdown pitches, physical abuse on the base paths, and racial epithets from the opposing dugouts throughout the 1948 season, though not as frequently as the previous year. Opponents were learning that the more they tried to provoke him, the better he played. In Philadelphia, for example, Robinson was the object of vitriolic bench-jockeying and responded with a base-stealing spree, including a swipe of home. "There was no doubt as to Jackie's talent," said pitcher Robin Roberts, who had been promoted to the Phillies in the spring of 1948. "From the first time I faced him that year it was clear that he was not only an exceptional base runner but also a solid hitter and an all-around ballplayer. I was so nervous just being called up to the big leagues that I had quite enough to worry about just trying to keep him off the base paths."[19]

Center fielder Richie Ashburn, also promoted to the Phillies that season, downplayed the racial overtones of the Phillies' bench jockeying. "[Manager Ben] Chapman wasn't the only one riding Robinson," he said. "Everyone on our team got on him, including me. And being from Nebraska I didn't have any racial feelings one way or the other. Heck, I was in there to play baseball and beat somebody, and most players were in there for the same reason."[20] But in a column he wrote for the *Philadelphia Bulletin* in 1973, Ashburn publicly apologized for his role in the Phillies' Robinson-bashing during that season. He admitted that his purposeful spiking of the Dodgers' second baseman on the base paths was done more out of peer pressure and to follow Chapman's orders than for himself. "I felt sorry for Jackie," he wrote. "Major league baseball is tough enough under ideal conditions, but Jackie had to battle the fans and the press as well as our club, which was exceptionally tough on him. Maybe I should have said something, but I wasn't a crusader. I was just a kid then, trying to beat the Dodgers."[21]

Instead of striking back, Robinson channeled the anger into his play. "After I spiked him," recalled Ashburn, "it only seemed to motivate him more. Jackie beat us like a drum that series, and there wasn't much bench jockeying after that."[22] Ben Chapman was fired a few weeks later. When Eddie Sawyer, a reserved former professor from Ithaca College, became the new manager, the Phillies treatment of Robinson improved dramatically.

By the end of June Jackie was "asserting himself with a vengeance," according to Durocher. It was clear that he was venting his rage through his aggressive play, but if he started just one fight he would risk losing all the progress he had made. Having failed repeatedly to rein him in, Durocher chose to look the other way, dismissing Robinson's fiery play as a matter of self-motivation and competitive drive. "Jackie was the kind of player who needed to be diving, scratching and yelling to be at his best," he said in his 1975 autobiography, *Nice Guys Finish Last*. "He doesn't just want to beat you, he wants to shove the bat up your ass. I could understand that. It was the way I played. Besides, he resented my trying to keep a rein on him."[23] Robinson insisted that was not the case. "I think Leo felt I had not given him my best effort that season and that I had worked harder for Shotton the year before," he recalled years later. "Although Leo and I got into a number of hassles and exchanged many verbal insults, I believe we never lost the respect we had for each other."[24]

By most accounts, Durocher was a difficult person to respect, let alone like. Ironically Robinson was somehow able to put aside his own strong moral code to respect a manager with a Las Vegas lifestyle replete with loose women, mobsters, gamblers, and other unsavory characters. In fact Robinson maintained few loyalties, though the ones he had were unconditional. Branch Rickey, for example, was certainly not a disinterested humanitarian in regard to the integration of baseball. If he was, he would not have disrespected the Negro League owners by refusing to compensate them for the contracts of the players he signed. Though Robinson might have understood the contradiction, he never acknowledged it. Instead he supported Rickey's contention that the Negro Leagues were a poorly run business and the contracts were not legally binding. David Falkner, author of *Great Time Coming: The Life of Jackie Robinson from Baseball to Birmingham*, believes that Robinson wrote an essay for *Ebony Magazine* in June 1948 condemning the black leagues in order to defend Rickey against charges by Negro League owners that he stole their players.[25] Nor did Robinson show much loyalty to Satchel Paige, one of the Negro League's greatest stars, who paved the way for his opportunity to integrate baseball.

When Paige signed with the Cleveland Indians on July 7, 1948, joining Larry Doby as the second African American player on that team, Robinson was asked to comment and replied that Paige was the "greatest Negro pitcher in the history of the game."[26] According to Doby, however, Jackie "detested Satch strongly." "Satch was competition for Jack," said Doby. "Satch was funny. He was an outstanding athlete, and he was black. He had three things going. Jack and I wouldn't tell jokes. We weren't humorists. We tried to show that we were intelligent, and that's not what most white people expect from blacks. Satch gave whites what they wanted from blacks—joy."[27]

Doby's observation that "Satch was competition for Jack" raises the question of jealousy. Baseball writers and historians have portrayed Robinson as being above such petty jealousies. They suggest that his attitude toward Negro Leaguers was patronizing because of his superior education and success at other sports. If Robinson was jealous of Paige because he was stealing the spotlight, it may also serve to explain the inevitability of his conflict with Campanella.

Campy returned to the Dodgers on Friday night, July 2, just in time to appear in a three-game series against the rival New York Giants. To make room for him, rookie catcher Gil Hodges was moved to first base.[28] As soon as he arrived at Ebbets, the clubhouse manager sized up his square physique and picked out jersey No. 39, promising to give him a better-fitting uniform after the three-game series ended. That night, Campy went three for three with a double and two singles. The following night he belted a triple and two singles, and in the Sunday afternoon finale he smashed two home runs and singled to collect four RBIs. Needless to say, he kept No. 39 for the rest of his career.[29] With Campanella in the lineup, the Dodgers won sixteen of the next nineteen games.

"One of Branch Rickey's concerns was the relationship my father would establish with a primarily white pitching staff," said Roy Campanella Jr.[30] Campy quickly eliminated those concerns by taking charge from the start. Hugh Casey, a moody South Carolinian, made the mistake of challenging the new catcher's authority. The first time Casey pitched to him, Campanella called for a curve ball, but Casey ignored the signal and threw a fastball instead. The hitter launched the pitch into the upper deck. On the way back to the dugout, Campanella told the offending hurler, "You should never shake off one of my signs. I'm smarter than you, and you should know I'm smarter than you. I'm smarter than most of the pitchers on this team. That's why I call the signals."[31] No sooner had Campy completed his lecture than shortstop Pee Wee Reese, the team captain, got in Casey's ear. "Hugh," said the Kentucky Colonel, "maybe we better listen to Campy when he calls for a curve ball."[32]

Elwin Charles "Preacher" Roe, a southpaw from Arkansas, was a more receptive pupil. Roe, who'd been a hard-luck pitcher for the Pittsburgh Pirates, turned his career around when he came to the Dodgers in 1948 because he listened and learned from the black catcher. "Campy immediately set himself in charge of things," recalled Roe. "He'd say: 'Now you just do what Ol' Campy tells ya and I guarantee we'll get by,' and it'd be that way."[33] With Campanella behind the plate, Roe became one of the Dodgers' greatest pitchers, compiling a record of ninety-three wins and thirty-seven losses for a .715 winning percentage, 632 strikeouts, and a 3.26 earned run average during his seven years in Brooklyn.[34]

Ironically Durocher, who pushed for Campanella's promotion, had already sealed his own fate with Brooklyn. Rickey had had enough of his manager's outspoken opinions, his off-field antics, and his antagonistic treatment of Robinson. On July 16, just two weeks after Campy's return, the Dodgers' president fired "Leo the Lip" and brought back the more sedate Burt Shotton, who had guided Brooklyn to the pennant the previous season. At the same time, Rickey quietly ensured that the fiery little manager would have a job in baseball by finagling an elaborate scheme with the rival New York Giants, who simultaneously fired their own manager, Mel Ott, in order to hire Durocher.[35] Over the next decade Leo and the despised Giants would offer the Dodgers their stiffest competition in the National League.

Rickey and Shotton almost immediately retooled the Dodgers' lineup. With Campanella behind the plate, Gil Hodges was made the regular first baseman, a move that strengthened the team at two positions. Campy went on to hit .258 with 9 home runs and 45 RBIs, while Hodges (.249, 11 home runs, 70 RBIs) provided consistency both at the plate and in the infield. Veteran Pete Reiser, whose arm was gone, was demoted to pinch hitter, and Gene Hermanski (.290, 15 home runs, 60 RBIs) took his place in the outfield. Shortly afterward, Duke Snider, a good-looking young power hitter, was called up from the Minors and contributed 21 homers to the offensive attack. Together with Hermanski and Carl Furillo (.297, 44 RBIs), Snider would form one of the strongest outfields in the National League. Rickey also promoted Carl Erskine, a compact five-foot-ten, 165-pound fastballer, from St. Paul. Erskine, who went 6-3 with an impressive 3.26 earned run average in just seventeen games that season, would prove to be one of the gutsiest pitchers in the game over the next decade.[36]

Finally, with Durocher off his back, Robinson managed to turn his season around. He went on a hitting tear, boosting his average to .296 and leading Brooklyn to a 31-15 record over a six-week period. His fielding also improved as he and shortstop Pee Wee Reese developed into a strong double-play combination. But Robinson's "personal highlight" came in a

18. Campy and Jackie at the Harlem YMCA, November 1948. (University of Minnesota Libraries)

game against Pittsburgh when he was ejected for "heckling an umpire." The incident occurred when Butch Henline, the home-plate umpire, called Gene Hermanski out on strikes. Several of the Dodgers began to protest what they believed was a bad call. He gave them a warning to quit, but Jackie continued to heckle him. Losing his patience, Henline tore the mask off his face and threw Robinson out of the game. There was nothing unusual about an umpire ejecting a player for overzealous bench jockeying, but that's exactly why Robinson valued it. "Henline didn't pick on me because I was black," he said. "He was treating me exactly as he would any ballplayer who got on his nerves. That made me feel great, even though I couldn't finish the game." One sportswriter titled the next day's story "Jackie Just Another Guy." "It was the best headline I ever got," said Robinson.[37]

By September 2 the Dodgers were in first place by half a game. Unfortunately the team went into a tailspin after that. Reese, the lead-off hitter, slumped, managing just two hits in forty-seven at-bats. Without their offensive catalyst, the Dodgers' attack came to a grinding halt. The Boston Braves won the pennant, with St. Louis finishing second and the Dodgers a half-game behind the Cardinals in third.[38] Nevertheless Rickey had assembled the core of a remarkably talented team. His anticipated dynasty was taking shape.

Just as important, Robinson found someone with whom he could share the burden of being a black player in a white man's game. With Campanella's promotion to the Dodgers, he had someone to talk with, to serve as a sounding board when he vented his anger, and to watch his back. "I roomed with Jackie when I first came up," said Campy. "We discussed [the racial abuse] every night when we'd go to bed. Jackie got into a few arguments, and I tried to tell him to just cool it. All we were out there to do is to prove we could play ball."[39] Robinson reciprocated by taking his younger teammate under his wing, spending time with him on the road, and preparing him for the life of a Major Leaguer.

The friendship blossomed over the course of the season. As the only African American Dodgers, they were not always given accommodations in the same hotels or restaurants as their white teammates, so they lodged and ate together on the road. When the Dodgers played in Philadelphia, a city notorious for segregated hotels, Campy invited Jackie and Rachel to spend the weekend at his parents' house on Kerbaugh Street. The two players also confided in each other. Jackie offered baseball advice, and Campanella often deferred to him out of affection as well as the tremendous respect he felt toward his teammate for all the racial abuse he suffered. They became closer in the off-season after Jackie accepted a position as athletic director at the Harlem YMCA. He persuaded Roy to join him in working with disadvantaged youth, teaching them good sportsmanship, refereeing basketball games, playing checkers, and occasionally shooting pool with them. In addition, Campanella and Robinson made frequent appearances at public schools across the city, conducting baseball clinics after school hours.[40] The teammates became so close that in January 1949, when the Campanellas purchased a house in the affluent Addisleigh Park section of St. Albans in southeast Queens, the Robinsons relocated there as well. Separated by just a few blocks, now even their families spent much of their time together.[41]

Baseball's noble experiment with integration appeared to be evolving just as Branch Rickey had planned. Other African American players were already in the Dodgers' farm system and would be promoted to Brooklyn in the near future. And Jackie and Campy would provide the leadership to ensure their success.

6

Striking Back

Jackie Robinson reported to spring training in March 1949 in great antici-pation of the coming season. Having shunned the winter banquet circuit, he weighed 190 pounds, thirty pounds lighter than at the start of the '48 campaign. The lighter weight enabled him to cover more ground defen-sively and improve his offensive production by stealing more bases and bunting for base hits. Jackie planned to show the National League his true worth not only as a player but as a man.

For two seasons Rickey had sworn his star second baseman to a Christ-like existence of turning the other check, and Robinson had responded with "courage far beyond what [Rickey] had asked." But at the end of the '48 season Rickey realized that it was time to "issue an emancipation proclamation" for Robinson. He knew that "burning inside Jackie was an intense pride and determination" that could be stifled no longer. Rickey had seen the "tensions build up over two years" and worried that his "fil-ial relationship with Robinson would break with ill feeling if . . . he didn't tell him he was on his own."[1]

"Jack knew by 1949 that he was going to be able to be himself," said Rachel Robinson. "I saw it in terms of his greater spirits because now he didn't have to take anything from anybody. He just started the season that way, and the greater freedom was clear in his play, too."[2] In fact Robinson didn't wait for the regular season to begin. He exhibited his newfound freedom in the very first intrasquad game that spring at Vero Beach, Flor-ida. The game pitted Pee Wee Reese's squad of veterans against a younger group of Dodgers captained by catcher Bruce Edwards. By the third in-ning, Reese's team was being shellacked and Gene Wade, a brash twenty-year-old rookie outfielder, began to ride the veterans. Robinson, assigned to Reese's squad, took exception and returned the fire. The jockeying and profanity became worse as the game progressed.

In the seventh inning, Chris Van Cuyk, a six-foot-five, 220-pound pitcher, entered the game for Edwards's squad. Van Cuyk, who had won fourteen games at Double-A Fort Worth the previous season, was considered a top prospect. He was also a vitriolic bench jockey who'd been riding the veterans throughout the game. When he took the mound, Robinson showed no mercy.

"You'll be a 20-year man in Class D," he mocked, standing in to face the rookie pitcher. After Van Cuyk threw him two quick strikes, Jackie lined the third pitch over third base for a single and tore down the line shouting insults at the young hurler. Then, taking a sizable lead off first, he proceeded to heckle Van Cuyk with further taunts as well as false breaks toward second. "You do a lot of talking, Chris," Robinson goaded. "Why don't you do a little talking off that mound and see what happens."

When Robinson came to bat again in the ninth, Van Cuyk brushed him back with a letters-high fastball. The next pitch was also tight, this one around the knees, and Jackie had to dance out of the batter's box. Infuriated that a rookie was trying to intimidate him, Robinson lashed out at the next pitch, popping up to the catcher. "That's where your power is, Robinson!" shouted Van Cuyk.

Jackie said nothing. But after the game, as the players headed for the clubhouse, he confronted the rookie pitcher and warned him not to throw at him again. Before fists could fly, Campanella, ever the peacemaker, interceded. Stepping between the two players, Campy defused the situation with his quick wit and a smile, something he would do often over the next seven months.[3]

Arch Murray of the *New York Daily News* learned about the altercation and was waiting for Robinson in the parking lot to get the scoop. When asked about the incident, Jackie confirmed that Branch Rickey had lifted the ban and that opposing teams had "better be rough on me this year because I'm sure going to be rough on them."[4]

Concerned about the veiled threat, Commissioner Happy Chandler visited the Dodgers' training camp to urge Jackie "not to spoil a good record." Robinson assured him that he "had no intention of creating problems," but that he was "no longer going to turn the other cheek to insults."

Chandler claimed to understand his position but cautioned him about the adverse implications of his behavior for other black players, like pitcher Don Newcombe, who had just been promoted to the Majors.[5] Chandler had put his job on the line by supporting the Dodgers' experiment with integration, and he didn't want Robinson to jeopardize his credibility with the owners. He emphasized the responsibility that the star second baseman had not only to himself but to other African Americans as well as to baseball itself.

Once the regular season began, Jackie, no longer saddled with Rickey's ban, protested calls and taunted opponents and umpires on a regular basis. Nor did he ever back down when challenged. Once, in Philadelphia, Robinson was caught in a run-down between third and home in a tie game against the Phillies. Phils third baseman Puddin' Head Jones and catcher Andy Seminick were already positioned along the third base line, as shortstop Granny Hamner, second baseman Mike Goliat, and pitcher Russ Meyer rushed over to prevent him from scoring. The Phillies threw the ball back and forth, but Jackie, anticipating their throws, lunged, leaped, and stopped, evading a tag. He stayed in the run-down for more than forty seconds. Then, after an errant throw, Robinson sprinted for home. Meyer, who was covering home plate, dropped to his knees and grabbed Jackie's legs to prevent him from scoring. Undeterred, the Dodgers' second baseman bounced a hip off Meyer's head and scored, saying, "What the hell are you trying to do?!"

"Under the stands, Robinson," said Meyer, challenging him to a fight.

"Right now," snapped Jackie.

But the Philadelphia police beat them to the proposed ring, and the game resumed.[6]

Such incidents only served to show that Robinson not only won games, but he infuriated the losers in the process. Opposing players considered him "thin-skinned," while teammates tended to look the other way.[7] "I saw the wraps come off and watched him fight back," said Brooklyn center fielder Duke Snider. "And, believe me, he could dish it out. He was mean, sarcastic and caustic. I was somewhat embarrassed by some of the things he did or said in retribution. Then I'd think back and remember what he had gone through, so I figured he earned the right to do and say those things."[8]

Snider's mixed emotions were shared by pitcher Carl Erskine, who was befriended by Robinson when he was promoted to Brooklyn the previous season. Although Erskine believed that the unattractive behavior was "overkill on Jackie's part," he was sympathetic toward Robinson "because he'd been trying to control his anger for so long."[9] Still, Erskine admitted that "even Rickey wound up thinking it was a mistake to lift the ban" when he did.[10]

Campanella tried to get Robinson to restrain himself. He encouraged his teammate to have his say and then back off, allowing the manager and coaches to fight his battles. But as the season progressed, Campy realized the futility of his efforts.[11]

Brooklyn fans, on the other hand, gave Robinson their full sympathy. Their blue-collar background celebrated rough-and-tumble heroes. "Retributive justice" was part of the game, especially if it was exacted against the hated Giants. "When I was six-years-old, Jackie Robinson filled my imagination," recalled Doris Kearns-Goodwin, the Pulitzer prize–winning historian. For Kearns-Goodwin, who first saw Robinson play in the summer of 1949, Jackie's umpire-baiting, taunts, and aggressive play against a racist opponent were indistinguishable from his competitive drive, which manifested itself in his "diving head-long to snag a line-drive and taking a huge lead to provoke the pitcher." She simply viewed his behavior as that of a "fiery second baseman" and swore that "with nine Jackie Robinsons we'd never lose a game."[12]

Others, like the noted author Roger Angell, a devout Dodgers fan, believed that Robinson's controversial behavior reflected the bitterness he harbored over the tremendous responsibility he was asked to accept as the first black player to integrate the game. Seated in the Ebbets Field bleachers that season, Angell watched as Robinson "tore into an umpire without warning" and "for no immediate reason that his teammates or the opponents could discern." "After that moment," Angell admitted, "I knew that we had asked him to do too much for us."[13] Still others empathized with Jackie. Louis Uhlberg, a deaf freelance writer, had felt the sting of discrimination all his life because of the hearing impairment. Once he attended a Dodgers-Cardinals game where Robinson was purposely spiked on the base paths. Brooklyn fans expressed their outrage by standing and screaming "JACKIE! JACKIE! JACKIE!" Uhlberg, following their lead, stood and joined the chorus. But since Uhlberg couldn't pronounce words clearly, his screams sounded like "AH-GHEE! AH-GHEE! AH-GHEE!" The incident made a profound impression on his young son, Myron:

> Fans in the neighboring seats looked at my father. He must surely have been aware of their stares, but he kept his eyes locked on Jackie, who just stood there, bright red blood streaming down his leg with a face as if it had been carved in black marble. Embarrassed, I looked down at my feet.
>
> On the subway ride home, my father signed, "I am a deaf man in a hearing world. All the time I must show hearing people that I am a man as well. A man as good as them. Maybe better. Very hard for a deaf man. Very hard for a black man."[14]

Louis Uhlberg, like other disabled fans, embraced Robinson because they too had experienced discrimination. They too had been made to feel less than human because of their condition. If Jackie sought retribution, they would understand and perhaps even admire him for it. Even heroes are human.

To be sure, there were times when Robinson's controversial behavior benefited his team. Once, in Chicago, Jackie taunted Cubs pitcher Sam Jones so severely that it altered the outcome of the game. "I'm going to get you, Sam," he threatened from the on-deck circle. "Just wait until I get in that batter's box."

After Duke Snider flied out, Robinson stepped up to the plate and continued to harass the Chicago hurler. "C'mon Sam," he chided, "throw that thing in here so I can do something with it, unless you're afraid."

Unnerved by all the taunting, Jones let fly a wild pitch that hit Robinson on the arm. It was exactly what Jackie wanted. Now on base, he could inflict even greater damage. Heckling Jones as he danced off first, Robinson forced the pitcher to make an errant pick-off throw. The ball rolled down the right-field line, enabling Jackie to reach third.

Having ruined Jones's concentration, Robinson closed in for the kill. Taking a huge lead off third, he watched as the embattled Cubbie threw a curve ball in the dirt. As the ball skidded past the catcher, Jackie trotted home with what proved to be the winning run.[15]

Robinson could be just as tough on teammates too. "If a guy didn't hustle," said Ralph Branca, who pitched for the Dodgers from 1944 to 1953, "Jackie would get on his case." Before that, he'd just mind his own business and keep quiet. But now that the ban was lifted, he could argue with umpires and get on the other team. It opened the door for him to just be natural."[16] At the same time, Jackie understood that his pioneering role was much larger than the national pastime. Embraced by the nation as an American sports hero, he graced the covers of magazines and was offered many opportunities to appear on national television. As a hero to millions, he needed to find a way to reinforce that awesome responsibility off the playing field. He found an outlet with the Harlem YMCA, a multimillion-dollar institution that served as an employer, hotel, soup kitchen, recreation center, and counseling office for literally tens of thousands of blacks in an impoverished community. Recruited by Rudolph Thomas, the director, Jackie agreed to serve as the Harlem Y's youth director working with at-risk children and encouraging them to improve their minds as well as bodies. The job not only protected the Dodgers' second baseman from charges that he cared only about himself and was exploiting his star power for his own gain, but it also gave him additional prestige within the civil rights movement.[17]

African Americans viewed Jackie as nothing less than a civil rights leader. They saw him breaking down the barriers that prevented them from securing equal opportunity in the workplace. Accordingly there were those blacks who applauded Robinson's combative behavior on the playing field, his outspokenness in the press, and his occasional challenge of Dodgers management. Others, black and white, did not appreciate his controversial style. Realizing that he needed the support of both races in order for integration to be successful, Robinson was extremely careful to draw the line at physical violence, even when provoked.[18]

"Jack was profoundly a nonviolent person," insists his wife, Rachel. "He never felt that violence was going to accomplish anything. He feared it, and rejected it as an option."[19] Robinson restrained himself when he realized that striking back could lead to physical violence. His mettle was first tested on April 8, when the Dodgers, playing their way north from spring training, were scheduled for a three-game exhibition series against the Atlanta Crackers of the Southern Association. Since Robinson and

Campanella were slated to start those games—and Don Newcombe would undoubtedly pitch in one—the first game would represent the first interracial athletic event in Georgia's history.

As early as January, when the exhibitions were first scheduled, Dr. Samuel Green, the Grand Dragon of the Ku Klux Klan, tried to stop them, contending that Georgia's segregationist laws prevented whites and blacks from playing with or against each other in a sporting contest. Governor Herman Talmadge gave Green his unconditional support. When Branch Rickey learned of the attempt to scuttle the games, he insisted, "No one anywhere in this country can tell me what players I can or cannot play."[20] Georgia's attorney general Eugene Cook backed Rickey, declaring that while the state had laws "dealing with segregation in the school system, transportation and marriage, there [was] no prohibition against Negroes playing baseball with white people." Nor were there any county or city ordinances barring interracial sporting competitions, though blacks were prohibited from attending such events as spectators. In addition, a local survey revealed that 90 percent of the Atlantans polled were eager to see the Dodgers play the hometown Crackers.[21]

Nevertheless when the Dodgers arrived at Atlanta's Ponce de Leon Park on April 8, the KKK was outside picketing them. With the assistance of city police, the team was escorted to the visitor's clubhouse, where Robinson was promptly handed a stack of death threats from local bigots. Dodgers manager Burt Shotton felt obligated to read one of the notices aloud: "Take the field and you're going to be shot!" Though he was accustomed to such threats, Robinson was deeply affected, but still he resolved to take the field.

"We were all scared and took the threats very seriously," recalled Carl Erskine. "This was different. It wasn't some heckler, a harmless nutcase in the bleachers. If ever a clubhouse of strapping young men was at a loss for words, this was the time. We couldn't believe anybody would want to kill somebody else for playing ball because of his race."[22] Stunned, the Dodgers sat in silence, not knowing what to say or do. Finally, outfielder Gene Hermanski offered some comic relief. "Why don't we all wear [Robinson's] No. 42?" he suggested. "Then the nut won't know who to shoot at!" The remark broke everyone up. Tensions eased, and the team began preparing for the game.[23]

African American spectators were forbidden from entering the park by a state ordinance that prohibited integrated attendance at a sporting event. But when Robinson, Campanella, and Newcombe protested, blacks were allowed to sit in the bleachers and in overflow sections in the outfield, which was cordoned off by ropes, and on a levee behind the right-field fence. To show their appreciation, the African American fans greeted the three black Dodgers with a roaring ovation when they took the field to warm up. Robinson, noticeably edgy, stood beside his double-play partner, Pee Wee Reese, near the batting cage. Reese tried to break the tension with some gallows humor. "Say, Jackie, do you mind moving over a few feet to your right?" he asked. "This guy might be a bad shot!"[24]

Despite Robinson's three-hit, two-RBI performance, he was both booed and cheered whenever he stepped to the plate. Still, the mixed response could not detract from his tremendous drawing power, even in the segregated South. More than 6,500 spectators jammed inside and around the periphery of Ponce de Leon Park, which seated only 4,000.[25] Jackie's huge popularity and his stature as a civil rights leader made him vulnerable to competing political interests. At a time when the United States was embroiled in a cold war against the Soviet Union, Congress feared the infiltration of Communist influences into American society. In the summer of 1949 the House Un-American Activities Committee (HUAC) conducted hearings to determine whether American minorities, especially blacks, were loyal to the United States. Alvin Stokes, HUAC's principal investigator, charged that the "Communist Party was setting up an independent Negro Soviet Republic in the South," asserting that the plot was "cunningly calculated to promote a civil war in which the Negro people would be sacrificed to the machinations of Moscow." Stokes insisted that the plan, as well as those African Americans who sympathized with Communism, posed a "serious national security threat." He also identified Paul Robeson, the well-known black athlete turned actor and singer, as one of the prominent African Americans who sympathized with Communism.[26] Robeson, an international celebrity, had recently inflamed matters at the Soviet-sponsored World Peace Conference in Paris when he suggested that African Americans would not go to war against a Soviet Union that staunchly opposed racial discrimination.[27]

To disprove Stokes's accusations, several witnesses testified about the sacrifices black soldiers had made during World War II, including Gen. Dwight D. Eisenhower, who was profoundly influenced by the racial discrimination he witnessed in the military ranks. "Our Negro population is fully worthy of its American citizenship," insisted Ike. "Negroes proved that loyalty on the battlefields of Europe and Africa."[28] Black witnesses who came before the committee went to great lengths to denounce Communism as well as Paul Robeson. Manning Johnson, who abandoned the American Communist Party and became a government informant, was the most damning witness. Calling Robeson a "Black Stalin," Johnson contended that the popular singer was under confidential orders from the Party "to work among the intellectuals, the professionals and artists they hoped to attract to their cause."[29] But HUAC, wanting to find an *African American* of Robeson's status to discredit him, turned to Jackie Robinson. Urged on by Branch Rickey and NAACP leaders Roy Wilkins and Lester Granger, Jackie reluctantly agreed to testify.[30]

Robinson's reservations were based, in part, on the deep respect he had for Robeson, who had achieved unprecedented star status as a college and professional athlete in the 1920s, as a lead actor in Hollywood in the 1930s, and as a concert singer in the 1940s. He used his popularity to speak out against racism and the racial stereotypes that undermined more positive images of blacks. In fact Robeson had been widely credited with paving the way for Robinson's quest to break baseball's color barrier with his public advocacy of integrating the game. A close friend and protégé of W. E. B. Du Bois, Robeson shared the scholar's belief that the race problem in America could be solved only through interracial cooperation, not separation. He actively promoted that philosophy in his public remarks and personal example. More important, Robeson's appeal transcended race, and as a result he was influential in the mainstreaming of African American culture and art forms. It was the very same kind of appeal that Robinson hoped to achieve for himself. Jackie was also keenly aware that his testimony would be used to pit one famous African American against another.[31] "Rachel and I had long talks about it," he recalled years later. "I knew that Robeson was striking out against racial inequality in the way that seemed best to him, but the newspaper accounts indicated that he was speaking for the whole race of black people. Even with all the respect I had for him, I didn't believe that anyone had the right to do that."[32] Jackie eventually agreed to testify before HUAC, fearing that his refusal might permanently damage his career.[33]

Appearing before HUAC on July 18, Robinson began his testimony by acknowledging that many people had urged him not to testify but that politics was something he could not avoid. Instead of focusing his remarks on Robeson's controversial statement, however, Jackie used the platform to attack American racism:

> Although I am no expert on communism, I am an expert on being a colored American with thirty years of experience at it. As I see it, there has been a terrific lot of misunderstanding on this subject of communism among Negroes in this country and it's bound to hurt my people's cause unless it's cleared up.
>
> What the public should understand is that every Negro is going to resent discrimination . . . and will use every bit of his intelligence to stop it. This has nothing to do with what communists may or may not be trying to do. The more a Negro hates communism because it opposes democracy, the more he is going to hate any other influence that kills off democracy in the country—and that goes for racial discrimination in the army and segregation on trains and buses, and job discrimination. . . . Negroes were stirred up long before there was a Communist Party and they'll be stirred up long after the party has disappeared. We can win our fight without the communists, and we don't need their help.

Shifting the topic to Robeson, Jackie expressed his doubts that the singer "could actually speak for fifteen million blacks" when he stated that African Americans would refuse to fight against the Soviets. "If he actually made the statement," Robinson added, "it sounds silly to me. But Mr. Robeson has a right to his personal views."[34]

Although Jackie tried to minimize the damage to Robeson by focusing on the issue of American racism, his HUAC testimony was a major media event. His carefully worded statement appeared on the front page of the *New York Times* the following day, precipitating questions about the relationship between the two prominent African Americans. Robeson took the high moral ground, declining to comment on Robinson personally. "I am not going to permit the issue to boil down to a personal feud between me and Jackie," he told a gathering of newspapermen. "To do that, would be to do exactly what the other group wants us to do."[35]

Jackie's remarks, however unintentional, destroyed any future success Robeson may have enjoyed in the United States. His concert engagements and movie contracts were canceled, and music stores stopped selling his records. Near summer's end, a symbolic lynching of Robeson took place at Peekskill, thirty miles north of New York City. A huge bonfire was lit by former fans to burn his sheet music. Others burned crosses. The protest quickly spiraled out of control as demonstrators began throwing rocks and overturning cars.[36] "Paul Robeson should have the right to sing, speak, or do anything he wants to do," said Robinson in an effort at damage control. "Those mobs make it tough on everyone. They say here in America, you're allowed to be whatever you want. I think those rioters ought to be investigated. Let's find out if what they did is supposed to be the democratic way of doing things."[37] But the damage had already been done.

Within months the federal government rescinded Robeson's passport, eliminating any possibility of his earning money abroad. Within three years Robeson's annual income plummeted from $104,000 to just $2,000.[38] The HUAC hearings had destroyed the prestige and influence Paul Robeson once enjoyed in the African American community by identifying him as a Communist. Unwittingly Robinson had contributed to Robeson's demise. Although he never expressed any regrets about his testimony, near the end of his life he stated that he had an "increased respect for Robeson, who sacrificed himself, his career and the wealth and comfort he once enjoyed because he was sincerely trying to help his people."[39]

Campanella never went on record about his teammate's appearance before HUAC, but it would have been against his nature to support Robinson's testimony. He purposely distanced himself from politics, not wanting to jeopardize the financial security and prestige a Major League career afforded him. That season he was elected to the National League All-Star Team, the first of eight straight appearances he made at the midsummer classic. Campy was now recognized as one of the very best catchers in the game. Nearly a decade of hardship in the Negro Leagues was beginning to pay off. That experience also taught him to do his talking on the playing field and otherwise keep his mouth shut. Campanella was unnerved by Robinson's outspokenness on civil rights issues and his combative behavior; he believed it did not project well on the few black players who had been promoted to the Majors and easily threatened the good life they currently enjoyed. While he tried to temper Jackie's controversial behavior, it was becoming increasingly difficult to do so. On August 2, for example, Jackie "threw his cap on the ground and went into a rage of disagreement" against the Chicago Cubs. Three weeks later, in Pittsburgh, he was ejected from a game by umpire Butch Henline for questioning a call and then suggesting that the arbiter was prejudiced.[40] Campy allegedly confronted Robinson after the latter incident, reminding him that his boorish behavior could jeopardize the cause of integration. "It may take ten years to go ahead, but you can fall all the way back in one," Campanella insisted. "It's nice up here [in the Major Leagues]. Don't spoil it."[41] Whether or not the confrontation actually took place, the sentiments expressed did echo Campy's true feelings. Years later he would tell baseball historian Jules Tygiel, "Everything we did stood out so much then [that we] couldn't afford to make a mistake."[42]

Campanella's anxiety over Jackie's behavior was heightened by the questionable influence he began to have on Don Newcombe. Newcombe had been Roy's teammate and closest friend in Nashua. When the young pitcher was promoted to the Dodgers in 1949, Campy, who had roomed with Robinson on the road, changed roommates. While Jackie may not have been happy about the arrangement, he understood the need for Newcombe to be reunited with his old teammate. "The matchup was perfect," according to Carl Erskine. "Campy soothed Newk, who was young, talented and brash."[43] Still, Robinson made an earnest effort to mentor the twenty-three-year-old rookie. At times Jackie was a positive influence, serving as a protector. During spring training in Vero Beach, for example, Newcombe got into an off-field altercation with Fermin Guerra, the Philadelphia Athletics' Hispanic American catcher. Because of Guerra's fair complexion, he was indistinguishable from white onlookers who rallied to his side. One of the observers handed the irate catcher a wooden post and told him "to kill the black [expletive] with it." Sam Lacy, a sportswriter for the *Baltimore Afro-American*, grabbed the Dodgers' rookie and hustled him off before any further damage could be done. "After that, there was talk that I was going to be lynched," Newcombe recalled. "Nobody took it lightly. At five in the morning, Jackie convened a meeting at Branch Rickey's house. Jackie, Mr. Rickey, Campy, Buzzie Bavasi, the mayor of Vero Beach, the sheriff and the chief of police were all there. They were prepared to get me out of town if they had to. The whole time they were talking they had an airplane waiting for me at the local airport. It was finally decided that I could stay, but I wouldn't be able to leave camp until the end of spring training."[44]

On other occasions Robinson could be a bully, challenging the young pitcher's character in order to motivate him on the mound. During the late spring, Newcombe started a game against the Pittsburgh Pirates and was enjoying an 11–1 lead in the fourth inning when he began having difficulty throwing strikes. He made matters worse by aiming the ball. After walking two straight batters, Jackie jogged in from second base and proceeded to goad him.

"Why don't you just go in and shower?" he said sarcastically. "You don't act like you want to win this one. See that bullpen out there? There are three guys who hope you leave. They want this easy win."

Newcombe was dumbfounded. He expected a pep talk. That's how Campy motivated him. But here was Jackie, dressing him down when he could use some encouragement. He didn't expect that, especially from another *black* teammate.

"Go on inside," continued Robinson. "Go shower, or reach back and throw the damn ball!" Infuriated by the suggestion that he was a quitter, Newcombe was burning up inside, but he didn't say a word. He just stood there on the mound and took it. After Robinson returned to his position, he relocated the strike zone and pitched himself out of trouble. The negative motivation had worked, but at what cost?

"Jackie always knew that getting inside Newk's head and rattling his cage a bit made him pitch better," explained Erskine. "But Campy was just the opposite. He would soothe Don in his own way. Cool and easy, Campy soothed Newk every time and emotionally stroked his confidence, like a balm on a wound."[45]

Campanella certainly wasn't going to goad Newcombe, or any pitcher for that matter. It wasn't his nature. He believed in the power of positive motivation. If he could help his pitchers relax, he knew he'd get peak performance from them, particularly Newcombe, who had a huge ego. Campy constantly stroked that ego, helping him to realize the tremendous potential he possessed. If Newcombe got himself into trouble during a game, Roy would settle him down with such encouraging phrases as "It's just you and me, roomie!," "You've got all it takes!," and "You're going to win this one!" If, on the other hand, Newcombe ignored the catcher's signals and needed to be disciplined, Campy registered the point in a humorous way: "Newk, you better do somethin' because when I signal for the express you throws me the local!"[46] It was as forceful as Roy was going to be with the young hurler. He couldn't afford to alienate Newcombe; it could destroy their friendship as well as hurt the team. Although Erskine insists that Newcombe benefited from both approaches, Newcombe felt differently.[47] "I'd call Campy a stabilizer," he said years later. "Roy stabilized fractious attitudes on the team, especially between Jackie and me."[48]

With Campanella's encouragement, Newcombe went on to pitch the Dodgers to a National League title that season. In the heat of the pennant race, he hurled thirty-two straight scoreless innings. At the end of the regular season, Newcombe had compiled an impressive 17-8 record with a league-leading five shutouts and a 3.17 earned run average. Duly impressed, the Baseball Writers Association of America voted him National League Rookie of the Year.[49] Slated to start the opening game of the 1949 World Series against New York at Yankee Stadium, Newcombe pitched shutout baseball through eight innings, allowing just three hits. But Yankee hurler Allie Reynolds was better, striking out nine and limiting the Brooklyn offense to just two hits to clinch a 1–0 victory. The lone run came in the bottom of the ninth, when Newcombe surrendered a game-ending homer to Tommy Henrich.[50]

Robinson, who extended his combative ways into the postseason, criticized plate umpire Cal Hubbard throughout the game for "calling so many bad strikes." He even went so far as to accuse the American League umpire of "calling a pitch-out a strike." After the game Commissioner Chandler ordered Jackie to stop "popping off" and to "behave himself," and, in a rare show of remorse, Robinson wired an apology to Hubbard.[51] But he got revenge in Game Two when he scored the lone run against Yankee pitcher Vic Raschi on a two-out single by Gil Hodges to win the game. Raschi later admitted that it wasn't Hodges who beat him, but Robinson, who was dancing off third base, bluffing for a steal of home. "I'd never seen anything like him before," said Raschi. "A human being who could go from a standing start to full speed in just one step. He did something to me that almost never happens—he broke my concentration and I paid more attention to him than to Hodges."[52] It proved to be Brooklyn's only victory in the Fall Classic, though, as the Yankees won the next three games to clinch the championship, four games to one.

Despite the loss, Robinson considered the season a success for the Dodgers. "There was a tremendous improvement in the closeness of our club," he said, oblivious to the anxiety his antagonistic behavior created for some teammates. "Racial tensions had almost completely dissipated and the club had been strengthened by the addition of talented players like Roy Campanella and Don Newcombe."[53] The 1949 campaign had also been a personal success for Jackie. He established himself as a strong defensive second baseman who could hit for both power and average. Playing in all 156 regular season games, Robinson compiled a .342 batting average, the best in the National League. He also led the league in stolen bases while collecting 203 hits, 16 home runs, 12 triples, and 28 doubles.[54]

When the Baseball Writers voted Robinson the National League's Most Valuable Player over Stan Musial of the St. Louis Cardinals by a thirty-eight-point margin, it appeared that the press was also willing to look the other way when it came to Jackie's combative behavior.[55] Rickey, an unconditional ally, also rewarded his star second baseman with a $35,000 contract for the upcoming season. Robinson added considerably more to his income by endorsing products, making public appearances, and signing a contract for a bio-pic, *The Jackie Robinson Story*, in which he costarred with Ruby Dee, who played the role of his wife, Rachel.[56]

In his eagerness to earn more money, however, Jackie alienated himself from Campanella. Campy and Newcombe, along with Larry Doby of the Cleveland Indians, made arrangements to join the Jackie Robinson All-Stars in a month-long postseason barnstorming tour through the South. All the players reportedly agreed to split the profits into four equal shares. But after the first few games, Campanella and Newcombe discovered that Robinson had made a separate deal with his promoter, Lester Dworman. According to the deal, Jackie would receive $5,000 up front, plus one-third of any profits over $70,000. The arrangement could potentially earn him three to four times as much as the $5,000 share Campy was promised and the $4,500 budgeted for Newcombe. Apparently Doby too cut a better deal for himself. He was guaranteed $5,000, an additional $25 for each of the first twenty games, plus 5 percent of the gross profits after expenses. But that didn't alleviate his anger when he discovered how much more Jackie stood to earn.[57] According to Campanella's biographer, Neil Lanctot, the three players considered leaving the tour but confronted Robinson instead. Jackie might have been embarrassed, but he was unapologetic and threatened to call off the tour. "I don't like what you're inferring here," he snapped. "I made my deal, you made your deal, and I can't be responsible because you are going to get five thousand dollars."[58] Dworman, the promoter, admitted that the tour "made a fortune" and that Campanella saw that the first night "when the audience was jammed." When Campy insisted on "a better deal," Robinson and Dworman, with Campy's signed agreement in hand, told him, "Go screw yourself, or get the hell outta here."[59]

Newcombe left the tour early to join a better-paying barnstorming trip on the West Coast. Doby gave Robinson the cold shoulder but remained with the tour. So did Campanella, though he was devastated by the betrayal of his close friend. Still, Roy played hard and extended himself to fans in his affable way. He even offered some effusive praise to an eighteen-year-old Willie Mays, who stole the show when the Robinson All-Stars played the Negro League's Black Barons at Birmingham's Rickwood Field on October 15. "The kid was playing centerfield," Campy recalled many years later. "We had Doby, a real speed demon, on third base. Somebody hit a fly ball to deep center and the kid made an over-the-shoulder bread basket catch. Then he wheeled and threw Doby out at the plate. I couldn't believe it." Campanella was so impressed with the play that he phoned Branch Rickey after the game and asked him to send a scout to watch Mays play.[60]

After three weeks Robinson, unapproachable and lethargic in his play, ended the tour with four games remaining on the schedule. More than 148,500 spectators had turned out for the tour, almost 50,000 more than expected. The tour did extremely well, earning Robinson $15,000.[61] Campanella returned home $5,000 richer but resentful of Jackie, who he felt had exploited him. Money had always been important to Campy. Although he realized that he did not command the popularity of Robinson, he still wanted to be treated fairly in terms of financial compensation. Shortly after the tour ended, Rickey learned about the falling out between his two star players and met with Campanella to discuss his contract for the upcoming season. The Dodgers' president handed a blank sheet of paper to his All-Star catcher, asking him to "write in the figure." Embarrassed, Campanella pushed the paper aside and requested to be "paid what I'm worth." But Rickey insisted. Taking pen in hand, Roy wrote $12,500, giving himself a $3,000 raise from the previous season. The amount was still $22,500 less than Robinson's salary but satisfied the catcher. Rickey called the contract "the best bargain in baseball."[62]

The year 1949 was indeed pivotal for Jackie Robinson. He had been freed from the restrictions of Branch Rickey's ban against striking back at racial discrimination on and off the playing field. He was able to express his anger and frustration against the bigotry of white society, though it was not always clear that his perception was accurate. Voted by the Baseball Writers the National League's Most Valuable Player, Robinson had proved that he belonged in the Majors, that his rookie season wasn't an aberration. It also reinforced his desire to prove his manhood, the same way that W. E. B. Du Bois equated professional success with full citizenship. Just as important, Jackie believed that the Dodgers as a team had overcome the racial tensions that had tarnished his first two seasons with the club. Maybe so, but all those things came at a price.

Robinson's uncontrollable desire to flex his newfound freedom created tension among his teammates and, at times, even jeopardized their lives. The obligation he felt as an African American celebrity to testify before the House Un-American Activities Committee helped to destroy the career of another black man who had commanded an even greater international status. And the desire to capitalize financially on his celebrity status alienated him from the closest friend he had in baseball. Robinson refused to accept any responsibility for these injustices, though they were clearly the consequences of his actions. Instead, near the end of his life, he chose to emphasize the "lesson" he learned "about racial hatred in America" during the 1949 season, specifically that "a black man, even after he has proven himself on and off the playing field, will still be denied his rights."[63]

Robinson was so focused on his own circumstances that he couldn't see the implications of his actions on those who were fighting for the very same rights. Any challenge, real or perceived, was interpreted as a "humiliation" that he suffered in order "to provide a better future for my own children and for young black people everywhere." When asked why he had been so combative, Robinson admitted that he was "grateful for all the breaks and opportunities I've had," but that he believed he "wouldn't have it made until the humblest black kid in the most remote backwoods of America has it made." It was a virtuous—and undoubtedly genuine—position. But it was also colored by Robinson's fierce desire to "stand up like a man" and strike back in order to avenge the resentment he felt for being considered an "uppity nigger."[64] Even if it came at the expense of others.

Like all heroes, Jackie Robinson was disappointingly human.

7

Collision Course

Between 1950 and 1954 Jackie Robinson established himself as a leader in the black struggle for civil rights. But he also generated negative press and created tension among some teammates with his outspokenness and constant retribution against racial abuse, both real and perceived. The close relationship he had forged with Roy Campanella became a casualty of his controversial behavior. During those five years the friendship slowly deteriorated into a bitter rivalry based on the diametrically opposed approaches of each man toward integration. While they suppressed their mutual resentment for the good of the team—and especially for their black teammates—there were other factors that heightened tensions between the two.

Both Robinson and Campanella sought to be the acknowledged leader of a team that had repeatedly clinched the National League pennant only to fall short of defeating the regal New York Yankees in the World Series. "Wait 'til next year" became a painful reminder of that almost perennial failure. As the team aged, the possibility of clinching a world championship became more remote. In addition Robinson distanced himself from the Dodgers' front office after 1950, when Branch Rickey decided to sell his share of the franchise to co-owner Walter O'Malley and join the Pittsburgh Pirates. O'Malley disapproved of Robinson's outspokenness on civil rights and made clear his preference for Campanella and his passive acceptance of the company line.

As these developments unfolded in Brooklyn, the civil rights movement was being transformed by a new generation of activists who fought to end legal (de jure) and customary (de facto) racial discrimination. Initially working through the courts, this younger, more impatient generation would eventually employ mass nonviolent confrontational tactics such as demonstrations, freedom rides, sit-ins, and boycotts. Many of the activists were inspired by Jackie Robinson's example, which insisted on immediate gains in the struggle for civil rights.

During the 1950s African Americans in northern cities grew increasingly active in opposing racial discrimination in housing, jobs, and education. Led by their ministers, educators, and other professionals, the activists had a greater awareness of the obstacles to their advancement than did blacks in the rural South. They also had greater freedom to associate with each other and to work through independent institutions to advance their cause. Realizing the effectiveness of collective action, they began with isolated, small-scale protests that gradually led to more militant movements.[1] Without such activism, the NAACP's strategy to work through Congress and the courts in achieving civil rights legislation would have enjoyed limited success. Even after the Supreme Court's landmark *Brown v. Board of Education* decision in 1954 mandating the desegregation of public schools, black activism was necessary to compel the federal government to implement the decision and extend its principles to all areas of public life rather than simply in schools.[2]

The civil rights movement also benefited from the new medium of television. Television provided constant reminders of the second-class citizenship blacks were forced to endure in a prosperous society dominated by whites. The images did not go unnoticed by white northern liberals. Black voters commanded a substantial influence within the Democratic Party, which mobilized to support the movement once it began. Civil rights became an issue that northern politicians could not ignore at home, while the cold war made racial injustice an embarrassment abroad. At a time when the United States was appealing to Africa for support and presenting itself as a model to other countries, racial discrimination contradicted its claim to be the leader of the free world.[3]

President Dwight D. Eisenhower was keenly aware of these developments. Though reluctant to act aggressively, Eisenhower worked behind the scenes to advance the cause of civil rights. He completed the desegregation of the military, begun by the Truman administration, by mandating the integration of the navy yards and veterans hospitals. Ike also appointed five pro–civil rights justices to the Supreme Court and forged a congressional coalition that passed the first civil rights legislation in eighty-two years, thereby paving the way for the *Brown* decision. While he personally believed that the "decision was wrong" and doubted that "the hearts of men could be changed with laws," Eisenhower accepted his constitutional obligation to carry it out when, in 1957, Central High School in Little Rock, Arkansas, refused the admission of black students. Eisenhower placed the National Guard under federal command, and black students entered the high school under military protection. It was the first time since the end of Reconstruction that an American president deployed federal troops to protect the rights of African American citizens.[4]

Despite the momentousness of these events, there was never any discussion of them among the Brooklyn Dodgers. As outspoken as he was, Robinson never raised the subject of civil rights with teammates. Don Zimmer, promoted to the Dodgers as an infielder in 1954, "never once heard a conversation about civil rights" in the clubhouse or off the playing field. "It just didn't go on with the players. We didn't think in terms of skin color. That team was like family. On the field it was all business. Off the field there was a lot of togetherness, but we never talked about the black-white thing."[5] Don Newcombe had different memories: "We had to be very careful about the guys in our own dugout. Jackie, Roy and me had to find out which guys were on our side and which weren't. We didn't socialize with the white guys. We never went out to dinner with white teammates. We never had breakfast in the hotel with them."[6] If that was the case, there certainly wouldn't have been any discussion of civil rights between the three black Dodgers and their teammates. But Newcombe is also prone to exaggeration because of the bitterness he still feels over his baseball career and the discrimination he experienced.[7] Carl Erskine, who'd begun his career with the Dodgers in 1948 and pitched with the club through 1957, disputed Newcombe's portrayal of a segregated team. In fact Robinson and Campanella considered Erskine one of their closest friends, white or black, on the team. But the white pitcher did agree that civil rights were never a topic of conversation throughout his tenure in Brooklyn. "Civil rights wasn't even a blip on the screen because it didn't exist when it came to playing baseball," said Erskine. "When we were in uniform we had one goal: to help each other win the ball game on that particular day. Jackie and Campy knew that and respected it."[8]

Nor were the Dodgers unique in their conscious effort to avoid any discussion of civil rights. "There was nothing unusual about that," said Monte Irvin, who played for the New York Giants. "Willie Mays, Hank Thompson, and I never discussed civil rights in the Giants' clubhouse either," he said, referring to his teammates on baseball's first all-black outfield. "Our white teammates loved us, but they weren't concerned with civil rights. Most of the guys were young and single. None of us were making much money since the minimum salary was $5,000. You didn't want to risk your career by bringing up a controversial subject like civil rights. And Willie, Hank, and I certainly weren't going to raise the topic with them."[9] But that didn't mean Irvin and other blacks who had made it to the Majors weren't concerned about the issue. Irvin suggested that most of the black ballplayers who were promoted to the Majors viewed their responsibility as being role models for other African American athletes and adopted a passive approach to civil rights. "We tried to set an example by playing well, by minding our behavior and not getting into trouble so we could make it better for those blacks who came after us," he said. "That was our way of making a contribution. Maybe it was, maybe it wasn't enough."[10]

Campanella's approach to civil rights was similar to Irvin's. While he resented being treated like a second-class citizen because of his race, he wasn't going to jeopardize his baseball career by protesting. Predictably Campy adopted a diplomatic attitude: "I've had to struggle all my life. I'm a colored man. I know there are lots of things I can do and things I cannot do without stirring up some people. But a few years ago there were many more things that I could not do than is the case today. So, I'm willing to wait [for change]. Everything that has happened [in the civil rights movement] is because of waiting. I believe in not pushing things. And a man's got to do things the way he sees them. No other way."[11] Content to let Congress and the courts determine civil rights issues, Campy focused on playing baseball to the very best of his abilities. His contribution to the movement would be as a "role model," not as an "activist." His example would be difficult to ignore as the decade unfolded.

Campanella was the consummate team player, a "gamer," an athlete who put the needs of the team before his own needs by playing through pain. Despite repeated injuries, he persevered. During the heat of the pennant race in 1950, he dislocated his right thumb but still insisted on catching every day. That off-season he almost lost his sight when the hot-water heater in his home blew up, blistering the cornea of each eye. His recovery lingered into the spring of 1951, when a foul ball split his thumb in an exhibition game. During the regular season, Campy suffered a severely bruised hip sliding into second base and later chipped an elbow during a collision at home plate. In a three-game playoff against the New York Giants to determine the National League pennant winner, Campanella reinjured his hip. In each case, he continued to strap on the catcher's gear and take charge of the team defensively while singlehandedly carrying the Dodgers' offense at various times during the season.[12] He compiled a .325 batting average—the highest of his Major League career—and collected the first of three Most Valuable Player Awards. Impressed by his play, Ty Cobb, the Detroit Tigers Hall of Fame outfielder, predicted, "Campanella will be remembered longer than any catcher in baseball history."[13]

Campy's selflessness earned him the unconditional respect of the Dodgers pitching staff. "No one dared shake Campy off," said Carl Erskine. "I rarely did. And the few times I did—I could count them on one hand over my entire career—I got burned. When I listened to Roy, I was successful. For all the pitchers, Roy was a pal, a confidant, a guiding light out there on the field."[14] Campanella also endeared himself to the position players with his infectious enthusiasm for the game. "Campy just brightened the clubhouse," said Duke Snider. "If we had won the day before, he'd walk in and shout, 'Same team that won yesterday is gonna win today!' He was a lot of fun to be around and helped us relax with all those stories of his days in the Negro Leagues."[15]

Fans also loved Campanella. Both black and white youngsters flocked to him because of his easygoing nature and his color-blind attitude toward race relations. In February 1950, for example, he was invited to speak at a predominantly white Episcopal church in Rockville Center, Long Island, to raise funds for the construction of a black Baptist church. Speaking on the topic "Delinquency and Sportsmanship," he voiced his belief that "children were not born with prejudice, but were infected with it by their elders." "The only way to combat this cycle of bigotry," he contended, "was to bring kids of different races together early on in social and recreational programs."[16] True to form, Campanella chose to emphasize the need for harmony between the races, suggesting that earlier generations of blacks

19. Robinson and Campanella pose with a young Japanese American admirer, Sam Yamashita, during an exhibition game in Hawaii. The two teammates were estranged by this time, as reflected in Robinson's noticeable glare at the Dodgers' catcher. (Private collection of Samuel Yamashita)

and whites were equally responsible for the bigotry that prevailed among their children. Only by exposing youngsters of different races to each other would the cycle be broken. It was a message that was palatable—if not appealing—for both black and white fans, and it allowed Campanella to transcend the racial boundaries that divided them.

After he captured his second MVP Award in 1953, Roy's popularity eclipsed Robinson's. When comedian Happy Felton began to conduct a pregame television show during Dodgers home stands, he expected that young contest winners would most want to meet Jackie Robinson. "But Campy was way out in front," recalled Felton. "He just has a special way with kids. He gets along with them without even trying."[17] Kids were able to sense Campanella's affinity for them. He shared many of their interests and hobbies, including model trains and tropical fish.[18] And he played baseball with the enthusiasm of a youngster. In fact Campy was credited with one of the most popular baseball quotations of the modern era: "You have to have a lot of little boy in you to play baseball for a living."[19] Jim McGowan, one of the winners in Felton's contest, recalled, "Even though Jackie was the hero of all the black kids in Brooklyn because he brought pride to our race, I wanted to meet Campy. Maybe that was because, like him, I had a white father and a black mother. But I knew a lot of black kids in my neighborhood who loved Campy because he was more approachable as well as a great ballplayer. Jackie was more distant, almost like a god."[20] On matters of race, Campanella was nonconfrontational. "One reason I've never had any trouble with white folks is because I've always tried to treat people like I wanted to be treated," he explained years later. "I try to think before I say anything to anyone. I don't want to hurt anyone's feelings because I don't want them to hurt mine."[21]

To be sure, Campanella's leadership of the Dodgers, his easygoing personality, and his refusal to speak out publicly against racial discrimination also endeared him to the white baseball establishment. But those same qualities irked Robinson. No doubt Jackie was jealous of Campanella's baseball success. As the catcher's star was rising, Robinson's was declining, especially after 1954, when his batting average and offensive production tailed off dramatically. His one and only MVP Award came in 1949, when he led the National League with a .342 batting average. Afterward he never captured another batting title or led the league in any offensive category except on-base percentage (.440), in 1952.[22] Campanella, on the other hand, captured three National League MVP Awards in 1951, 1953, and 1955, and during those years he finished among the league leaders in batting average, home runs, RBIs, and slugging average.[23]

What disturbed Robinson more was Campanella's refusal to speak out against racial injustice. Jackie considered his teammate an "Uncle Tom" because of his behavior as an agreeable black man in a white society.[24] Campy got along with everybody and liked it that way, while Robinson didn't care if he was accepted by others, particularly the white establishment. He realized that his outspokenness alienated him from most whites, but he refused to remain silent because he understood the stark difference between perceived equality and full equality. That is why he could live in the affluent St. Albans section of Queens, Long Island, with such celebrity neighbors as Count Basie, Lena Horne, and Ella Fitzgerald and still criticize publicly the second-class citizenship of black people. Robinson saw no contradiction in owning a home in an affluent suburb because he had earned the right to live there. But he also wanted other African Americans to enjoy the same right, which would only come with full citizenship. Conversely, Campanella, who lived in the same neighborhood, kept quiet about civil rights because he didn't want to jeopardize his own status. He simply refused to put his financial success and popularity on the line for other black people. While Robinson may have interpreted his teammate's example as cowardly, Campy viewed it as practical given the racial climate of the time. "Jackie was militant," noted Duke Snider. "He knew that history had placed him in a special role, and he never ducked from that role. That's why he played the game with a chip on his shoulder, why he spoke out against race discrimination; things Campy could never have done."[25] "Jack would get impatient with Campy because he wanted him to speak up more," recalled Rachel Robinson. "Campy would get impatient with Jack because he thought he spoke up too much, and that is a fact of life."[26] Their different approaches put the two players on an inevitable collision course as the decade of the 1950s unfolded.

Branch Rickey might have been able to mediate the controversy, but he left the Dodgers at the end of the 1950 season. When John L. Smith, a pharmaceutical mogul who owned 25 percent of the team, died in July, Rickey's days in Brooklyn were numbered. As long as Smith was alive, he could stave off co-owner Walter O'Malley's efforts to take control of the franchise, perhaps even one day hand the reins over to his son, Branch Jr., who in 1947 had been promoted to the position of assistant general manager. But when Smith succumbed to cancer at age fifty-eight, Rickey became vulnerable to O'Malley's machinations. The two men disagreed on everything from personnel to contract negotiations, and if Rickey didn't leave he might find himself working for O'Malley after his contract expired in October. The Dodgers' president also found himself strapped for cash since he had borrowed heavily on his life insurance to buy into the team in 1943 and his stock portfolio had not performed well. When John W. Galbreath, chairman of the Pittsburgh Pirates and a fellow Ohioan, asked Rickey to take over the Pirates, he sold his quarter-interest in the Dodgers for $1 million and moved to Pittsburgh.[27]

About the same time, Happy Chandler, the commissioner who had backed Rickey's experiment with integration, was forced out of his job by the owners. When they elected Chandler to succeed the autocratic Judge Landis, the owners believed that he would be willing to follow their lead. Instead he proved to be independent. While he defended ownership's right to the reserve clause, Chandler distanced himself from the moguls by arguing for a minimum players' salary and a pension plan to be paid from World Series profits and vetoing a plan to raise admission prices because he believed it to be unfair to the fans. Still, the owners tolerated these measures. But Chandler's active support for Rickey's plan to integrate the game was, for them, unforgivable. Accordingly when the former Kentucky senator asked for an early extension of his seven-year contract as a vote of confidence, the owners voted it down by a 9–7 margin. Chandler resigned in midseason of 1951 and was replaced by National League president Ford Frick.[28] As a result, by 1952 Robinson had lost his two most loyal supporters, and his relations with baseball's white power structure quickly deteriorated.

During spring training in 1952, O'Malley, acting on hearsay, accused Jackie of faking an injury in order to skip an exhibition game. He phoned the second baseman and asked to meet with him and Rachel to discuss the matter. It was unusual for Rachel to be involved in any matters concerning her husband and the team, but she agreed to attend. It may have been a ploy to intimidate Rachel so that she would persuade her husband to temper his behavior or risk losing his job. If that was his intention, he was sorely disappointed. During the meeting O'Malley, who had never been happy with Robinson's outspokenness or his combative play, sought to lay down the law. He reprimanded Jackie for missing the exhibition game, saying that it was "unfair to the fans." He also told his second baseman that he had no right to complain about being assigned to a separate hotel while the team was in Florida. "A separate hotel had been good enough for you in 1947," he added. Insulted by the remark, Robinson exploded. He told O'Malley that he was "dead wrong" if he thought that he was going to tolerate the same deplorable conditions he had been forced to endure in the past. Challenging O'Malley's character, Jackie added that if O'Malley "had more guts," he "wouldn't have to experience such indignities." As for missing the exhibition game, Robinson said he "resented the implication that he was pretending to be injured" and accused O'Malley of being "more interested in the few extra dollars he could gain" from the exhibition contest than "protecting the health of the team for the [regular] season." O'Malley had heard enough. He told Robinson that he was behaving like a "cry baby" and to stop being a "prima donna." The remark shocked Rachel. Now it was her turn to vent. If O'Malley thought she was going to be an unwitting ally, he was wrong, and she spared no criticism:

> Mr. O'Malley, I've seen Jack play with sore legs, a sore back, sore arms, even without other members of the team knowing it. He did it not for praise, but because he was thinking about the team. Nobody worries about this club more than Jackie Robinson and that includes the owners. I live with him, so I know. . . . Jack's heart and soul is in the baseball club and it pains me deeply to have you say what you just said.
>
> You know, Mr. O'Malley, bringing Jack into organized baseball was not the greatest thing Mr. Rickey did for him. It was sticking by him to the very end. He understood Jack. He never listened to the ugly little rumors you've mentioned to us today. If there was something wrong, he'd go to Jack and ask him about it. He would talk to Jack and they would get to the heart of it like men with a mutual respect for each other's feelings.

Stunned by her remarks, O'Malley realized that he wasn't making any headway and softened his tone. Insisting that he "meant no harm," he retreated from his accusatory approach and made a simple request: "Just try to come out [to the game] and play today."[29]

"O'Malley's attitude towards me was viciously antagonistic," recalled Jackie near the end of his life. "I learned that he had a regular habit of calling me, 'Mr. Rickey's prima donna.' To put it bluntly, I was one of those 'uppity niggers' in his book."[30] Making matters worse was O'Malley's obvious respect and loyalty to Campanella, which reinforced Robinson's growing resentment of his teammate.

Despite the fact that Campy had gained weight and his batting average dropped to .269 in 1952, O'Malley predicted that Roy had at least five more years as "the best catcher and one of the greatest clutch hitters in baseball."[31] O'Malley even suggested that Campy's "intelligence, level-headedness," and "popularity with the other players" ensured a place for him in the Dodgers organization when his playing days were over.[32] Robinson, who had entertained thoughts of managing in the future, interpreted the remark as a personal snub. He never forgave O'Malley for forcing Rickey out of Brooklyn, and he interpreted all of his actions through the prism of that negative bias. O'Malley reinforced Robinson's suspicions by trading away many of the players Rickey had developed. Some of those transactions were most likely motivated by ego and the desire to assert his authority, just as Jackie suspected. At the same time, baseball was a business, and the need to rebuild the Dodgers by developing younger players and replacing aging stars was necessary for any franchise that hoped to remain competitive. Thus O'Malley was no different from any other owner. Still, Robinson's relationship with him continued to deteriorate. And O'Malley's was not the only authority Jackie challenged.

As the 1950s unfolded, Robinson became more antagonistic toward the National League umpires, sometimes at his own expense. Jocko Conlan, widely respected for his accuracy and fairness, earned the second baseman's wrath in 1950 when he called him out on strikes. When Jackie glared at him disapprovingly, Conlan remarked, "It was right over the middle!" Robinson lashed out in a hailstorm of abuse before being thrown out of the game. The ejection ended a streak of hitting safely in sixteen straight games and a streak of reaching base in fifty-five consecutive games.[33] In April 1951 Robinson was called out on strikes by umpire Dusty Boggess. Throwing his bat down at home plate, Jackie trotted out to his position at second base, shouting a derogatory remark. Either Boggess didn't hear Robinson or simply ignored him. But Babe Pinelli, who was umpiring behind third, refused to let the remark go unnoticed and berated Robinson. Tempers flared, and Dodgers manager Charlie Dressen had to intervene. Later, when asked about the incident, Jackie insisted that the umpires were "out to get me." "I know what they're doing," he said. "I'm not blind. One of the umpires even went up to Dressen before the season started and told him that I'm trying to show them up and they weren't going to stand for it." Although he claimed that he wasn't trying to "show anyone up," he insisted that he was "entitled to make a beef as much as anyone else." Even some of his closest friends began to lose patience with him. Clyde Sukeforth, the scout who discovered Robinson, reminded him that he had been a model player with the umpires during his first two years in the Majors and asked, "So why can't you be quiet now?"[34] By 1953 Robinson had created so many enemies among the umpires that the National League's new president, Warren Giles, had no sympathy for him. When Giles censured Brooklyn for unmercifully riding umpire Frank Dascoli for a controversial call, he singled out Robinson as "particularly offensive," even though Dascoli ejected just one Dodger, Chris Van Cuyk, from the game.[35]

If the umpires were baiting Jackie, he had nobody but himself to blame. He tended to overreact to any call that went against him, interpreting those judgments as being racially motivated. Robinson had tremendous difficulty separating his role as a civil rights pioneer from the arbitration of the game, even when his prickliness jeopardized personal or team success. His personal makeup wouldn't allow him to respond any other way. Jackie's fiery attitude and indomitable spirit—the very same qualities that made him the most attractive candidate to break the color barrier—worked against him after he was freed from the "no striking back" ban. In fact, unwittingly or perhaps consciously, Robinson was telling baseball's white establishment that they "couldn't have it both ways" each time he challenged an umpire's decision. Just because the color barrier had been broken didn't mean that human nature had also been reformed. Umpires were only human, and no doubt many still harbored racist feelings. To expect those umpires to divorce their decision making process from personal prejudice was just as naïve as expecting Robinson to simply dismiss any call that went against him. Essentially Jackie was placed in an impossible situation, but he only made it worse by challenging any umpire who ruled against him.

Robinson's antagonistic attitude toward the umpires, his outspokenness on civil rights, and his growing difficulties with Walter O'Malley did not escape the scrutiny of the sportswriters, who became increasing critical of him. They were accustomed to dealing with accommodating black athletes like Joe Louis, the heavyweight boxing champion, and Jesse Owens, the Olympic track star. Predictably they flocked to Campanella, who was considered "one of the boys," according to Jack Lang, who covered the Dodgers in the 1950s for the *Long Island Press*. "Campy was just a fun-loving guy," said Lang. "He got along with everybody. All the writers loved him."[36] Similarly Arthur Daley of the *New York Times* regarded Campanella as a "delightfully warm and wonderful guy."[37] Campy endeared himself to the sportswriters by providing insightful analyses of games and humorous quotes. He also knew which writers to cultivate, like Dick Young of the *New York Daily News*, the most scrutinizing of all the city's scribes. After Campanella won his first MVP Award in 1951, Young approached him about a biography. Not only did the catcher agree to several interviews, but he refused to accept any of the royalties after the book was published.[38] Because they favored him, the press protected him. When, for example, he requested that the sportswriters avoid any mention of his quitting high school because he didn't want his children to know, they readily complied.[39]

On the other hand, the writers viewed Robinson as "oversensitive," "hot-tempered," and "irrational."[40] With the exception of Roger Kahn of the *Herald Tribune*, who believed that Jackie's "bellicosity" was a more accurate reflection of "what black attitudes should be," Robinson had no close friends among the beat writers.[41] They could not relate to his constant effort to make baseball a platform for civil rights or his tendency to interpret any difference of opinion as racially charged. In 1952, for example, when Jackie publicly accused the Yankees of racism in their hiring practices because they were the only New York team without a black player, he was excoriated in the national press as a "soap box orator" and a "rabble rouser" who should limit his activities to "ball playing" instead of being a "crusader."[42] Even the black press had difficulty with some of Jackie's actions. After the 1953 season, while barnstorming in Birmingham, Alabama, against the Indianapolis Clowns of the Negro Leagues, Robinson, who was managing an integrated team of Major League All-Stars, benched three white players—Gil Hodges, Ralph Branca, and Bobby Young—in compliance with the city's ordinance against sports competitions between blacks and whites. When he announced his intention to abide by the ordinance, the African American *Birmingham World* criticized him for the decision:

> It's up to Jackie Robinson and his promoters to cancel the scheduled
> engagement or challenge the "unconstitutional" sports segregation
> ordinance which will force him to bench his three white players.

Branch Rickey set a bold precedent by introducing Negro players to the major leagues. He stood up and fought, bypassing cities which were not enlightened enough to permit fair competition. Has J.R. forgotten this?

Jackie Robinson is an international symbol of decent sports. He is respected and loved by fair-minded Americans everywhere. All of this is at stake in the Birmingham engagement. Money is not as precious as a good name.

Is Jackie Robinson going to let Branch Rickey down? Is he coming to Birmingham to give aid and comfort to bigotry?[43]

Ignoring the criticism, Robinson went ahead and banned the three white players from the game.[44] While he might have had valid reasons for doing so, the contradiction between his decision and the very same principle of integration for which he stood alienated him further from the press.

Dick Young was Robinson's greatest critic. Once, in an effort to reconcile their differences, the *Daily News* scribe approached him and explained that he only wanted to "discuss baseball," but "sooner or later we always get around to social issues."

"If I couldn't talk about race relations," Jackie replied, "we'd probably have to stop any serious discussion." Young bristled at the remark. "Listen," he continued, "I'm telling you as a friend, that a lot of newspapermen like Campanella because he doesn't talk about civil rights. But you wear your race on your sleeve and that makes enemies."

"Dick, we might just as well get this straight," said Robinson. "I like friends just as much as other people. But if it comes down to a question of respect or friendship, I'll take their respect. I know a lot of the writers don't like me because I discuss things that get in the way of their guilt complexes, but I'll bet you they respect me."

Realizing that he wasn't making any headway, Young simply tried to encourage Jackie to be more like Campanella, who was just happy to be playing in the Majors and never spoke out on racial discrimination. "Personally, Jackie, whenever I talk to Campy, I almost never think of him as a Negro," said Young. "But any time I talk to you, I'm acutely aware of the fact that you're a Negro."

Young's effort to use Campanella as an example backfired. "I want to be thought of as the kind of Negro who's not going to beg for anything," snapped Robinson in a veiled reference to his Dodgers teammate. "I want to be the kind of Negro who'll be reasonable, but is damned well tired of being patient. If that makes me the kind of guy they can't like, that's tough."[45]

The conversation reflected Robinson's inability to find a middle ground between his "kind of Negro" and others, like Campanella, who he considered "whining, handkerchief-heads with their hat in their hands expressing eternal gratitude for whatever benefits or rights that the white man gave him."[46] In other words, if you weren't 100 percent in agreement with Jackie Robinson, you were against him. Young, realizing the futility of his effort, never again bothered to reconcile their differences. And Robinson, to his last days, considered the sportswriter a "racial bigot."[47]

Despite their differences on race relations, Robinson and Campanella shared an infamous reputation as bench jockeys and indulged in the practice on a daily basis. Carl Erskine recently described their jockeying as "a form of eloquent professional hatred rolled up into a ball of biting, irreverent humor that would have made anyone laugh at the mere shock of hearing the comments."[48] No opponent was a better target than the New York Giants. Throughout the 1950s the two teams were perennial rivals, competing against each other for the pennant down the stretch. The New York newspapers exploited the rivalry by fueling the emotions of blue-collar fans with controversial quotations from the players and provocative game reports. "There was some real animosity between the players too," admitted Monte Irvin, who played for the Giants from 1949 to 1955. "We didn't like them [the Dodgers] off the field and we hated them on the field. The feud between Jackie and [Giants manager] Leo Durocher was especially nasty. Leo used to tell Jackie he was swell-headed, and Jackie would call Leo a 'traitor' for leaving the Dodgers. Sometimes it got very personal."[49] One especially vicious exchange occurred when Robinson, playing second base, began needling Durocher about his wife, Lorraine Day, a Hollywood actress. Durocher, who was standing in the third-base coaching box, lost his cool and charged Jackie, screaming a steady stream of racial epithets. Dodgers shortstop Pee Wee Reese stepped between the two men and broke up the argument. When Durocher regained his composure he saw two of his own black players, Monte Irvin and Hank Thompson, standing on second and third base, respectively. Only then did he realize how shamefully he had acted. Hanging his head, "Leo the Lip" walked back to the coaching box, unable to even look at his own players. Realizing the awkwardness of the situation, Irvin, in an effort to help his manager save face, shouted out, "Go get him Skip! He had no right to say that to you. Anything you say goes double for me."[50] The incident underscored just how complicated the issue of loyalty was for the game's first black players.

But back in the 1950s, when the issue of race was involved, black ballplayers' loyalties were sometimes divided. There were so few blacks in the Majors that if one of them was ostracized, the others felt a moral obligation to come to his defense, whether or not they played on the same team. On the other hand, the etiquette of the game demanded loyalty to one's team, first and foremost, especially when the verbal barbs were unacceptable even by baseball's lax ethical standards. Thus Irvin's defense of his manager was justified because Robinson had violated those standards when he attacked Durocher's wife. There were other occasions when the Dodgers-Giants rivalry pitted the black players on the two teams against each other. Campanella, for example, was especially hard on Giant outfielder Willie Mays. During Mays's rookie year, 1951, Campy made it a point to agitate him by asking questions whenever he came up to bat. "What do you say, pup?" "Are you getting [laid] much?" "When you getting married?" The banter was meant to break the young ballplayer's concentration so he wouldn't get a hit. But it was also extremely personal and it unnerved Mays. Newcombe could be just as bad. Once, after learning of Mays's comment that he "wouldn't have trouble hitting against him," Newcombe threw at the Giants' outfielder, knocking him down each time he came to bat. After the third knockdown pitch, Irvin came to his teammate's defense: "If you want to pick on somebody, Don, why don't you pick on a veteran like me? Somebody who can defend himself for Christ's sake!"[51]

Although Robinson spoke highly of Mays as a ballplayer, he didn't have much respect for him personally. Jackie viewed the young Giants' center fielder much like Campanella: as a docile, uneducated black who shirked his responsibility to advance the cause of civil rights because he didn't want to jeopardize his career. Mays later claimed that while Robinson mentored young black players from other teams, he never had a mean-ingful conversation or significant encounter with him.[52]

Irvin admitted that the bitterness of the Dodgers-Giants rivalry af-fected his relationships with the black Dodgers. "We weren't too friendly with each other," he recalled. "Jackie and I were never close, on or off the field, though I admired the fact that he'd taken so much abuse without cracking the first couple of years in the Major Leagues. Newcombe and I mostly stayed away from each other. But Campy was my friend all the way back to our days in the Negro Leagues. I knew he was the kind of guy who wanted to beat your brains out on the field, but after the game was over we'd forget about it. The bottom line was that on the field, I was loyal to the Giants. If I hadn't been, then there would have been a dou-ble standard, and that would have damaged the cause [of integration]."[53] However, the rivalry didn't prevent Irvin or the other black Giants from barnstorming with Robinson and Campanella after the season ended. Between 1950 and 1954 Jackie or Roy organized and led a group of Ma-jor League All-Stars that toured the South each October and early No-vember, playing games against local semiprofessional teams and Negro Leaguers. Among the regulars on those barnstorming trips were Irvin, Mays, Thompson, Newcombe, and Doby.[54] The additional income those trips afforded each player was undoubtedly incentive enough to join the tour, but the fact that black Major Leaguers from other clubs were rou-tinely invited indicates that Robinson and Campanella were looking out for them and their financial interests.

Robinson and Campanella also went out of their way to mentor young black players from other rival teams. Both Dodgers made a conscious ef-fort to befriend Ernie Banks of the Chicago Cubs, before he reached the Majors. In 1950 Robinson invited Banks, then a shortstop with the Kansas City Monarchs, to join his All-Star team on a barnstorming trip through the South. Banks, who idolized Jackie, jumped at the opportunity to serve as his double-play partner. Before a game in Meridian, Mississippi, Rob-inson approached Banks to compliment him. "Young man," said Jackie, "I've been watching you and you really can pull that inside pitch. You hit very well." Afterward Jackie worked with Banks to help him get rid of the ball more quickly on double plays.[55] Campanella, also on the tour, was noticeably impressed with Banks as well and, along with Robinson, promoted the youngster with Brooklyn's front office. "'Ernie,' they said to me, 'you can play in the major leagues, and we're going to recommend you,'" recalled Banks years later. "I thought they were kidding, but they did recommend me to the Dodgers. They were friendly. They wanted to see me and other young black players make it to the majors."[56] The encouragement continued after Banks cracked the big leagues. In 1953, when Banks was a rookie with Chicago, Campanella went out of his way to drive him from Ebbets Field to his Manhattan hotel after a day game. During the ride Campy emphasized the responsibility that young black players had to do their best when they made the Majors to pave the way for other prospective Negro Leaguers. Complimenting Banks on his playing ability, he cautioned, "Just remember this, and at your age it's easy to forget. The higher you climb in baseball, the greater your responsibility will be all up and down the line, both on and off the field."[57]

Robinson and Campanella also mentored Hank Aaron when he was promoted to the Milwaukee Braves in 1954. After spring training that year, the Dodgers and Braves barnstormed together on the way north, stopping off to play games at Mobile, New Orleans, Birmingham, Memphis, Louisville, and Indianapolis. "The black players stayed at the same hotels during that trip," recalled Aaron in a recent interview.

Jackie and Roy invited me to join them and the other black Dodgers. We'd sit around Jackie's room playing cards and talking. They talked about how to cope with the racial situation, what to do if a guy spit on you, or whether to join in if there was a fight on the field. Those sessions were my college. They taught me that the job [of integration] was never done. I learned that some players and some fans would hate me no matter what I did, and that I had a choice. Either I could forget that I was black and just smile and go along with the program until my time was up, or I could remember that I had a special responsibility that went beyond playing ball. And that was to be the very best player I could be and serve as an example for other black ballplayers [who were] coming up.[58]

For Aaron, who idolized Jackie Robinson as a youngster, the attention was overwhelming. Growing up in Mobile, Alabama, he dreamed of becoming a Major League baseball player. But his father discouraged the dream, reminding him that there were no "colored ballplayers" in the Majors. All that changed in 1947, though. And the following year, when Robinson visited Mobile, fourteen-year-old Aaron skipped school to hear his hero speak. "Truthfully, I went to hear his baseball stories," he admitted. "Jackie encouraged us to stay in school, get a good education, and make sports a second choice. But I came away determined more than ever to be in the big leagues before he retired. Jackie had that kind of effect on all of us. He gave us our dreams. He breathed baseball into the black community, kids and grown-ups alike."[59]

While Robinson's relationship with Banks and Aaron was supportive, his effort to mentor younger black teammates could be problematic, especially when Campanella was trying to do the same thing. Both Jackie and Campy actively sought to be acknowledged by teammates as the leader of the Dodgers. One of the ways they did this was to cultivate younger black teammates. It was a responsibility both men accepted as African American veterans, and they embraced it because of the broader influence they could exercise on the team itself. Joe Black, a twenty-year-old pitcher, roomed with Robinson when he was promoted to the Dodgers in 1952. "There were days on the road when I was too tired to do anything but play baseball," recalled Black in a 1997 interview. "But Jackie wouldn't let me. He'd get me out of bed early in the morning so I would go with him to a school to talk to the kids there. Usually, the school would schedule an assembly for one or two hours. Jackie would talk about the importance of education and tell them that they had to be ready when the opportunity for a good job came their way. At the time, I didn't realize how much those visits meant to the kids, or how he was teaching me to be a role model."[60]

Robinson also prepared Black for the racial abuse he would suffer when the Dodgers played on the road. Once, when the Dodgers traveled to Philadelphia to play the Phillies, a leather-lunged fan spotted Black following Robinson onto the playing field and yelled out, "Hey! There's Robinson, King of the Niggers, with a little baboon right behind him!" Black, noticeably upset by the remark, turned to Jackie, who calmed him down. The fans in other cities would mockingly sing the Negro spiritual "Old Black Joe" when the rookie pitched. Black, an imposing six-foot-three-inch hulk, would become agitated, but Jackie always managed to refocus him.[61] "If it wasn't for those talks with Jackie," admitted Black, "I don't think I could have turned the other cheek so many times.[62] Campanella, briefly a teammate of Black's on the Elite Giants, also endeared himself to the rookie pitcher by warning him about the ever-present vices of loose women and alcohol. He also taught the youngster how to pitch under pressure. "It didn't take long for Joe to love Campy," said Carl Erskine. "All of the veteran pitchers gave Joe the same advice. We told him to listen to Roy, follow whatever he says, and throw with confidence. Both Jackie and Roy took young Joe under heir wings and made him an instant star."[63] With pitching ace Don Newcombe serving in the military overseas in Korea, Black stepped up in 1952. He won fifteen games for the Dodgers, saved another twenty-five, and was voted Rookie of the Year by the sportswriters.[64]

There were occasions, however, when Campy and Jackie gave mixed signals to their protégés because of their diametrically opposed approaches to civil rights. At the beginning of the 1953 season, for example, Brooklyn manager Charlie Dressen moved Robinson from second to third base to make room for a younger black infielder, Jim Gilliam. Dressen, a big Robinson fan, was looking out for his star player as well as hoping to improve the team offensively. He realized that Jackie was getting older and having trouble with his knees, which limited his mobility. Playing third wouldn't be as stressful on his legs because he wouldn't have to turn the double-play, and Dressen could still keep his productive bat in the lineup. Gilliam, on the other hand, had a talent for getting on base and stealing, ideal qualities for a lead-off hitter. Though he didn't have a real strong arm and could not turn the double-play smoothly, the rookie would make up for it with his sure-handed fielding and intelligence. In fact Gilliam would go on to become the National League's Rookie of the Year in 1953. The odd man out was thirty-four-year-old Billy Cox, considered the best defensive third baseman in the game, but a .250 hitter at the time. Cox was infuriated by the move, especially being replaced by a black man. Nor were his roommate, Preacher Roe, a southerner, and Carl Furillo, a fellow Pennsylvanian, very happy about Dressen's decision. Although all three players had, at one time or another, expressed their disenchantment about playing on the same team with blacks, they made a concerted effort to get along with their African American teammates until now. Apparently spring training was an especially tense period when Robinson and the others made veiled and accusatory references about the situation. Finally, Campanella, having heard enough, took it upon himself to bring the focus back to the team. "You guys can be wrong, but don't be loud wrong," he snapped behind the closed doors of the clubhouse. "Settle it now and get out on the field because we have a game to win." Shortly afterward Cox returned to third base and Robinson shifted to left field.[65] But the incident underscored the differences between Campanella, who placed team success above individual differences, and Robinson, who could be prickly with anyone who snubbed him. It also revealed the latent animosity that existed over integration among some of the Dodgers and couldn't help but send mixed signals to the younger black players on the team.

On another occasion, Robinson, in an effort to show leadership, reinforced the infamous reputation he's established for baiting umpires. During a 1954 game against the Cubs at Wrigley Field, Duke Snider hit what appeared to be a home run into the left-field bleachers. But the ball bounced back onto the field, and umpire Bill Stewart ruled it a double. Robinson believed that a fan had interfered with the ball and that the hit should be ruled a homer. Charging the field to protest, Jackie assumed his teammates would follow him out of the dugout. To his surprise, no one did. Walter Alston, the Dodgers' new manager, stood in the third-base coaching box, hands on hips, staring angrily at Robinson. Regrouping, Robinson trotted out to Stewart, said a few quiet words, and returned to the dugout. He later admitted that it was a "humiliating moment" that only served to reinforce the "hothead, umpire-baiting label" that had been imposed on him by the press. Angered by Alston's refusal to support him, Jackie swore that it would be the last time he would "fight the team's battles."[66]

The most troubling incident, however, came during the Dodgers' trip to St. Louis that season. Whenever the team played in St. Louis the white players stayed at the Chase Hotel, which refused to accommodate African Americans. Robinson, Campanella, and the younger black players were forced to stay at the Adams Hotel, a black establishment with no air-conditioning or any of the other conveniences of the Chase. Perhaps inspired by the NAACP's challenge that same year to overturn the separate-but-equal doctrine in *Brown v. Board of Education*, Jackie decided to challenge Jim Crow. "Jack got off the train in St. Louis," recalled

Pee Wee Reese, "and said to me, 'I'm going to the Chase with you.' Roy Campanella, Newk and Gilliam told him not to do it. They said they were doing all right and asked him not to rock the boat. But Jackie said, 'You do whatever you want, but I'm going to the Chase.' Then he got on the bus with all the white players, went right into the hotel and tried to register."[67] Robinson told a different story, though.

According to Jackie, he only confronted Campanella, and it was 1955, the year *after* he'd challenged the Chase and won. Newcombe and the other black Dodgers decided to join him at the Chase, but Campy still refused as a "matter of principle since they hadn't wanted [him] in the past." Robinson, frustrated, told Campanella that he "had no monopoly on pride" and that "baseball hadn't wanted him in the past but that he was in the game now." He added that "winning a victory over the Chase Hotel" meant that all the Dodgers were "really becoming a team [since] all members would be treated equally." Robinson also insisted that integrating the Chase allowed "all blacks, not just those in baseball, to stay in a decent hotel." But Campy dismissed him, muttering, "I'm no crusader."[68]

Years later Campanella agreed that the incident took place in 1955, after Robinson had integrated the Chase. But he insisted that the hotel still prohibited blacks from eating in the dining room, sitting in the lobby, or swimming in the pool. Campy also stated that Newcombe and Gilliam decided to stay with him at the Adams, and when Robinson approached them, he replied, "I'm not talking for anybody else; only for myself. It's got to be the whole hog or nothing for me. As long as there's any kind of discrimination, you can leave me out. Besides, I've been coming to St. Louis for seven years and if they didn't want me all this time, then I don't want them now."[69]

There is yet another version of the story, according to Don Newcombe, who claims that both he and Robinson integrated the Chase in 1954. Newcombe, angered at being treated like a second-class citizen after he had served in the military, insists that he was the one who came up with the idea of challenging Jim Crow and that Jackie joined him. "We walked right through the front door," recalled Newcombe, "and everyone was looking at us as we waited for the manager. He took us into the dining room and offered us a cup of coffee."

"Do you know why we're here?" asked Jackie.

"I think I have an idea," replied the manager, "but why don't you tell me."

"Don and I want to know why after all these years we haven't been able to stay at your hotel," Robinson explained. "Don just got back from two years of service to his country. He's mad, and he wants to know. So do I."

Embarrassed, the manager said, "The only thing I can think of, gentlemen, is we don't want you in the swimming pool."

Amused by the response, Jackie admitted that he didn't know how to swim. "I never swim during baseball season," added Newcombe. "Afraid to hurt my arm." "And just like that," according to the Dodgers' ace pitcher, "the manager allowed us to stay at the Chase."

Newcombe insisted that he and Jackie invited Campanella and Gilliam to join them, but they both refused on principle.[70] "So me and Jackie moved into the Chase," said Newcombe. "The thing is, then, and in all the years we stayed there after that, they never gave us a room on the side of the hotel where the pool was located. We had our ideas why. That bigot didn't want us looking at those pretty white women walking around in their bikinis. But what he didn't know was that I had women in my room all the time. Black women, white women, all kinds. That bigot should have come to my room one night and seen what was going on."[71]

Monte Irvin questions the validity of Newcombe's account. "It doesn't sound like Newcombe," said Irvin when he learned of the black pitcher's alleged attempt to integrate the Chase with Robinson. Newcombe had plenty of disagreements with Jackie. He preferred to just play with him on the field and then go his own way. Like Campy, Newcombe didn't appreciate Jackie's attitude. They both saw him as aggressive and "stand-up-ish" and they resented his efforts to make them "the same way he was."[72]

Regardless of which version of the story is accurate, the Chase Hotel incident was the breaking point in the Campanella-Robinson relationship. It underscored the incompatibility of the two players and their different approaches to integration and threatened to divide the black Dodgers into two rival camps: those who supported Campanella and his accommodationist philosophy and those who sided with Robinson and his belief that racial discrimination must be challenged directly whenever possible. Afterward neither man even pretended friendship. They tolerated each other on the playing field for the good of the team and kept their distance from each other off the diamond in order to avoid further acrimony. Making matters worse was the reality that both players were aging and they still had yet to win a World Series.

"Wait 'til next year!" might have been a rallying cry for the Dodgers faithful, but it was a perennial reminder that the team couldn't defeat the New York Yankees in the Fall Classic. In fact, by 1955 the Dodgers hated the Yankees as much as if not more than they hated their National League rivals, the New York Giants. In 1947, Robinson's rookie year, the Dodgers lost to the Bronx Bombers in an exciting seven-game series. The two teams met again in the 1949 Fall Classic, and Brooklyn went down to defeat in just five games. It took the Dodgers three more seasons before they could face the Yanks again. Although Brooklyn held a 3–2 lead after five games, the Yankees came back to take the final two and clinch the world championship. In 1953 the Dodgers posted a club record 105 wins and cruised to the pennant by thirteen games. But again the Yankees took the World Series in six games. Manager Charlie Dressen's patience was wearing thin. Despite the fact that he had piloted the club to two straight World Series appearances, Walter O'Malley offered him nothing more than the usual one-year contract. In 1954 Dressen said he wouldn't stay on unless he was given a three-year deal. O'Malley let him go and signed Minor League skipper Walter Alston, who wasn't so demanding.[73]

While Campanella was elated to be reunited with his old manager from Nashua, New Hampshire, Robinson and Alston clashed from the start. Jackie had difficulty respecting the authority of a manager whose entire Major League career consisted of one at-bat and whose decisions he considered "boneheaded."[74] In addition, Alston, a man of few words, did not create a favorable impression when, prior to spring training, he met with his veteran team and told them, "I've read a lot of clippings about how great this team is. But I haven't seen it. You guys know what it takes to win. I don't give pep talks. You either do it, or we get someone else. Meeting's over."[75]

Robinson was uncertain if he had the physical or emotional stamina to play baseball. At thirty-five, he was past his prime as an athlete, and an ongoing battle with diabetes was taking its toll. He was also tired of all the acrimony that had surfaced between him and Campanella. Nor did he have much patience for O'Malley or the intrusive press. Realizing that the prospect of securing an administrative position with the Dodgers— or any other team—was slim, Jackie began to ponder life after baseball.

Hoping to find employment that would be financially rewarding as well as allow him to continue his active role in civil rights, Jackie instructed his lawyer, Martin Stone, to put out feelers in private industry.[76] The man who broke baseball's color barrier was planning to retire from the game whose history he had forever changed.

8

Breakup

The 1955 Brooklyn Dodgers were not only one of baseball's greatest teams, but they have also been mythologized in history as "America's team." They symbolized the community and its values as well as the success of integration. During the spring, summer, and early fall, residents flocked to Ebbets Field to cheer on their beloved "Bums" and enjoy the circus-like atmosphere. Others sat on the front steps of their brownstones and listened to the game, babysitting their kids and their neighbors'. The Dodgers, who fielded white, black, and Hispanic role models, lured teenagers away from crime and juvenile delinquency. Even during the winter months, when baseball was dormant, Brooklynites seemed to talk about nothing but the game in anticipation of what the upcoming season might bring. Brooklyn took the Dodgers to their hearts; as a result, an ethnically and racially diverse community was able to transcend the bigotry and prejudice that plagued the rest of the nation. As the first integrated team in the Majors, the Dodgers became easy targets for the intolerance of opposing teams and their fans. Determined to see the noble experiment succeed, Brooklyn's "Boys of Summer," rallied together for support. In the process Ebbets Field became a microcosm of the American Dream, where an integrated community of fans enjoyed a common interest in which everyone could be on an equal footing. The love affair reached a climax in 1955, when the Dodgers captured their first and only World Series. The mythology still endures more than half a century later, a reminder of an integrated America's unlimited potential for social justice.[1]

In fact the 1955 Dodgers were a veteran team with star players past their prime. With the exceptions of Sandy Amoros, Jim Gilliam, and Duke Snider, who were in their mid-to-late twenties, the average age of the starting

20. The 1955 world champion Brooklyn Dodgers (season record: 98-55). Seated: batboy Charlie DiGiovanni. Bottom row (*left to right*): George Shuba, Don Zimmer, coach Joe Becker, coach Jake Pilter, manager Walter Alston, coach Billy Herman, captain Pee Wee Reese, Dixie Howell, Sandy Amoros, Roy Campanella. Middle row (*left to right*): clubhouse attendant John Griffin, Carl Erskine, Sandy Koufax, Lee Scott (in suit), Roger Craig, Don Newcombe, Karl Spooner, Don Hoak, Carl Furillo, Frank Kellert, trainer Harold "Doc" Wendler. Top row (*left to right*): Russ Meyer, Jim Gilliam, Billy Loes, Clem Labine, Gil Hodges, Ed Roebuck, Don Bessent, Duke Snider, Johnny Podres, Al Walker, Jackie Robinson. (National Baseball Hall of Fame Library, Cooperstown, New York)

line up was thirty-four.[2] Four of the eight regulars—Robinson, Campanella, Snider, and Gil Hodges—had been signed and developed by Branch Rickey, who departed five years earlier for Pittsburgh. Another regular, Pee Wee Reese, the thirty-six-year-old team captain, had been the Dodgers' starting shortstop for fifteen years and was on the downside of his playing career. Robinson, also thirty-six, was a "tiring third baseman" with a portly physique. The constant racial abuse he suffered—and provoked— had taken its toll physically. His hair had grayed and his legs, the foundation of his success as a base stealer, were betraying him.[3] Jackie kept his diabetes a secret from teammates as well as Dodgers ownership and management, fearing that knowledge of it would jeopardize his career.[4]

He refused to take that risk as long as baseball was his livelihood and a critical forum for civil rights. He was proud of his role in integrating the national pastime and could see the fruit of his effort on the Dodgers' roster, which featured six players of color, including himself, Campanella, Don Newcombe, Joe Black, Gilliam, and Amoros. Jackie also knew that each of those players deserved to be in the big leagues, with three MVP Award winners and four Rookies of the Year among them.[5] As a result, he entered the '55 campaign struggling with mixed emotions over whether he could do more for civil rights as a ballplayer or in the private sector.

Campanella, at age thirty-three, was also struggling. Hampered by hand injuries that had limited his playing time the previous year, he saw his batting average slip to .207. Without Campy's powerful bat, the Dodgers finished a disappointing five games behind the New York Giants, who went on to face the Cleveland Indians in the 1954 World Series. No doubt his five-foot-nine-inch frame was beginning to feel the effects of his 220 pounds in the ongoing battle he waged against his weight. Sportswriters were beginning to wonder if the constant physical demands of catching had finally taken their toll.[6] Though O'Malley had recently signed him to a $45,000 contract, Campy, probably embarrassed by the off-year, told the Dodgers' owner that he'd "play for nothing if he had to."[7]

More troubling, the Dodgers struggled with the personal animosity Jackie Robinson and Roy Campanella harbored against each other. The feud had become a cold war, the two star players largely ignoring each other off the field and barely tolerating each other on it. Teammates and the beat writers were well aware of their mutual disdain, which exacerbated the inevitable tensions that surface among twenty-five players with different backgrounds over the course of a 154-game season.[8] The feud affected at least one other relationship on the team, that between Robinson and manager Walter Alston, a big fan of Campanella. It began during an exhibition game in Montgomery, Alabama, when Jackie was benched for a younger third baseman, Don Hoak. Disgusted by the move, he asked sportswriter Dick Young, who had a talent for getting the inside scoop, if he had heard how Alston was planning to use him that season, but Young said he had not. "When I'm fit," said Robinson, "I've got as much right to be in the line-up as any man on this club, and Alston knows that. Or maybe he doesn't know that." The next day the discussion appeared in the *New*

York Daily News. Alston was enraged: "If Robinson has any complaints, why the hell doesn't he come to me and not tell them to a writer? Only two days ago he said he had a sore arm and wanted to go to a doctor in New York. If he was ready to play, why not tell me?"

Instead of dropping the matter, Robinson fanned the flames by responding, "I believe it's the manager's job to know the physical condition of his players. I've been in shape all spring. I just can't play one day and then sit on the bench four days and do a good job."

Alston was in a precarious position. He realized that if he didn't stand up to Robinson, he'd lose the respect of all his players. On the other hand, if he did challenge Jackie, he'd lose face among the veterans. Determined to cut his losses, Alston, known for his brute strength, challenged Robinson to a fight. Words were exchanged as the two men positioned themselves for blows before Campanella interceded. "When are you guys going to grow up?" he asked. "We came here to play ball not fight."[9]

Throughout the 1955 season the two men remained resentful of each other. Alston, who believed that the aging Robinson should be a utility man, platooned him at third base with Hoak, limiting Jackie's playing time to 105 games. The decision infuriated Jackie, who already viewed Alston as a "usurper," the man who "stole" his friend Charlie Dressen's job. Sometimes Jackie was openly critical of the manager, complaining about his "boneheaded judgments," his inability to "remain cool under pressure," and his leniency with umpires. On other occasions he was silently resentful of Alston, which could be worse since Robinson's emotions were always close to the surface.[10]

Interestingly another team conflict seemed to unite the black Dodgers, marginalizing the impact of the Robinson-Campanella feud, at least for a time. It involved rookie pitcher Sandy Koufax, a Jew and an extremely talented prospect. Signed by the Dodgers for an annual salary of $6,000 with a $14,000 bonus—a considerable amount considering the total Brooklyn payroll was just $500,000—Koufax instantly created jealousy among some of the veterans who were paid less.[11] Despite his request to go to the Minors, the young hurler, like all "bonus babies," had to remain on the Major League roster or the Dodgers would risk losing him to another team. Koufax's very presence triggered the widespread anti-Semitism that existed in baseball itself and divided the team along racial lines. Some white teammates spurned him as a "moneyed kike," while the black Dodgers rallied to his defense, having been the victims of prejudice themselves. Robinson, Campanella, Gilliam, Black, and Newcombe went out of their way to protect Koufax. Robinson was especially critical of Alston, who rarely used the rookie pitcher in spite of his potential. According to Tom Villante, a member of the Dodgers' broadcast team, Jackie "appreciated Sandy's talent" and he "already disliked Alston, so it was easy for him to take [Koufax's] side." "The fact that Sandy would every so often show this terrific flash of brilliance and pitch a terrific game," said Villante, "and then Alston wouldn't pitch him again for thirty days irked Jackie. It only confirmed, in Jackie's mind, just how dumb Alston really was."[12] The other black Dodgers were more subtle in their support of the young Jewish star. They embraced him as one of their own, inviting him to socialize with them and offering him constant encouragement. Some were astounded that after everything the team had experienced with the integration process there were still white Dodgers who openly discriminated against a teammate. "I couldn't understand the narrowness of some of our star players who talked about Sandy as a 'Jew bastard who's gonna take somebody's job,'" recalled Newcombe. "They hated Jews as much as they hated blacks. You think of crackers being from the South, but these guys were from California and other places. It was because of that bigotry that we took care of Sandy."[13] Despite the problems with team chemistry, Brooklyn somehow managed to record its most productive season ever.

The Dodgers opened the 1955 season by reeling off ten straight wins and taking twenty-two of their first twenty-four games. By July 4 they found themselves in first place with a twelve-and-a-half-game lead. Not even a mid-August slump could dislodge them as they completed the season thirteen and a half games in front of second-place Milwaukee.[14] "We were no challenge to the Dodgers," recalled Hank Aaron of the Braves, who reluctantly admitted to keeping a scrapbook of the team. "Don Newcombe was the best pitcher in the League that season, and with Campy and Jackie they were never out of first place."[15] Indeed Newcombe was the ace of a formidable pitching staff, posting a 20-5 record for an .800 winning percentage. With a devastating fastball and a curve that broke so sharply umpires suspected him of throwing a spitter, Newk hurled seventeen complete games and recorded 143 strikeouts and a 3.20 earned run average. The only pitcher to come close that season was the Phillies' Robin Roberts, who went 23-14 with a .622 winning percentage. Either one would have been worthy of the Cy Young Award if it had existed at the time.[16] Carl Erskine, famous for his overhand curveball, contributed another eleven victories and pitched 195 innings, recording 84 strikeouts with a 3.78 ERA. Twenty-two-year-old Johnny Podres went 9-10 with 114 strikeouts and a 3.96 ERA, and Clem Labine, known for a sinking fastball, was the league's top reliever, with thirteen victories and eleven saves in sixty appearances.[17] Campanella anchored the team, both offensively and defensively. He hit .318, and his short, powerful swing connected for 32 home runs and 136 RBIS, impressive statistics that secured a third MVP Award.[18] Although Robinson batted just .256, the lowest of his career to that date, he still contributed 81 hits, including 8 home runs and 36 RBIS.[19] But the key to the Dodgers' success was their .365 on-base percentage, which was 11.3 percent better than the .328 league average. Six of the eight regulars posted on-base percentages over .370. Seven of them, Hodges being the exception, walked at least as often as they struck out.[20] As a result the Dodgers did not have to rely on power hitting as much as manufacturing runs by utilizing the bunt, hit-and-run, and base-stealing. The small-ball strategy allowed the team to compile a 98-55 record, earning them another shot at the New York Yankees in the Fall Classic.[21]

The Dodgers were a stronger team statistically than the Yanks, but they simply didn't have luck or fate on their side. In the previous five years Brooklyn's hopes for that first world championship went down in flames. Twice they lost the pennant in the last inning of the final game. The defeats were legendary, especially the loss in the 1951 playoff to Bobby Thomson and the Giants. On two other occasions, they won the pennant only to lose the Series to the Bronx Bombers. By comparison, the Yankees won all but two American League pennants between 1947 and 1958 and an unprecedented five straight world championships from 1949 to 1953. After those achievements Yankees manager Casey Stengel, who failed to make the Dodgers winners, was hailed as a genius by the baseball establishment. It seemed the Brooks were cursed.

But in 1955 Robinson had an additional incentive to win. In April the Yankees fielded their first African American player, catcher Elston Howard. Eight years after Jackie had broken the color barrier the Bronx Bombers had finally integrated. Now only three all-white teams remained: the Phillies, Tigers, and Red Sox.[22] Instead of celebrating the event, however, Stengel insulted his black catcher. When asked what he thought of Howard's early performance, the Yankees' manager remarked, "Well, when they finally get me a nigger, I get the only one who can't run."[23] It was a feeble attempt to be funny, but the remark was abusive and did not escape notice by Robinson, who had been openly critical of the all-white Yankees years earlier. On that occasion he was reprimanded by the National League president for his remarks. This time Jackie held his tongue and let his on-field performance do the talking in the World Series.

Newcombe faced New York's ace, Whitey Ford, in Game One at Yankee Stadium on September 28. Neither hurler had their best stuff, but the Yanks took a 6–4 lead into the eighth inning. With two outs, Robinson on third base, and Dodgers pinch hitter Frank Kellert at bat, Jackie decided to take matters into his own hands. Anticipating that Yankees catcher Yogi Berra wouldn't expect him to steal home, Robinson inched off third as Ford went into his wind-up. He broke for the plate before the hurler released the ball. Snagging Ford's pitch in front of the plate, Berra allowed Jackie to slide into his tag. The image was instantly freeze-framed in the national conscience: Jackie Robinson, consumed by rage and pride, once again defying all odds and stealing home. That image still endures as a lasting reminder of the black man's vindication. When umpire Bill Summers called Robinson safe, Berra, incensed by the call, jumped up and down, screaming in protest. It remains one of the most controversial decisions in baseball history.

Although Jackie brought the Dodgers to within one run of the Yanks, New York held on to win the game, 6–5.[24] The Yankees won again the following day, 4–2, and it appeared as if Brooklyn was going to be bridesmaids once again. No team had ever come back from being down two games to none to win the best-of-seven Series. Predictably Brooklyn fans resumed their familiar chant: "Wait 'til next year!"

Seated in the visitors' clubhouse, heads in hands, the Dodgers were dejected until Robinson perked up. "We gotta win Game Three," he snapped. "If we lose again, they'll be calling us choke-up guys the rest of our lives. Do we want that?"[25] The implication of going down in baseball history as choke artists was powerful motivation. The tone of the Series changed

21. Jackie steals home against the New York Yankees in Game One of the 1955 World Series. The catcher is Yogi Berra. (National Baseball Hall of Fame Library, Cooperstown, New York)

dramatically when the scene shifted to Ebbets Field on September 30 for Game Three. Alston sent twenty-three-year-old Johnny Podres to the mound against Bob Turley. Podres had finished just 9-10 during an injury-plagued season but had shown promise early on. "I started off that year with seven wins by June," recalled Podres. "Even though I got hurt, it ended up pretty good for me. I hadn't pitched many innings by the fall because of the injury, so I was fresh. It was like coming out of spring training. I had a good fastball, and I was raring to go."[26] Alston's hunch proved to be correct. Campanella led the Dodgers' attack with three hits and three RBIS. But Robinson sparked the team's comeback. With the scored tied 2–2 in the bottom of the second, Jackie put the Dodgers ahead for good when he singled with one out, went to second when Amoros was hit with a pitch, and advanced to third on a bunt single by Podres. Turley became unnerved with Robinson dancing off third, threatening to steal home. He walked Reese, forcing in Robinson with the go-ahead run. Later in the game, Jackie suckered Elston Howard, who was playing the outfield, into an extra-base hit by purposely overrunning second base on a steal. When Howard threw to second, Robinson easily scampered to third. Brooklyn won 8–3, as Jackie finished the game with two hits and played a flawless third base with seven chances.[27]

Rejuvenated by Podres's complete-game victory, the Dodgers came back the next day to tie the Series at two-all with an 8–5 victory behind the clutch pitching of Clem Labine and homers by Campanella, Snider, and Hodges. Snider was the hero of Game Five, belting two home runs off Yankees pitcher Bob Grim for a 5–3 Dodgers win. When the Series returned to Yankee Stadium on October 3, Whitey Ford took the mound and coasted to a 5–1 victory. Once again the momentum shifted, and the Yankees were confidant that they'd clinch another championship. Alston chose Podres to start Game Seven against the Yankees' Tommy Byrne. Confident after his stellar performance in Game Three, Podres told his teammates, "Just get me one run. That's all I need. Just one!"[28] Years later the Dodgers' hurler insisted that the deciding Game Seven was no different from any other game he pitched. "It really didn't matter that we were playing the Yankees and the Dodgers had never beaten them before," he said.

> Hell, I'd beaten the Giants, Cardinals, and Reds that year, and they all had good ball clubs. Sure we were down. The Yankees had tied up the Series the day before and we were playing at their place. But we knew we had a good ball club, so there wasn't much pressure on me. When you're playing with Jackie Robinson, Roy Campanella, Duke Snider, and Gil Hodges, you know you're going to get a lot of runs. I figured if I pitched my normal game, I'd be fine. Besides, if I had good stuff, I'd beat 'em. That's the way it always worked.[29]

The deciding game of the Series was played at Yankee Stadium on October 4. Robinson, scratched from the lineup with a pulled Achilles tendon, would have to watch from the dugout what would become the greatest single game in Brooklyn's history. The contest remained scoreless until the fourth, when the Dodgers scored a run on a double by Campanella and a single by Hodges. The Dodgers added another run in the sixth on a sacrifice fly by Hodges. The only danger Podres experienced came in the sixth. With two men on and no outs, Yogi Berra hit a long fly ball down the left-field line. Since Berra usually hit the ball to right, Dodgers left fielder Sandy Amoros, who had just entered the game, had positioned himself toward center. He had to make a long run to the left-field corner and it looked as if the ball would fall in for a double, allowing both runners to score. But Amoros dashed to the line and at the last possible moment stuck out his glove to make the catch. Whirling around, he threw the ball back into the infield, where shortstop Pee Wee Reese caught Yankees runner Gil McDougald off first base for an easy double play. Podres surrendered just one hit after that, retiring the Yankees in order to give the Dodgers their very first world championship.[30]

Sportswriter Shirley Povich captured the magnitude of the victory when he called in his story to the *Washington Post*: "October 4, 1955. Please don't interrupt, because you haven't heard this one before . . . honest. At precisely 4:45 p.m. today, in Yankee Stadium, off came the 52-year slur on the ability of the Dodgers to win a World Series, for at that moment the last straining Yankee was out at first base, and the day, the game, and the 1955 Series belonged to Brooklyn." But the most memorable headline graced the front page of the *New York Daily News*, which displayed the caricatured face of a nearly toothless hobo and the caption "WHO'S A BUM!" Before either newspaper hit the streets, Dodgers fans went crazy. Caravans of cars honked their horns up and down Flatbush Avenue and Ocean Parkway. Brooklynites, young and old, marched through the streets of their neighborhood banging garbage cans lids, hugging each other, and crying. Telephone circuits between the boroughs collapsed from overload. Confetti showered down from the upper floors of office buildings. The owners of restaurants, candy stores, and butcher shops gave away their wares for free.[31]

Overwhelmed by emotion, Walter O'Malley, known for his tight purse strings, increased Campanella's salary to $50,000, making him the highest paid player in Dodgers history. He would come to regret the action the following year, when the catcher, hampered with injuries throughout the season, would suffer one of his worst performances. The '56 campaign was in the distant future, though. The present was a time to celebrate. A few weeks later the baseball writers voted Campy his third MVP Award.[32] It couldn't get any better for the kid who began his career on the crude sandlots of North Philadelphia.

During their final year together, Campanella and Robinson found it difficult to hide their disdain for each other. Roy's status as a three-time MVP and the highest-paid Dodger intensified the jealousy Jackie already harbored against him. In turn Robinson believed that Campanella was jealous of his pioneering role in baseball. "I'm the only stumbling block against his moving into a better position in the Brooklyn organization," he told sportswriter Carl Rowan. "Nothing will make him more happy than if I was off the club and he would be the number one man."[33] Robinson's feelings were confirmed by an incident that took place during spring training that year. When a black youngster approach Campanella hoping for a tryout as a catcher, Roy told him, "I'm not running the camp, but if I was, Robinson would be the first son of a bitch to get rid of." After learning of the remark, Jackie confronted the catcher, but nothing came of it. He then asked general manager Buzzie Bavasi to trade him, anticipating that "this thing was going to develop into a real problem."[34] Shortly afterward Robinson, in a private letter to his wife, wrote, "The more I see of Camp the less I like him. . . . He's like a snake, ready to strike at the best possible moment."[35] Deceitfulness wasn't his only complaint. Jackie, who could be priggish as well as sanctimonious, was also disturbed by Campanella's womanizing. No doubt Campy was subject to the same temptations as most Major Leaguers. In fact when the Dodgers were on the road, they enjoyed their own entourage of groupies. Known collectively as "the Varsity," the women met them at train depots, hotel lobbies, and the ballparks. Initially O'Malley tended to look the other way, but eventually he threatened a $500 fine for any player who consorted with the group. It was his way of discouraging the possibility of an interracial coupling, which could lead to a publicly humiliating, if not disastrous incident.[36] Although Campanella had a reputation for flirting with other women, the only evidence of an extramarital affair comes from Robinson. "It seems Campy has a girl here," he wrote to Rachel that spring. "The fellows keep kidding him about her and it has gotten under his skin. Camp is always kidding the other guys but can't take it himself."[37] More often, however, Robinson's criticism focused on Campanella's passive approach to civil rights rather than his personal conduct.

The year 1956 marked the beginning of the modern civil rights movement. After the Supreme Court's *Brown v. Board of Education* decision, black activists, fed up with second-class citizenship, mobilized to end de facto segregation in the South. The first significant protest occurred in Montgomery, Alabama, in December 1955, when Rosa Parks, a seamstress at a local department store, challenged the city's discriminatory seating policy in public transportation. Parks was arrested for the crime of refusing to give up her bus seat to a white man who demanded it. Her arrest catalyzed Montgomery's black community leaders, who selected Dr. Martin Luther King Jr., a twenty-five-year-old Baptist minister, to lead a citywide bus boycott. The boycott placed economic pressure not only on Montgomery's bus company but on many of the city's merchants who relied on black customers. What ensured the success of the movement, however, was a class-action lawsuit brought against Montgomery city officials a few months after the boycott began.

Four black women who, like Rosa Parks, also defied segregated seating, challenged the constitutionality of both city and state segregation ordinances. The case, argued in federal courts by NAACP attorneys, referenced the *Brown* decision. After considerable deliberation, a special three-judge panel in the U.S. District Court declared Alabama's state and local laws requiring segregation on buses unconstitutional. The Supreme Court affirmed the judgment, ending the 381-day boycott. The Montgomery boycott propelled King to the forefront of the fledgling civil rights movement. During the next year he, along with other leading black clergymen, established the Southern Christian Leadership Conference as an institutional vehicle to coordinate an ongoing campaign of nonviolent social protest, including sit-ins, interstate bus rides, and voter registration drives. King's inspirational example also served to mobilize other black activists, who began to escalate their protests against segregation and inequality. White backlash soon followed, and several black churches in the South were fire-bombed.[38]

When Campanella was asked for his reaction to the bombings, he said that such violence could be prevented if blacks "stopped pressing to get too far too fast." He simply couldn't understand why blacks felt compelled to challenge civil law, even if those laws violated their constitutional rights. His own experience taught him that acceptance by white society was the reward for patience and conformity. Robinson was infuriated. "I'm irked that Campy, a Negro with children, should blame the bombings on Negroes who were asking only for their constitutional rights," he told the sportswriters. "If I had a room jammed with trophies and awards," he added, referring to his teammate's baseball achievements, "and a child of mine came to me and asked what I had done in defense of black people, and I had to tell that child that I had kept quiet, I would have to mark myself a total failure in the whole business of living." Jackie's personal jealousy of Campanella had become tied to his disillusionment with the catcher's passive stand on civil rights. O'Malley joined the fray by taking Campy's side and criticizing Robinson for making "ill-timed and intemperate" comments in the press.[39] Routinely put off by Jackie's outspokenness, O'Malley seized the opportunity to let the star third baseman know that his patience was wearing thin. He preferred more docile blacks, like Campanella, who sometimes willingly, sometimes unwittingly, supported white racism. Stronger criticism came from Bill Keefe, sports editor of the *New Orleans Times-Picayune*, who wrote that the Supreme Court's "new law [banning segregated seating on buses] received a push from the insolence of Jackie Robinson." Identifying the Dodgers' star as "the most harmful influence the Negro race has suffered," Keefe mused, "The surprising part is that he wasn't muzzled long ago."[40]

As the 1956 season unfolded, Robinson distanced himself from his teammates, with the exceptions of Reese, Hodges, and Erskine. "Jackie didn't let many people get close to him to begin with," recalled teammate Don Zimmer. "He was closest to Pee Wee. Some of the players might have had differences with him, but you could understand why Jackie was careful after all the things he went through. It was also his last year, and his feud with Alston seemed to simmer in the background that season. The two of them never really got along."[41] In fact Robinson could be a snob, considering many of his teammates "boorish" and "ignorant." He especially disliked their locker-room humor, profanity, and promiscuity.[42] On the other hand, the few he liked commanded both his respect and unflinching loyalty. Erskine, one of his closest friends, struggled with severe arm problems early in the season but continued to pitch with the pain. Robinson felt bad for him and was angered by a quotation he read in the New York newspapers on Saturday, May 12. According to Tom Sheehan, the chief scout of the New York Giants, the Dodgers were "over the hill" and Erskine couldn't "win with the garbage he's been throwing up there."

Jackie cut out the column and saved it. That afternoon Erskine was sched-uled to pitch against the Giants at Ebbets Field. Willie Mays stepped up to the plate in the fifth inning of a scoreless game and blistered the ball down the third-base line. Robinson dove to his right, speared the ball, and threw Mays out at first. It proved to be the pivotal defensive play of the game. Erskine went on to pitch a rare no-hit-no-run masterpiece. "After I retired the Giants in the ninth," recalled the Dodgers' pitcher, "Jackie rushed to the mound, shook my hand, and then turned and raced to the Giants' dugout, where Tom Sheehan was seated. He reached into his hip pocket, pulled out the clipping, and waving it at Sheehan, shouted, 'How do you like that garbage?'"[43]

Before a Sunday afternoon game at Milwaukee in late August, Braves pitcher Lew Burdette began taunting Robinson from the dugout with the term *watermelon*. First baseman Gil Hodges, interpreting the remark as a racial slur, told Burdette to "knock it off." When the Braves' hurler de-cided to berate Hodges as well, Robinson, who was taking ground balls at second base, purposely fired a ball over the first baseman's head right at Burdette in the Milwaukee dugout. Then he challenged the pitcher, "Meet me outside the park after the game."[44]

Jackie's friendship with Pee Wee Reese was the strongest, dating to his first year in the Majors, when the shortstop repeatedly defended him in the clubhouse and publicly on the playing field. Realizing that their play-ing days were numbered, Robinson began promoting the Dodgers' cap-tain as a managerial candidate among the sportswriters. "Pee Wee Reese is one of the finest men I have ever met," he insisted. "Pee Wee sees things in everyone. He remembers everyone he meets. I've learned so many things from him. He knows the temperament of all the guys and treats them ac-cordingly. That's an important feature of a manager, and I hope Pee Wee becomes one. He knows baseball. He knows people."[45]

Brooklyn managed to eke out another pennant in 1956 to face the Yan-kees one last time in the Fall Classic. The Dodgers won the first two games at Ebbets Field by scores of 6–3 and 13–8. But their fortunes turned when the Series shifted to the Bronx, with the Yanks taking the next two con-tests, 5–3 and 6–2. With the Series tied at two games apiece, Game Five, played on October 8 at Yankee Stadium, would prove to be one for the re-cord books. Sal Maglie started for the Dodgers and held the Yanks hitless until Mickey Mantle's two-run homer in the fourth. But New York's Don Larsen was even better, hurling a 2–0 shutout for the first perfect game in World Series history. Refusing to be denied, the Dodgers bounced back the following day, in Game Six. The game was a pitcher's masterpiece as Brooklyn's Clem Labine and Yankee Bob Turley held each other in check for nine innings in a scoreless deadlock. With two outs in the bottom of the tenth, Robinson lined one of Turley's fastballs over the head of the left fielder, scoring Jim Gilliam from second base and forcing a decisive Game Seven. Unfortunately for Brooklyn, the finale was anticlimactic. The Dodgers suffered a 9–0 whitewashing, and once again, the Yankees were world champs. Campanella, unable to throw well or hold a bat comfortably because of a calcium deposit protruding from his right thumb, hit just .182 with 7 strikeouts. Robinson was more effective, hitting .250 with 6 hits, 2 RBIs, and 1 home run, though he struck out to end the Series.[46] It would be the last time either man appeared in the Fall Classic.

Even before the 1956 World Series had begun, Robinson had had his fill of baseball. He'd been secretly negotiating with Bill Black, president of Chock full o' Nuts, to become vice president in charge of personnel for the restaurant chain, which employed a sizable African American labor force. About the same time, *Look* magazine approached Jackie and offered him $50,000 for an exclusive story on his impending retirement.[47] Since neither deal had been finalized, though, Robinson said nothing of his plans to Dodgers president Walter O'Malley or general manager Buzzie Bavasi. Instead he continued to tell the press that he intended to return to the Dodgers for the 1957 season.[48] On December 12 he agreed to terms with Chock full o' Nuts. Although he was scheduled to meet with O'Malley the following day to discuss his future with the club, Bavasi phoned him to say that he'd been traded to the New York Giants for $30,000 and pitcher Dick Littlefield.[49]

Cheated out of the opportunity to preempt Dodgers ownership, Robinson would later consider the trade O'Malley's penultimate insult.[50] Stunned and angry, he wanted to tell Bavasi that he was "no longer the Dodgers' property to be traded," but he held his tongue so that *Look* could break the story.[51] To that end, he contacted Horace Stoneham, owner of the Giants, and unsuccessfully tried to persuade him not to announce the trade. As soon as the deal was made public, Dodgers fans rallied indignantly to Jackie's side and teammates paid him endless tributes.⁵² One of the shrewder tributes came from Jimmy Cannon of *Newsday*, who managed to capture Robinson in all of his complexity: "You are Jackie Robinson, who is consumed by rage and pride. You're a complicated man, persecuted by slanderous myths, using anger as a confederate. No athlete of any time has been assaulted by such aching loneliness which created your personality and shaped your genuine greatness."⁵³

Jackie could have reconsidered retirement. *Look* had not gone public yet. Besides, the Giants were a perennial contender and had a brighter future than the aging Dodgers. Willie Mays, the young star of the team, was ecstatic about being united with his boyhood idol. Mays craved a mentor like Jackie, and the Giants planned to make them roommates.⁵⁴ But Robinson had no intention of playing for the Giants, whom he despised. He also likened Mays to Campanella, a docile, uneducated black ballplayer who refused to take a public stand on civil rights, fearing that it might jeopardize his success in baseball.⁵⁵ After all the acrimony with Campy, Jackie certainly didn't want a similar situation with Mays. Thus Jackie prepared for the inevitable announcement that he was through with baseball.

In early January a *Look* employee leaked Robinson's decision to retire. Jackie was excoriated for his duplicity. Red Smith of the *Herald-Tribune* criticized him for misleading the Dodgers, the Giants, the fans, and the press by selling the news of his retirement to *Look* and holding the announcement for the publication's deadline. "Robinson has embarrassed the Dodgers, dislocated the plans of the Giants and deceived the fans as well as the working newspapermen who thought they had his confidence," wrote Smith. "Of all the qualities Robinson displayed in the past, the most attractive was candor. In the end, it was candor that he sacrificed to mislead the club that brought him into baseball and paid him for eleven years, the club that committed itself in good faith to pay him this year, the fans and the individual members of a press who have contributed hugely to his fame."⁵⁶ Predictably O'Malley now dismissed Robinson as a "mercenary" and "ingrate" who was "always seeking publicity." Bavasi, who apparently believed that he had no obligation to inform Robinson that he was about to be traded to the Giants, scorned the *Look* article as a ploy by Jackie to pilfer more money out of the Giants. Insulted by the suggestion of greed, Robinson insisted that no amount of money would make

22. Jackie visits Ebbets Field after retiring from the Dodgers, 1957. (National Baseball Hall of Fame Library, Cooperstown, New York)

him "ever play baseball again" and that Bavasi's "unwarranted criticism in the press insulted my integrity."[57]

On June 8, 1957, *Look* ran "Why I'm Quitting Baseball" by Jackie Robinson. There were no more rumors; Robinson's retirement was now official. Although the Giants pleaded with him to reconsider and offered him a $35,000 contract, Jackie informed Stoneham that he was "too old to help the Giants" and dismissed the notion that his decision to retire was based on being "traded to [the Giants] organization." Instead Robinson stated his intention to "devote his full time to the business opportunities that have been presented to [him]." After receiving the letter, Stoneham wished Jackie success and happiness, adding his regret over "not having you on our side for a year or two."[58]

"The Dodgers should have allowed Jack to retire with dignity and honor and celebration instead of selling him for thirty pieces of silver to the Giants," insisted Rachel Robinson some forty years after the trade. "I just thought that was a violation of some kind of code of honor. But he expected it to happen, so when he was told he was traded, Jack already had a job with Chock full o' Nuts. It was exciting to be able to defend himself and not have to do something he didn't want to do, which was play for the enemy Giants."[59] Naturally Robinson was more defensive. "The way I figure it," he wrote in his 1972 autobiography, "I was even with baseball and baseball was even with me. The game had done much for me and I had done much for it."[60]

Robinson's retirement should have marked the end of his feud with Campanella. Instead the former teammates continued to snipe at each other in the newspapers. Appraising the Dodgers' prospects for the upcoming season shortly after his retirement, Robinson gave an interview to Dick Young of the *New York Daily News*, expressing doubts about Campy's ability to rebound from an injury-plagued season and saying he was "washed up." Always eager to capitalize on—as well as create— controversy, Young reported the observation to Campanella, who admitted that he "wasn't surprised by the remark." Insisting that Robinson "doesn't know what he's talking about," Roy said he was "far from through with baseball," predicting that he'd "catch five more years for Brooklyn and at least 100 games in each of the next three years." Then he proceeded to launch a reprisal:

A guy like Jackie should have gone out of baseball with a lot of friends. Instead, he made a lot of enemies. He was always stirring this stuff up in the clubhouse, too, making a lot of trouble. Instead of being grateful to baseball, he's criticizing it. Everything he has, he owes to baseball. That beautiful house of his and that new job of his, too. Does he think those Chock Full 'o Nuts people would have anything to do with him if he had never played baseball?

Jackie better learn to talk differently to those people who are working for him in that director of personnel job of his. If he talks to some of them the way he talked in baseball, they'll wrap something around his neck and walk out. Jackie will find out how quick you can be forgotten when you're out of baseball. It has happened to greater players than him.[61]

Robinson learned of Campanella's diatribe while in St. Louis on a speaking engagement for the NAACP. Stating that he didn't remember calling Campy "washed up," Jackie clarified his position, contending that the Dodgers were right in worrying about the catcher's condition after his hand operation. "It's no secret," he added, "that the club has for years been looking for a No. 2 catcher just in case Campy reaches the end of the line." When asked to comment on Campanella's remark that he was a "trouble-maker," Robinson attributed the remark to jealousy, insisting that his former teammate had "always been envious of me for being the first Negro in baseball." He also took a swipe at sportswriter Dick Young, a longtime nemesis: "It's unfortunate that Campy let himself be suckered into this situation. But I'd like to congratulate Young for making such a sucker out of Campy."[62]

Four days later Campanella responded. Citing Robinson's undignified exit from baseball, he told the *Daily News*, "Jackie can't hurt me. . . . He's made quite a few cracks since retiring, but he doesn't know everything. When it's my turn to bow out of baseball, I certainly don't want to go out like he did. It just wasn't the dignified way to do it." Campy also admitted what others had long known: that the two stars hadn't been friendly since the early 1950s. "You can play with a guy, but not want to live with him. I always steered clear of Jackie when he was popping off in the clubhouse, and after a while, I just steered clear of him."[63]

Apparently Robinson decided not to go public with any more opinions of Campanella after that. The breakup was complete.

Epilogue

Life was not kind to either Jackie Robinson or Roy Campanella after they parted ways in 1956. Both men struggled with poor health and family problems, while attempting to redefine themselves and their careers. At the same time, those struggles allowed each man to become more sympathetic to the other's views on civil rights, enabling them to restore their friendship nearly a decade later.

After his retirement from baseball, Robinson channeled his energies into a new career as a businessman and community leader. In both capacities he became an important figure in the civil rights movement. Acting as a spokesman and fundraiser for the NAACP, he encouraged African Americans to become more active in business enterprises. Naturally he led by example, participating in black-owned ventures like the Freedom Bank in Harlem and the Jackie Robinson Construction Company in Englewood Cliffs, New Jersey. He also became an important advisor to Martin Luther King Jr. and assumed an active role in Republican Party politics in order to ensure that civil rights issues were a major consideration in that party's platform. But Robinson's support for presidential candidate Richard Nixon in 1960 and later New York governor Nelson Rockefeller placed him at odds with the NAACP, which favored the Democratic Party, and reinforced the widespread impression that he was a political conservative.[1]

When the leadership of the civil rights movement changed during the 1960s Robinson struggled to adjust. No longer were traditional organizations like the NAACP and the Urban League as influential among black activists as newer groups like King's Southern Christian Leadership Conference and the Student Non-violent Coordinating Committee, composed of black college students. By the mid-1960s more radical men were challenging King for leadership of the movement, including Malcolm X of the Nation of Islam and Huey P. Newton and Stokely Carmichael of the Black Panthers. Advocating black separatism and militancy, these groups distanced themselves from the integrated and nonviolent approach championed by King. They appealed to a younger, more assertive generation of blacks who had grown impatient with the inability of Congress and the courts to rectify race-related issues of poverty and other economic problems that were left unaddressed by simply ending segregation. They demonstrated their anger and frustration by rioting during the long hot summers of 1964–67.[2]

Robinson found himself caught in the wide chasm between the nonviolent direct action he once pioneered and the growing militancy of these groups. Although he continued to head the NAACP's Freedom Fund drive, he alternatively rebuked and defended the younger, more militant generation of black activists. In 1962, for example, he challenged a small group of black nationalists who were picketing a recently opened Jewish-owned restaurant. Chanting anti-Semitic slogans, the nationalists, who viewed the store as unfair competition for local black merchants, demanded that the Jewish owner relocate. Robinson condemned the group in the newspapers, stating that "black supremacy is just as bad as white supremacy" and that black people had been "fighting against this same thing all his life."[3] Similarly in 1969, when asked what he thought about black militants who advocated separatism, Robinson insisted that the militants "don't represent the mass of American blacks." Opposing the growing belief among urban blacks that "the whites of today should carry the burdens of their fathers and grandfathers," he declared that the African American community must identify a "talented tenth of business leaders to uplift other, [less advantaged] blacks" and provide them with constructive employment instead of rioting and looting.[4] His words not only echoed those of W. E. B. Du Bois two generations earlier but created a growing impression among younger black activists that Jackie was, as they said on the streets, an "Uncle Tom."[5] Ironically this militant generation perceived Robinson the very same way he viewed Campanella during their playing days in the 1950s. Jackie's efforts to reconcile his differences with his estranged teammate during the 1960s may very well have been due to a newly discovered sympathy for Campy.

On the other hand, there were times when Robinson defended the young black nationalists. In September 1968, when ten Black Panthers were beaten up by a mob of off-duty Brooklyn police officers, Robinson excoriated the police as "trigger happy" and white people in general as having "their heads way down in the sand, hoping that things will pass over as long as we don't rock the boat." Stating that he too "could have become a Black Panther as a teenager," Robinson insisted that the goals of the Panthers were "no different than those of other major civil rights groups: self-determination, protection of the black community, decent housing and employment, and express opposition to police abuse."[6] Robinson reinforced this message the following year, speaking before the National Conference of Christians and Jews in New York City and before a gathering of Black Panthers in Brooklyn.[7] Perhaps his sympathy for their cause was due to his trying experience with his eldest son, Jackie Jr., a Vietnam veteran who became addicted to drugs and was in and out of trouble with the law after his discharge.[8]

Robinson blamed himself for the trouble, believing that he had neglected his son as a child, spending more time with baseball and civil rights. Through his son's painful addiction and legal problems, he came to see the world through the eyes of a troubled young black man struggling to survive. Over a three-year period, Jackie Jr. recovered from his addiction only to die in a car accident.[9] Devastated by the loss, the fifty-two-year-old Robinson, barely able to walk and blind in one eye because of diabetes, soldiered on.

During the last year of his life, Jackie returned to baseball. With the exception of his Hall of Fame induction in 1962, he had stayed away from the game after his retirement.[10] But in 1972 he agreed to attend the ceremonies when the Los Angeles Dodgers officially retired his uniform No. 42 that summer and, in the fall, when Major League Baseball honored him on the twenty-fifth anniversary of his first season. The latter event took place on October 15, 1972, just prior to the second game of the World Series between the Reds and the A's at Cincinnati's Riverfront Stadium. Unwilling to ignore the fact that a quarter of a century had passed and there were still no African Americans in management positions, Jackie remarked that he was "extremely proud and pleased" to be honored, but that he'd be "tremendously more pleased and more proud when I look at that third base coaching line one day and see a black face managing in baseball."[11] Just nine days later he died of a massive heart attack at his home in Stamford, Connecticut.

Campanella's post-playing career was also marred by tragedy. His last year with the Dodgers came in 1957, their final season in Brooklyn. At thirty-six he looked forward to the Dodgers' move to Los Angeles, but a car accident on January 28, 1958, ended his career. The crash nearly severed his spinal cord and left him paralyzed from the shoulders down. Unable to move his arms or lower body, Campanella spent the next three months strapped to a bed with a metal brace attached to his head and neck. Another six months of rehabilitation followed, during which time he learned to move around in a wheelchair and to feed himself. He remained paralyzed for the rest of his life.[12] After he returned home in November 1958, Campanella was beset with family problems. His fifteen-year-old stepson, David, was arrested for burglary and other juvenile offenses. His wife, Ruthe, blamed Roy for her son's problems, insisting that David felt the burden of "living in the shadow of a celebrity."[13] Unable to adjust to her husband's new lifestyle, Ruthe left him in 1960. Shortly afterward Roy filed for divorce. She died of a cerebral hemorrhage three years later.[14] Struggling for money, Campy was forced to sell his Glen Cove, Long Island, house at auction. He relocated to a Harlem apartment where he could be close to his liquor store, a business he had opened during his playing career. Estranged from his first wife, Bernice Ray, and their two daughters, Roy did his best to care for the three children he had with Ruth: Roy Jr., Tony, and Ruth.[15]

On May 5, 1964, Campy married his nurse, Roxie Doles, and his life finally took a turn for the better. The couple moved to suburban Westchester, New York, where they raised his three children and her two. He earned money through his liquor business, doing radio and television shows, and working for the Dodgers during spring training.[16] It was also during this time that Campanella reconciled with Robinson.

In 1963 Jackie offered an olive branch to Roy when he asked his former teammate to be interviewed for a forthcoming book on black ballplayers' experiences since integration. Titled *Baseball Has Done It*, the book reflected Campy's disillusionment with the lack of progress in civil rights, a sentiment he never would have voiced during his playing days:

We never thought it would be like this. I didn't think [the discrimination] would go on for years and years and years. I thought things would gradually change. . . .

It's a horrible thing to be born in this country and go along with all the rules, laws and regulations and have to battle in court for the right to go to the movies—to wonder which stores my children can go in in the South to try on a pair of shoes or sleep in a hotel.

I am a Negro and I am part of this. . . . I feel it as deep as anyone and so do my children. This struggle has mushroomed into something much more powerful than the hydrogen bomb. This is the biggest explosive the United States has. It's in the open and it'll never be closed up again.[17]

Far from being an epiphany, Campanella's newfound assertiveness was the result of the often violent backlash to the civil rights protests of the 1960s. Television images of black protestors being beaten unmercifully by southern policemen for simply riding an integrated bus across state lines and schoolchildren being fire-hosed for demonstrating against segregated public facilities made Campy realize that little had changed since his days in the Negro Leagues. He even began to speak out against the segregation that still existed in the Florida towns that hosted spring training camps, insisting, "If you play like a major leaguer, you should be permitted to live like one."[18] Campy's conversion was also influenced by his son Roy Jr.'s more aggressive position on civil rights. An intelligent, articulate young man, Roy Campanella Jr. was attracted to Malcolm X's emphasis on black pride, though he did not go so far as to advocate black separatism. After graduating from Harvard University, where he majored in anthropology, Roy Jr. became a successful television director and documentary film maker who focuses on issues of African American culture and interest.[19]

On May 16, 1964, Jackie visited his former teammate at Campy's Harlem liquor store and handed him an autographed copy of his recently published book. Campy "greeted Robinson warmly," and they conducted a two-hour discussion on race relations in America. During the discussion it became clear to Jackie that the two men now shared the same philosophy, namely, that there was no place for segregation, black separatism, or violence in the civil rights movement. Equal opportunity would

23. Jackie presents Campy with an autographed copy of his book *Baseball Has Done It*. Their May 12, 1964, reunion marked the end of a nearly decade-long estrangement. (Bettmann/Corbis/AP Images)

come only through candid dialogue and active cooperation between the races. Attributing their former feud to the intrusiveness of the New York press, Robinson insisted that "Roy's contribution to the cause can be as vital" because "what he is saying here today is an inspiration to kids all over the nation."[20]

Another personal highlight of these years came in 1969 with Roy's induction into the National Baseball Hall of Fame. Although he was often mentioned as the best candidate for baseball's first black manager, Campy, who possessed the knowledge, experience, and temperament for the job, never realized that dream because of his paralysis.[21]

In 1978 the Campanellas relocated to California, where Roy joined his former teammate and friend, Don Newcombe, in the Dodgers' Community Service Department. That same year Campanella was named to the National Baseball Hall of Fame's recently expanded Veterans Committee. Along with Monte Irvin, who was also on the committee, Campy made sure that several worthy Negro League players were enshrined at Cooperstown.[22] In the years that followed, Campanella served as a popular speaker throughout southern California and an annual catching instructor for the Dodgers during spring training. During the regular season he was the team's biggest supporter, attending every home game, offering his encouragement to the players and disabled fans who came to meet him.[23] Throughout these years Campanella wrestled with periods of depression, but he retained an optimistic attitude that was buttressed by his enduring love for baseball. "People look at me and get the feeling that if a guy in a wheelchair can have such a good time, they can't be too bad off after all," Campy told a sportswriter near the end of his life.[24] He died of a heart attack on June 26, 1993, at his home in Woodland Hills, a suburb of Los Angeles. He was seventy-one years old.[25]

Sportswriter Red Smith tried to capture the difference between these two civil rights pioneers shortly after their playing careers ended. "In the great social contribution which baseball has made to America since 1946," he wrote, "Jackie Robinson was the trail blazer, the standard bearer, the man who broke the color line, assumed the burden for his people and made good. Roy Campanella is the one who made friends."[26] While Smith celebrated Robinson's example, anticipating the popular deification that followed his death, he was tremendously unfair to Campanella. In fact Campy's great achievement was destroying the stereotype of the talented black athlete who buckled under pressure. He demonstrated the athletic prowess, intelligence, and determination that opened the door for many other talented African American athletes in professional sports. Like Robinson, he also furthered the integrationist and egalitarian goals of the civil rights movement, and did so in a national pastime that captured the attention of most Americans in the post–World War II era.

To diminish either man's contribution because of their different approaches to civil rights is just as irresponsible as idolizing them. The civil rights movement would not have been successful without accommodation *and* direct action. While Robinson and Campanella assumed the role of pioneers, their examples would have meant little without popular support, both black and white, for civil rights. When we idolize them we fail to recognize their humanity. When we criticize them, we fail to acknowledge the meaning of their contributions as well as their sacrifices. Neither man would want that. Therefore if we seek to do justice to the examples of Jackie Robinson and Roy Campanella, we must look at the condition of contemporary race relations and ask ourselves, "What can I do?"

Notes

Introduction

1. Branch, *Parting the Waters*, 203–4.
2. The most complete biography of Martin Luther King Jr. is Oates, *Let the Trumpet Sound*.
3. Martin Luther King Jr. to Wyatt Tee Walker, quoted in Falkner, *Great Time Coming*, 237.
4. King to Walker quoted in Chris Lamb, "Blackout: The Untold Story of Jackie Robinson's First Spring Training," *American Legacy*, Spring 2007, 20.
5. Roy Campanella quoted in Tye, *Satchel*, 189.
6. According to Don Newcombe, Dr. King did credit other black Dodgers for their contributions to integrating baseball. Twenty-eight days before he was assassinated, King dined with Newcombe and his family and confided to the retired Brooklyn pitcher, "Don, I don't know what I would've done without you guys setting up the minds of people for change. You, Jackie, and Roy will never know how easy you made it for me to do my job." Newcombe quoted in Fussman, *After Jackie*, 61.
7. Robinson and Duckett, *I Never Had It Made*, 17–18.
8. Rampersad, *Jackie Robinson*, 34, 50–52, 65–66, 102–3.
9. Rampersad, *Jackie Robinson*, 154–155, 180, 255.
10. Tom Gallagher, "Jackie Robinson," in Shatzkin, *The Ballplayers*, 927–29.
11. Steven Greenfield, "Roy Campanella," in Shatzkin, *The Ballplayers*, 149–50.
12. Sam Lacey quoted in Rampersad, *Jackie Robinson*, 291–92.
13. Bob Broeg, "Campy, a Man Paid to Play a Boy's Game," *Sporting News*, July 24, 1971, 18; Dick Young, "'Campy Envied Me,' Busy Robby Hastens to Explain," *New York Daily News*, January 19, 1957; Dick Young, "Campy Ridicules Robinson: 'I'll Catch 5 More Years,'" *New York Daily News*, January 20, 1957.
14. Jackie Robinson to Rachel Robinson quoted in Rampersad, *Jackie Robinson*, 292.
15. A. S. "Doc" Young, "A Feud Grows in Brooklyn," *Los Angeles Sentinel*, January 27, 1957.

16. Washington, *Up from Slavery*.

17. Booker T. Washington, "Atlanta Exposition Speech" (1895), quoted in Franklin and Higginbotham, *From Slavery to Freedom*, 296.

18. Franklin and Higginbotham, *From Slavery to Freedom*, 297–98.

19. Du Bois, "Of Mr. Booker T. Washington and Others," in *The Souls of Black Folk*, 87. Du Bois failed to recognize that Washington anticipated a future where full integration of the races would be achieved. He only advocated vocational education as the means by which blacks would achieve that integration. See Washington quoted in Franklin and Higginbotham, *From Slavery to Freedom*, 298.

20. Du Bois, "The Talented Tenth," in Washington, *The Negro Problem*, 31–32.

21. Franklin and Higginbotham, *From Slavery to Freedom*, 300–303.

22. For a more complete account of Du Bois's life, see Lewis, *W. E. B. Du Bois: Biography of a Race*; Lewis, *W. E. B. Du Bois: The Fight for Equality*; Balaji, *Professor and the Pupil*.

23. Neil Lanctot, who has written the most comprehensive account of Roy Campanella's life and baseball career, contends that Rickey seriously considered making Campy the first Negro Leaguer to integrate the Majors. While Lanctot also acknowledges Campanella's and Robinson's contrasting approaches to civil rights, he focuses more on the personal feud between the two teammates, largely a result of a dispute over postseason barnstorming. See Lanctot, *Campy*, 207–13, 310–11. Roger Kahn acknowledges that the "contrasting styles" of Robinson and Campanella "fed an ironic rivalry" and that both players, "in the competition of seasons, forgot that their divergent roads led toward one goal." Kahn also admits that those sportswriters who covered the Brooklyn Dodgers were "driven toward one or the other" and that he "drew closer to Robinson because his bellicosity fit my preconception of what black attitudes should be" (*The Boys of Summer*, 356–57). Similarly Michael Shapiro contends that the rift was "not surprising" because Campanella and Robinson "had nothing in common but baseball and race." Even so, they "did not polarize the team" because they "wanted to win too much to allow that" to happen. See Shapiro, *The Last Good Season*, 162–68.

    Conversely Carl Erskine, a Brooklyn Dodgers teammate, insists that "Campy and Jackie saw eye to eye on everything; only their methods differed." The press "kept pining for divisions between the two" but could "never find them because the two loved and respected each one another" (Erskine and Rocks, *What I Learned from Jackie Robinson*, 107).

1. Brooklyn's Bums

1. McGee, *Greatest Ballpark Ever*, 63–64.

2. McGee, *Greatest Ballpark Ever*, 59–62.

3. Snyder-Grenier, *Brooklyn*, 236–37.

4. McGee, *Greatest Ballpark Ever*, 64–65.

5. Ritter, *Lost Ballparks*, 51–52.

6. McGee, *Greatest Ballpark Ever*, 69.

7. McGee, *Greatest Ballpark Ever*, 65–66.

8. *Brooklyn Daily Eagle*, April 6, 1913.

9. *Brooklyn Daily Standard Union*, April 6, 1913.

10. McGee, *Greatest Ballpark Ever*, 24–28.

11. John Day quoted in McGee, *Greatest Ballpark Ever*, 28–29.

12. Jackson, *The Encyclopedia of New York City*, 148–49.

13. Jackson, *The Encyclopedia of New York City*, 151.

14. Simon, *Jackie Robinson and the Integration of Baseball*, 33–34.

15. Robert Gruber, "It Happened in Brooklyn: Reminiscences of a Fan," in Dorinson and Warmund, *Jackie Robinson*, 43.

16. Jackson, *The Encyclopedia of New York City*, 152; Robbins and Palitz, *Brooklyn*, xv.

17. Snyder-Grenier, *Brooklyn*, 232–33.

18. *Brooklyn Daily Eagle*, January 23, 1897.

19. Snyder-Grenier, *Brooklyn*, 233–234.

20. Voigt, *American Baseball*, 164, 238.

21. Voigt, *American Baseball*, 238, 267.

22. Frederick Ivor-Campbell, "Brooklyn Dodgers' Team History," in Thorn and Palmer, *Total Baseball*, 70.

23. Snyder-Grenier, *Brooklyn*, 235.

24. Frank Graham Jr., "Casey Comes to Town," in Robbins and Palitz, *Brooklyn*, 20–21.

25. Snyder-Grenier, *Brooklyn*, 236–37.

26. Kavanaugh and Macht, *Uncle Robbie*; Golenbock, *Bums*, 20.

27. Ritter, *Lost Ballparks*, 54–55; McGee, *Greatest Ballpark Ever*, 107.

28. Rice, *Seasons Past*, 213.

29. White, *History of Colored Baseball*, 31.

30. Chadwick, *When the Game Was Black and White*, 29–30.

31. Clark and Lester, *The Negro Leagues Book*, 27.

32. Wilder, *A Covenant with Color*, 131–32.

33. Willensky, *When Brooklyn Was the World, 1920–1957*, 103–4.

34. Snyder-Grenier, *Brooklyn*, 45–46.

35. Pritchet, *Brownsville, Brooklyn*, 26–52.

36. U.S. Bureau of the Census, *Negroes in the United States, 1920–32*, 62.

37. Wilder, *Covenant with Color*, 113; Snyder-Grenier, *Brooklyn*, 53.

38. Wilder, *Covenant with Color*, 121.

39. McCullough, *Brooklyn*, 198–99; Snyder-Grenier, *Brooklyn*, 43.

40. Wilder, *Covenant with Color*, 145.

41. Snyder-Grenier, *Brooklyn*, 53.

42. Wilder, *Covenant with Color*, 162.

43. Bill Reddy quoted in Golenbock, *Bums*, 155–56.

44. Joe Flaherty quoted in Golenbock, *Bums*, 155–56.

45. Interview of James A. McGowan, Newtown PA, January 5, 2005.

46. Snyder-Grenier, *Brooklyn*, 239.

47. Snyder-Grenier, *Brooklyn*, 240; McCullough, *Brooklyn*, 174.

48. Golenbock, *Bums*, 185.

49. Dan Parker, "Leave Us Go Root for the Dodgers," *New York Daily Mirror*, 1942.

50. Ivor-Campbell, "Brooklyn Dodgers' Team History," 70.

51. Thorn and Palmer, *Total Baseball*, 822.

52. *New York Herald Tribune*, October 6, 1941.

53. *Brooklyn Eagle*, October 7, 1941.

54. Golenbock, *Bums*, 185.

55. Snyder-Grenier, *Brooklyn*, 240.

56. Golenbock, *Bums*, 186.

57. Ritter, *Lost Ballparks*, 55.

58. Ward and Burns, *Baseball*, 275.

59. Golenbock, *Bums*, 75–80.

60. Branch Rickey quoted in *New York Times*, February 12, 1943.

61. Lowenfish, *Branch Rickey*, 325–26.

2. Rickey's Choice

1. Lowenfish, *Branch Rickey*, 323.

2. Ward and Burns, *Baseball*, 284.

3. Lowenfish, *Branch Rickey*, 14–16.

4. Interview of Branch Rickey III, Colorado Springs CO, July 21, 2008.

5. Branch Rickey quoted in *Baseball: The Game*, part 1, Heritage Public Affairs Interviews, produced by WQED-TV, Pittsburgh, 1959; Ward and Burns, *Baseball*, 128.

6. Lowenfish, *Branch Rickey*, 22–24.

7. Rickey quoted in Mann, *Branch Rickey*, 216. When asked about the incident in the 1950s, Charles Thomas, who had become a dentist in Albuquerque, claimed that it was "exaggerated" and that he was "quite sure that Mr. Rickey didn't say what the reporters enlarged upon" (Falkner, *Great Time Coming*, 105).

8. Lowenfish, *Branch Rickey*, 24–38.

9. Ward and Burns, *Baseball*, 129–30, 149, 179.

10. Branch Rickey quoted in *Baseball: The Proving Ground of Civil Rights*, part 3, Heritage Public Affairs Interviews, produced by WQED-TV, Pittsburgh, 1959.

11. Lester Rodney, "White Dodgers, Black Dodgers," in Dorinson and Warmund, *Jackie Robinson*, 93.

12. Branch Rickey and George McLaughlin quoted in Mann, *The Jackie Robinson Story*, 11; Ward and Burns, *Baseball*, 284.

13. Mann, *Branch Rickey*, 213; Lowenfish, *Branch Rickey*, 326.

14. Merl F. Kleinknecht, "The Negro Leagues: A Brief History," in Clark and Lester, *The Negro Leagues Book*, 15–19. Among the best treatments of Negro League players are Hogan, *Shades of Glory*; Peterson, *Only the Ball Was White*. In addition there are several fine film documentaries on the Negro Leagues: *There Was Always Sun Shining Someplace: Life in the Negro Leagues*; *Before You Can Say Jackie Robinson: Black Baseball in America in the Era of the Color Line*; *Black Diamonds, Blues City: Stories of the Memphis Red Sox*; *Kings on the Hill: Baseball's Forgotten Men*.

15. Chadwick, *When the Game Was Black and White*, 16; Bankes, *The Pittsburgh Crawfords*, 63

16. Campanella, *It's Good to Be Alive*, 94–95.

17. Veeck and Linn, *Veeck as in Wreck*, 171–72. According to David M. Jordan, Larry R. Gerlach, and John P. Rossi, Veeck "falsified the historical record" in order to "polish his own place in baseball history," among other reasons. In fact, Veeck "did not have a deal to buy the Phillies. He did not work to stock any team with Negro League stars. No such deal was squashed by Landis or Frick" ("Bill Veeck and the 1943 Sale of the Phillies," 3–13). On the other hand, Veeck's claim might have some validity since he was the first owner to integrate the American League; in the summer of 1947 he signed Negro Leaguer Larry Doby to a contract with the Cleveland Indians.

18. Mann, *Jackie Robinson Story*, 12.

19. Interview of Gene Benson, Philadelphia, December 9, 1998.

20. Interview of Stanley Glenn, West Chester PA, December 7, 1999.

21. Tye, *Satchel*, 182, 190–199.

22. Interview of Mahlon Duckett, West Chester PA, May 12, 1999.

23. Frommer, *Rickey and Robinson*, 96; Tye, *Satchel*, 199; Holway, *Josh and Satch*, 180; "Joshua Gibson," in Clark and Lester, *The Negro Leagues Book*, 41–42. Josh Gibson died on January 20, 1947, in Pittsburgh. He was thirty-five.

24. Franklin and Higginbotham, *From Slavery to Freedom*, 451–52, 458–60.

25. Franklin and Higginbotham, *From Slavery to Freedom*, 454–55, 466–67.

26. Franklin and Higginbotham, *From Slavery to Freedom*, 492–93.

27. Dickson, *The Unwritten Rules of Baseball*, 20.

28. Albert "Happy" Chandler quoted in Polner, *Branch Rickey*, 174.

29. Cool Papa Bell quoted in Adomites et al., *Cooperstown*, 213.

30. For the most complete account of Monte Irvin's life, see Irvin and Riley, *Nice Guys Finish First*.

31. Interview of Monte Irvin, Houston, August 21, 2007.
32. Campanella had been exempted from the draft because he was married and the father of two children (Campanella, *It's Good to Be Alive*, 93).
33. Campanella, *It's Good to Be Alive*, 103–6.
34. Branch Rickey III interview.
35. According to Neil Lanctot, Campanella's biographer, Campy, though married, had a well-known reputation for carrying on extramarital affairs, which resulted in two broken marriages. See Lanctot, *Campy*, 65–66, 76, 345, 369, 371, 399, 400–401.
36. Rampersad, *Jackie Robinson*, 292.
37. Falkner, *Great Time Coming*, 96.
38. Smith learned that Isadore Muchnick, a liberal Jewish council member from Boston, had been pressuring the Red Sox and Braves to integrate. Muchnick threatened to impose Sunday blue laws on the two teams if they didn't offer tryouts to Negro Leaguers. Not wanting to be deprived of Sunday baseball—the most profitable day of the week—the two teams agreed. See Falkner, *Great Time Coming*, 101; Tye, *Satchel*, 185–86.
39. Interview of Marvin Williams, Conroe TX, August 4, 1999.
40. Williams interview.
41. Robinson and Duckett, *I Never Had It Made*, 41–42.
42. Robinson and Duckett, *I Never Had It Made*, 41–42.
43. Williams interview.
44. Kelly E. Rusinack, "Baseball on the Radical Agenda: The *Daily Worker* and *Sunday Worker* Journalistic Campaign to Desegregate Major League Baseball, 1933–1947," in Dorinson and Warmund, *Jackie Robinson*, 75–85.
45. Franklin and Higginbotham, *From Slavery to Freedom*, 492–95. See also Naison, *Communists in Harlem*.
46. Franklin and Higginbotham, *From Slavery to Freedom*, 496.
47. Franklin and Higginbotham, *From Slavery to Freedom*, 496–97.
48. Excerpts of the Mayor's Report on the Integration of Baseball quoted in Dan Daniel, "New York Report Criticizes Negro Leagues in Probe of Organized Baseball Color Bar," *Sporting News*, November 29, 1945. In November 1945 the committee made public its findings: there is "no difference between the potential ability of Negro and white youth," and the only reason blacks are excluded from Organized Baseball is "sheer prejudice"; "'moral principle' demand[s] that Negroes not be excluded from Organized Baseball"; there is "no rule in Organized Baseball prohibiting Negroes from the game" and thus Organized Baseball has a "responsibility of taking positive, aggressive activity [toward integration]." Although these findings were released after Jackie Robinson had already been signed by the Brooklyn Dodgers, they forced the owners to come to terms with the reality that the complete integration of

Major League Baseball was only a matter of time. See New York City Council, "Report of the Major League Steering Committee: November 20, 1945," National Baseball Library, Cooperstown, New York.

49. Rodney, "White Dodgers, Black Dodgers," 90–91.

50. Rusinack, "Baseball on the Radical Agenda," 80–81.

51. *Daily Worker*, September 19, 1939, September 17, 1940, January 25, 28, 1943; *Sunday Worker*, October 15, 1939.

52. Rampersad, *Jackie Robinson*, 123.

53. Wendell Smith made his opposition to the American Communist Party known as early as 1943, when a delegation of Negro newspaper publishers persuaded the baseball owners to hear an appeal for integration from Paul Robeson. According to Sam Lacey, a black sportswriter for the *Chicago Defender* and later the *Baltimore Afro-American*, Robeson's appearance before the owners was a strategic blunder on the part of the black press. His affiliation with the Communist Party was not popular with the American public and could be used to the owners' advantage in defending the "gentlemen's agreement." See Falkner, *Great Time Coming*, 100; Roberts and Klibanoff, *The Race Beat*, 20.

54. Wendell Smith quoted in Falkner, *Great Time Coming*, 109.

55. Clyde Sukeforth quoted by Dave Anderson, "The Days That Brought the Barrier Down: 50 Years Later, Robinson's First Manager Recalls the Integration of the Majors," *New York Times*, March 30, 1997.

56. Sukeforth quoted by Anderson, "The Days That Brought the Barrier Down"; Falkner, *Great Time Coming*, 106.

57. Craig Muder, "Branch Rickey Takes Control of the Dodgers," *Inside Pitch: Newsletter of the National Baseball Hall of Fame*, August 13, 2010, 1.

58. Robinson recounted in detail his first meeting with Rickey in his autobiography. See Robinson and Duckett, *I Never Had It Made*, 42–47. But historians consider Jules Tygiel's *Baseball's Great Experiment* the definitive account of the Robinson-Rickey meeting (65–67).

59. "Rickey Claims That 15 Clubs Voted to Bar Negroes from Majors," *New York Times*, February 18, 1948.

60. Sukeforth in Anderson, "The Days That Brought the Barrier Down."

61. Robinson and Duckett, *I Never Had It Made*, 42–43.

62. Tygiel, *Baseball's Great Experiment*, 66.

63. Robinson and Duckett, *I Never Had It Made*, 43–44.

64. Robinson and Duckett, *I Never Had It Made*, 46; Rampersad, *Jackie Robinson*, 126–27.

65. David Falkner argues that there were at least two different meetings between Rickey and Robinson before the Dodgers actually signed the Negro League star (*Great Time Coming*, 106–12).

66. Sam Lacey quoted in Jerelyn Eddings, "Special Report on Race," *U.S. News & World Report*, March 24, 1997, 54.

67. Irvin interview.

68. Branch Rickey III interview.

69. See interviews of Monte Irvin; Gene Benson; Marvin Williams; Mahlon Duckett; Bill Cash, West Chester PA, April 18, 1999; Stanley Glenn, West Chester PA, December 7, 1999; Wilmer Harris, Philadelphia, December 9, 1999.

70. Robinson and Duckett, *I Never Had It Made*, 10–11.

71. Branch Rickey III interview.

3. Jackie and Campy

1. Campanella, *It's Good to Be Alive*, 109–12.

2. Campanella, *It's Good to Be Alive*, 120.

3. Robinson and Duckett, *I Never Had It Made*, 16–18.

4. Rampersad, *Jackie Robinson*, 34.

5. Robinson and Duckett, *I Never Had It Made*, 18–20; Rampersad, *Jackie Robinson*, 32–33.

6. Ray Bartlett quoted in Rampersad, *Jackie Robinson*, 36.

7. Rampersad, *Jackie Robinson*, 47–49.

8. *Pasadena Star-News*, April 4, 1987.

9. Rampersad, *Jackie Robinson*, 51, 82.

10. Robinson and Duckett, *I Never Had It Made*, 23.

11. Rachel Robinson quoted in *Jackie Robinson: Breaking Barriers*.

12. Robinson and Duckett, *I Never Had It Made*, 24–37; and Rampersad, *Jackie Robinson*, 90–110.

13. Falkner, *Great Time Coming*, 92.

14. Jackie Robinson, "What's Wrong with Negro Baseball?," *Ebony*, June 1948, 116–37.

15. Falkner, *Great Time Coming*, 94.

16. Robinson and Duckett, *I Never Had It Made*, 35–36.

17. Interview of Monte Irvin, Houston, August 21, 2007.

18. Ron Fimrite, "Triumph of the Spirit," *Sports Illustrated*, September 24, 1990, 102.

19. Warner, *The Private City*, 161; Arthur P. Dudden, "The City Embraces Normalcy," in Weigley, *Philadelphia*, 588.

20. Warner, *Private City*, 172–173; Dudden, "City Embraces Normalcy," 588.

21. Campanella, *It's Good to Be Alive*, 29–30; Wolf, *Philadelphia*, 264.

22. Ida Campanella quoted in Fimrite, "Triumph of the Spirit," 102.

23. Davis, *Who Is Black?* Historically the term *black* was used in the United States to refer to "any person with any known African black ancestry" and reflected the "long experience with slavery." *Mulatto*, on the other hand, was original-

ly used to mean the offspring of a "pure African Negro" and a "pure white." These definitions were established by the U.S. government in the nineteenth century for legal purposes. They were retained until the 1960s, when civil rights legislation rendered them obsolete.

Davis argues that most American blacks, though racially mixed, are "physically distinguishable from whites, but they are also an ethnic group because of the distinctive culture they have developed within the general American framework." Such an inclusive definition suggests that the terms *black* and *mulatto* should be used to designate "racial," "cultural," and "ethnic" traits.

24. Campanella, *It's Good To Be Alive*, 43.

25. Campanella, *It's Good To Be Alive*, 29.

26. Lanctot, *Campy*, 14–15.

27. Broeg, "Campy," 16.

28. Interview of Roy Campanella by Lee Allen, Cooperstown NY, July 15, 1969, National Baseball Library.

29. Harry Bacharach (1873–1947) was a Jewish politician and mayor of Atlantic City, New Jersey, for two terms (1916–20 and 1930–35). In 1914 he was tried for election fraud in the 1910 mayoral election. See "Harry Bacharach," obituary, *Time*, May 26, 1947.

30. "The Man: Roy Campanella," *Black Sports*, November 1972, 24.

31. Dixon quoted in Broeg, "Campy," 16.

32. There is a discrepancy between Campanella's recollection of the game and the account that appeared in the *Beach Haven Times*. According to Campanella, Dixon started the game behind the plate, but after he tore a fingernail loose Campy was inserted as catcher. He also recalled that the final score was 3–1 in favor of the Bacharachs. However, the *Beach Haven Times* reported that Campy started the game and went zero for three with an error in a 17–6 win. See Lanctot, *Campy*, 22–23.

33. Lanctot, *Campy*, 25–26.

34. Campanella, *It's Good to Be Alive*, 49–51, 57–58.

35. Dixon quoted in Campanella, *It's Good to Be Alive*, 55–56.

36. Paul Lawrence Dunbar explained the accommodationist approach of this generation of blacks in his lyric poem "We Wear the Mask," about oppressed black Americans forced to hide their pain and frustration behind a façade of happiness and contentment. Dunbar, the son of slaves, wrote the poem in 1896, when racial prejudice was an inherent part of American social, economic, and political culture. The poem suggests that for blacks to reveal publicly their true feelings about whites' maltreatment of them would have been to risk dangerous retaliation. Instead most blacks wore a mask that suggested happiness and contentment but concealed acute distress and pain. See Braxton, *The Collected Poetry of Paul Laurence Dunbar*.

37. Campanella, *It's Good to Be Alive*, 65.

38. Campanella, *It's Good to Be Alive*, 70–73.

39. "Baltimore Elite Giants," Negro League Baseball Players Association website.

40. Fimrite, "Triumph of the Spirit," 98.

41. Quote is taken from interview of Monte Irvin, Houston, August 21, 2007. Campanella credited Biz Mackey with influencing him "on and off the field" in Red Smith, "From Jim Crow to Cooperstown," *New York Times*, February 14, 1978.

42. Clark and Lester, *The Negro Leagues Book*, 26.

43. "Roy Campanella, 71, Dies," *New York Times*, June 28, 1993; Broeg, "Campy," 16. According to Neil Lanctot, Campanella's biographer, Campy discovered that Bernice was pregnant in December 1938 and did the honorable thing by marrying her on January 3, 1939. The couple gave birth to a daughter, Joyce, seven months later. See Lanctot, *Campy*, 54–55.

44. Roy Campanella quoted in Murray Chass, "Campanella Recalls Negro League Days," *New York Times*, August 3, 1969; Campanella quoted in Halberstam, *Summer of '49*, 258.

45. Comparison of Negro League and Major League salaries taken from interviews of Bill Cash, West Chester PA, April 18, 1999; Gene Benson, Philadelphia, December 9, 1998; and Monte Irvin.

46. Campanella, *It's Good to Be Alive*, 80–81.

47. Clark and Lester, *Negro Leagues Book*, 27, 247–48.

48. Campanella, *It's Good to Be Alive*, 86–87.

49. Campanella, *It's Good to Be Alive*, 87.

50. Irvin interview.

51. Broeg, "Campy," 16.

52. Broeg, "Campy," 17.

53. Clark and Lester, *Negro Leagues Book*, 272.

54. Campanella quoted in Broeg, "Campy," 16.

55. Dave Anderson, "In Roy Campanella, the Heart of a Hero," *New York Times*, June 28, 1993; Roy Campanella, *It's Good to Be Alive*, 107. In addition to David, Ruthe's son from a previous marriage, the couple had three of their own children: Roy Jr., Tony, and Princess.

56. Campanella, *It's Good to Be Alive*, 96–97.

57. Interview of Mahlon Duckett, West Chester PA, May 12, 1999.

58. Broeg, "Campy," 17.

59. Campanella, *It's Good to Be Alive*, 104–6; Frommer, *Rickey and Robinson*, 109–10.

60. Trouppe, *20 Years Too Soon*, 155.

61. Merl Kleinknecht, "Gene Benson," in Shatzkin, *The Ballplayers*, 69.

62. Interview of Gene Benson, Philadelphia, December 9, 1998. Benson also taught Robinson how to hit the curve ball, though he was too humble to accept the credit for it. Ironically the two men were completely different in their approach to hitting. Benson sported one of the most unusual batting stances in the game. Turning his body almost a full 90 degrees so that he was facing the pitcher, he held the bat near his waist. This allowed him to keep his hands still as long as possible, waiting until the last second to drive pitches to the opposite field, which enabled him to become a great curve ball hitter. Despite his unorthodox style, available records indicate that Benson's lifetime batting average was over .300, with a peak mark of .370 in 1945. Robinson, on the other hand, held the bat over his right shoulder. Although he was more of a lunge hitter, Robinson also kept his hands back as long as possible, just as Benson counseled. Because of that skill, Jackie became one of the greatest curve ball hitters of his generation. See Falkner, *Great Time Coming*, 121.

63. Campanella, *It's Good to Be Alive*, 113–14.

64. Tygiel, *Baseball's Great Experiment*, 144–45.

65. Tygiel, *Baseball's Great Experiment*, 145–46.

4. Breaking the Color Line

1. Robinson and Duckett, *I Never Had It Made*, 54–55.

2. Billy Rowe quoted in Lamb, *Blackout*, 17.

3. Harold C. Burr, "Give Negroes Fair Play Rickey Urges," *Sporting News*, March 7, 1946. Wright had won thirty-one games for the Homestead Grays in 1943 before joining the U.S. Navy, where he posted a 15-4 record and had the lowest ERA of any pitcher in the armed forces.

4. Branch Rickey quoted in *Baseball: The Proving Ground of Civil Rights*.

5. Mann, *The Jackie Robinson Story*, 142.

6. Clay Hopper quoted in Lloyd McGowan, "Negro's Steady Play Wins Okay of Pilot Hopper and Montreal Fans," *Sporting News*, June 5, 1946.

7. Robinson and Duckett, *I Never Had It Made*, 60.

8. Lamb, *Blackout*, 88, 135–36, 140; "Royals' Game Off at Jacksonville," *New York Times*, March 23, 1946.

9. Lamb, *Blackout*, 104.

10. "Jackie Makes Good," *Time*, August 26, 1946.

11. Bill Young, "Jackie Robinson and the Montreal Royals, 1945–1946," *Sherbrooke Record* (Quebec), October 24, 2005.

12. Robinson and Duckett, *I Never Had It Made*, 114.

13. "Having a Hand in Baseball History," *Chicago Tribune*, April 17, 2006.

14. Robinson and Duckett, *I Never Had It Made*, 56–57; Tygiel, *Baseball's Great Experiment*, 3, 7.

15. Plaschke with LaSorda, *I Live for This!*, 157. Campanis would go on to become the Los Angeles Dodgers' general manager and be remembered for a racist statement he made in a live television interview on ABC's *Nightline* on April 6, 1987. When asked about the scarcity of black managers and executives in the Majors, the seventy-year-old Campanis suggested that they did not have the intelligence to hold those positions. See Eric Johnson, "'Nightline' Classic: Al Campanis," April 12, 2007, www.abcnews.go.com/Nightline/ESPNSports/story?id=3034914.

16. McGowan, "Negro's Steady Play."

17. Mel Jones quoted in Lloyd McGowan, "Robinson Topping International Hitters, Rated Ready for Dodgers in '47," *Sporting News*, August 21, 1946.

18. Tygiel, *Baseball's Great Experiment*, 139.

19. Tygiel, *Baseball's Great Experiment*, 137.

20. Tom Meany, "What Chance Has Jackie Robinson?," *Sport*, January 1947, 13.

21. Clay Hopper quoted in Monteleone, *Branch Rickey's Little Blue Book*, 85.

22. *Pittsburgh Courier*, October 12, 1946.

23. Buzzie Bavasi quoted in Campanella and Young, *The Roy Campanella Story*, 26.

24. Roy Campanella quoted in "Campanella's Big Gamble," *New York Journal*, September 21, 1953.

25. Roy Campanella quoted in Maury Allen, "Campy: Time for a Black Pilot Is Now," *New York Post*, February 9, 1972.

26. Newcombe quoted in Tygiel, *Baseball's Great Experiment*, 147.

27. Tygiel, *Baseball's Great Experiment*, 145.

28. Tygiel, *Baseball's Great Experiment*, 149.

29. Bob Oates, "Q & A with Roy Campanella," *USA Today*, June 17, 1985. Campanella's one-game stint as Nashua manager made him the first African American to manage in organized baseball.

30. Campanella, *It's Good to Be Alive*, 120–24; Tygiel, *Baseball's Great Experiment*, 152.

31. Don Newcombe quoted in *At Nightfall: The Roy Campanella Story*.

32. Tygiel, *Baseball's Great Experiment*, 151.

33. See "Lynchings: By State and Race, 1882–1968," University of Missouri-Kansas City School of Law, http://www.law.umkc.edu/faculty/projects/ftrials/shipp/lynchingsstate.html (retrieved July 26, 2010).

34. Dray, *At the Hands of Persons Unknown*; Wexler, *Fire in a Canebrake*.

35. Donovan, *Conflict and Crisis*, 332–37. Truman's commission was established, in part, to address white resistance to integration in such cities as Gary, Indiana; Athens, Alabama; and Philadelphia.

36. President's Committee on Civil Rights, *To Secure These Rights*, 9; Anthony Leviero, "Guidelines for Civil Rights Proposed by Truman Board," *New York Times*, October 30, 1947.

37. Hamby, *Beyond the New Deal*, 214–15, 247.

38. Chambers, *Witness*, 799.

39. "McCarthyism v. Trumanism," *Time*, August 27, 1951; Reeves, *The Life and Times of Joe McCarthy*, 224, 237.

40. Shortly after Branch Rickey signed Robinson to a professional baseball contract in November 1945, the *Daily Worker* emphasized the significant role of the American Communist Party in that development. See *Daily Worker*, October 26, 1946. Nat Low, who succeeded Lester Rodney as the sports editor of the newspaper, continued to highlight Robinson's on-field achievements as well as the discrimination he faced throughout the late 1940s and early 1950s. See Rusinack, "Baseball on the Radical Agenda," 82.

41. Falkner, *Great Time Coming*, 119.

42. See U.S. Department of Justice, "Jack R. Robinson," September 2, 1958, FBI Document No. 100-428850-2, FBI Freedom of Information Act Unit, Office of Public and Congressional Affairs, Federal Bureau of Investigation, Washington DC.

43. See Harold C. Burr, "Robby Faces Slow Climb: Owners Opposed to Bringing Negro Up," *Brooklyn Eagle*, January 14, 1947; Polner, *Branch Rickey*, 188.

44. Rickey quoted in Meany, "What Chance Has Robinson?," 12.

45. Fred Down, "Robinson Makes Swift Progress in Hard Task," *New York Times*, August 21, 1947.

46. Branch Rickey quoted in Arthur Daley, "In Havana, Where the Robinson Saga Began," *New York Times*, October 26, 1972.

47. Robinson and Duckett, *I Never Had It Made*, 69.

48. Marshall, *Baseball's Pivotal Era*, 142; Robinson and Duckett, *I Never Had It Made*, 69.

49. Pee Wee Reese, "What Robinson Meant to an Old Friend," *New York Times*, July 17, 1977.

50. Durocher and Linn, *Nice Guys Finish Last*, 203–5.

51. *New York Times*, April 13, 1947; Anderson, "The Days That Brought the Barriers Down." Durocher's managerial tenure in Brooklyn had been troubled by umpire baiting, foul language often heard by fans, his association with gamblers and organized crime, and a very messy and public divorce. When Brooklyn's Catholic Diocese began a campaign to have him dismissed, Rickey turned to his trusted assistant Clyde Sukeforth as an interim until he secured Burt Shotton's services. See Marzano, *Brooklyn Dodgers in 1940s*, 130–34, 142.

52. Bobby Bragan quoted in *Jackie Robinson: Breaking Barriers*.

53. Marzano, *Brooklyn Dodgers in 1940s*, 136.

54. Higbe, *The High Hard One*, 107.

55. Marzano, *Brooklyn Dodgers in 1940s*, 142.

56. Branch Rickey quoted in Mann, *The Jackie Robinson Story*, 160–65. Rickey made these remarks before a gathering of African American civic leaders at the predominantly black Carlton branch of Brooklyn's YMCA. They greeted his remarks with applause.

57. Robinson quoted in Meany, "What Chance Has Robinson?," 12–13.

58. Tygiel, *Baseball's Great Experiment*, 178.

59. Tygiel, *Baseball's Great Experiment*, 182–87; Kuklick, *To Every Thing a Season*, 145–47; William Ecenbarger, "First among Equals," *Philadelphia Inquirer*, February 19, 1995, 14.

60. Parrott, *The Lords of Baseball*, 194.

61. Robinson and Duckett, *I Never Had It Made*, 71–72.

62. Ecenbarger, "First among Equals," 14.

63. Tygiel, *Baseball's Great Experiment*, 182–83.

64. Chapman quoted in *Sporting News*, May 14, 1947.

65. *Sporting News*, May 14, 1947.

66. Jackie Robinson quoted in *Pittsburgh Courier*, May 3, 10, 1947.

67. Eddie Stanky quoted in Ward and Burns, *Baseball*, 291.

68. Branch Rickey, quoted in Rowan and Robinson, *Wait till Next Year*, 181–84; "Robinson Reveals Threats," *New York Times*, May 19, 1947.

69. Parrott, *Lords of Baseball*, 192.

70. Tygiel, *Baseball's Great Experiment*, 373. Tygiel cites Parrott as the only source for the controversial phone conversation between Rickey and Pennock. Since then the conversation has been cited repeatedly as fact by several writers, including Ecenbarger, "First among Equals," 14; Mark Kram, "The Nightmare That Was Philly," *Philadelphia Daily News*, April 9, 1997 (special supplement on Jackie Robinson), 10; Kuklick, *To Every Thing a Season*, 147; Rampersad, *Jackie Robinson*, 175.

71. Pennock died of a cerebral hemorrhage on January 30, 1948, at the relatively young age of fifty-four. Rickey passed away at the age of eighty-four on December 9, 1965.

72. Robinson and Duckett, *I Never Had It Made*, 74.

73. Rachel Robinson quoted in John Manasso, "Racial Issues Tarnish Tribute to Jackie Robinson," *Philadelphia Inquirer*, April 6, 2007.

74. Westcott and Bilovsky, *Phillies Encyclopedia*, 89.

75. Interview of Andy Seminick, West Chester PA, April 14, 2000.

76. Parrott, *Lords of Baseball*, 192.

77. Chapman quoted in Wayne Martin, "'Sure, We Rode Jackie,' Says Chapman," *Sporting News*, March 24, 1973.

78. Rowan and Robinson, *Wait till Next Year*, 184.

79. Interview of Harry Walker, Leeds AL, May 20, 1997.

80. Interview of Ken Raffensberger, York PA, April 25, 2000.

81. Interview of Howie Schultz, West Stillwater MN, April 26, 2000.

82. Glenn interview.

83. Interview of Bill "Ready" Cash, Philadelphia, April 18, 1999; interview of Mahlon Duckett, West Chester PA, May 12, 1999; Harris interview.

84. *Philadelphia Inquirer*, May 9, 10, 1947; *Philadelphia Daily News*, May 9, 10, 1947.

85. Ben Chapman quoted in *Pittsburgh Courier*, May 10, 1947.

86. Chapman quoted in Martin, "Sure, We Rode Jackie."

87. Interview of Clyde King, Goldsboro NC, February 1, 2009.

88. Interview of Gene Hermanski, Homosassa FL, August 19, 2007; Snider, *The Duke of Flatbush*, 24.

89. Reese, "What Robinson Meant to an Old Friend."

90. Marzano, *Brooklyn Dodgers in 1940s*, 138; Erskine and Rocks, *What I Learned from Jackie Robinson*, 62. Reese originally made this sympathetic gesture to Robinson during an away game against the Boston Braves, and repeated it later in the season at Cincinnati's Crosley Field.

91. Robinson and Duckett, *I Never Had It Made*, 76–77.

92. Snider and Pepe, *Few and Chosen*, 34.

93. Robinson and Duckett, *I Never Had It Made*, 78; Peter Golenbock, "Men of Conscience," in Dorinson and Warmund, *Jackie Robinson*, 18.

94. Robinson and Duckett, *I Never Had It Made*, 76.

95. Rachel Robinson quoted in *Jackie Robinson: Breaking Barriers*.

96. Robinson and Duckett, *I Never Had It Made*, 78–79; Jack Spector, "A Brooklyn Boy Remembers," *School Bank News*, April 1973, 3.

97. Rachel Robinson quoted in Eddings, "Special Report on Race," 54.

98. Erskine and Rocks, *What I Learned from Jackie Robinson*, 17–18.

99. *New York Herald Tribune*, May 9, 1947.

100. Ford Frick quoted in *New York Herald Tribune*, May 9, 1947.

101. Bob Considine, "The Will to Overcome," *Boston Herald*, October 27, 1972.

102. Greenberg with Berkow, *Hank Greenberg*, 189–91. The most comprehensive treatment of Robinson and Greenberg is Cottrell, *Two Pioneers*.

103. Mayer, *Notes of a Baseball Dreamer*, 23.

104. Jack Ryan, "Comiskey Cup Another Wedge for Jackie in '48 Salary Talks," *Sporting News*, November 15, 1947. Until 1947 voting for Rookie of the Year was limited to the Chicago Chapter of Baseball Writers. Robinson, who beat out New York Giants pitcher Larry Jansen, was the first to be honored nationally. Previous winners were Lou Boudreau (1940), Pete Reiser (1941), Johnny Beazley (1942), Bill Voiselle (1943), Bill Johnson (1944), Dave Ferriss (1945), and Eddie Waitkus (1946).

105. Bobby Bragan quoted in *Jackie Robinson: Breaking Barriers*.

106. Wolff, *The Baseball Encyclopedia*, 2672.

5. Teammates

1. See Veeck and Linn, *Veeck as in Wreck*, 170, 179. Doby was signed by Bill Veeck, owner of the Cleveland Indians, in 1947, eleven weeks after Jackie Robinson broke the color barrier with the Brooklyn Dodgers in the National League. In his rookie season Doby hit five for thirty-two in twenty-nine games. In 1948 he became the first black player to hit a home run in a World Series to help the Indians defeat the Boston Braves. He also helped the Indians win 111 games and the American League pennant in 1954. He was inducted into the National Baseball Hall of Fame in 1998. See Moore, *Pride against Prejudice.*

2. See Tommy Holme, "Jackie Robinson Is No Longer Unique," *Brooklyn Eagle*, July 21, 1947. Willard Brown struggled with racism and with the lack of talent on the St. Louis Browns. After batting .179 in twenty-one games, he left the Majors, but not before becoming the first black player to hit a home run in the American League. See Larry Lester, "Willard Brown," in Shatzkin, *The Ballplayers*, 126–27.

   Hank Thompson was the first African American player for both the Browns and the New York Giants. His best season came in 1953 when he hit .302 with twenty-four home runs. The following season he helped the Giants capture the National League pennant and went on to hit .364 in the World Series against the Cleveland Indians. See Rich Marazzi, "Hank Thompson," in Shatzkin, *The Ballplayers*, 1083.

3. See Marzano, *The Brooklyn Dodgers in the 1940s*, 150. Bankhead was the first black pitcher in the Major Leagues. After a strong career in the Negro Leagues playing for the Memphis Red Sox, he was signed at age twenty-four by Branch Rickey to play in the Brooklyn Dodgers' farm system. Bankhead was promoted to the Majors for parts of the 1947, 1950, and 1951 seasons. He hit a home run in his first Major League at-bat, on August 26, 1947, against Fritz Ostermueller of the Pittsburgh Pirates. In 1951, his final year in the Majors, he appeared in seven games, losing his only decision, with an ERA of 15.43. See Edward G. Maher, "Dan Bankhead," in Shatzkin, *The Ballplayers*, 45.

4. Lanctot, *Negro League Baseball*, 314–15. Veeck paid the Newark Eagles the unprecedented sum of $15,000 for Doby's contract. Muckerman paid the Kansas City Monarchs $5,000 for the contracts of Brown and Thompson, with the promise of more money if the two players lasted more than a month in the Majors.

5. Broeg, "Campy," 17.

6. See Trucks, *The Catcher*, 87–107. Baseball's early catchers "expected to be the center of attention." Natural leaders, they were rugged individualists in the same mold as frontiersmen and cowboys. During the twentieth century the

catcher evolved into a less glamorous position, "content to play a crucial but understated role." Morris, *Catcher*, 25–26, 277. Campanella represented a hybrid of the nineteenth- and twentieth-century catcher. While he was viewed as a team member, his easygoing personality and natural ability often took over the game. In this respect Campy was a transitional figure, paving the way for the twentieth-century athlete as hero and role model.

7. Roy Campanella Jr. quoted in *At Nightfall: The Roy Campanella Story*.

8. Roy Campanella quoted in *At Nightfall: The Roy Campanella Story*.

9. Broeg, "Campy," 17.

10. Durocher and Linn, *Nice Guys Finish Last*, 206–7.

11. Marzano, *Brooklyn Dodgers in 1940s*, 142, 163. Stanky was traded to the Boston Braves on March 6, 1948, in exchange for infielder-outfielder Bama Rowell and first baseman Ray Sanders.

12. Durocher and Linn, *Nice Guys Finish Last*, 206.

13. *New York Times*, May 2, 1948.

14. Herbert Goren, "Robinson Finds Going Rough," *New York Times*, April 9, 1948.

15. *New York Daily Mirror*, May 26, 1948.

16. Marzano, *Brooklyn Dodgers in 1940s*, 164.

17. Durocher and Linn, *Nice Guys Finish Last*, 206–7.

18. Bill Roeder, "Robinson on Batting Rampage Revives Flatbush Pennant Fever," *Brooklyn Eagle*, June 15, 1948.

19. Interview of Robin Roberts, West Chester PA, April 14, 2000.

20. Interview of Rich Ashburn, Philadelphia, June 11, 1996.

21. Rich Ashburn, "Honoring Jackie Robinson," *Philadelphia Bulletin*, April 21, 1973.

22. Ashburn interview.

23. Durocher and Linn, *Nice Guys Finish Last*, 208; Durocher quoted in Falkner, *Great Time Coming*, 176.

24. Robinson and Duckett, *I Never Had It Made*, 85.

25. Falkner, *Great Time Coming*, 93. Robinson criticized the indulgent lifestyles, miserable conditions, and low salaries of the Negro Leagues as well as the owners' failure to negotiate any kind of contract at all. See Robinson, "What's Wrong with Negro Baseball?"

26. Robinson quoted in *Pittsburgh Courier*, July 8, October 16, 1948.

27. Larry Doby quoted in Moore, *Pride against Prejudice*, 169.

28. Campanella, *It's Good to Be Alive*, 130–31.

29. Broeg, "Campy," 17.

30. Roy Campanella Jr. quoted in *At Nightfall: The Roy Campanella Story*.

31. Roy Campanella quoted in *At Nightfall: The Roy Campanella Story*.

32. Pee Wee Reese quoted in *At Nightfall: The Roy Campanella Story*.

33. Preacher Roe quoted in *At Nightfall: The Roy Campanella Story*.

34. Snider and Pepe, *Few and Chosen*, 161.

35. *Sporting News*, July 28, 1948; Falkner, *Great Time Coming*, 189.

36. Thorn and Palmer, *Total Baseball*, 1005, 1118, 1177, 1185, 1412, 1684.

37. Robinson and Duckett, *I Never Had It Made*, 87–88.

38. Marzano, *Brooklyn Dodgers in 1940s*, 169–72.

39. Roy Campanella quoted in *At Nightfall: The Roy Campanella Story*.

40. Campanella, *It's Good to Be Alive*, 148; Lanctot, *Campy*, 161.

41. Lanctot, *Campy*, 174–75.

6. Striking Back

1. Branch Rickey quoted in *Baseball: The Proving Ground of Civil Rights*.

2. Rachel Robinson quoted in *Jackie Robinson: Breaking Barriers*.

3. Bill Roeder, "Milquetoast Days over for Jackie," *New York World Telegram*, March 11, 1949.

4. Jackie Robinson quoted in Arch Murray, "Robbie Warns He Won't 'Take It' This Year," *New York Daily News*, March 11, 1949.

5. Albert Chandler and Jackie Robinson quoted in "Robinson Warned about Rough Play," *New York Sun*, March 14, 1949.

6. Ward and Burns, *Baseball*, 317–18.

7. Falkner, *Great Time Coming*, 213.

8. Snider and Pepe, *Few and Chosen*, 39.

9. Interview of Carl Erskine, Anderson IN, August 14, 2007.

10. Erskine quoted in Falkner, *Great Time Coming*, 214.

11. Durocher and Linn, *Nice Guys Finish Last*, 208.

12. Goodwin, *Wait 'til Next Year*, 44.

13. Angell, *Five Seasons*, 54.

14. Uhlberg, *Hands of My Father*, 202–4.

15. Snider and Pepe, *Few and Chosen*, 41.

16. Branca quoted in *Jackie Robinson: Breaking Barriers*.

17. Falkner, *Great Time Coming*, 192–93.

18. Falkner, *Great Time Coming*, 218–19.

19. Rachel Robinson quoted in *Jackie Robinson: Breaking Barriers*.

20. Rickey quoted in "Dodgers Schedule Exhibition in Atlanta," *New York Herald Tribune*, January 15, 1949.

21. "Klan's Howl Held to be Groundless," *New York Times*, January 18, 1949.

22. Erskine interview; Erskine and Rocks, *What I Learned from Jackie Robinson*, 20–21.

23. Interview of Gene Hermanski, Homosassa FL, August 19, 2007. Hermanski stated that he originally made the suggestion in a 1947 game against the Reds at Cincinnati's Crosley Field. On that occasion, Shotton informed the team

not only of the death threats but also that there were FBI agents in the park to protect Robinson.

24. Reese quoted in Erskine and Rocks, *What I Learned from Jackie Robinson*, 21.
25. "Robinson Received Mixed Reviews in Atlanta," *New York Times*, April 8, 1949.
26. Alvin Stokes quoted in U.S. House of Representatives, Un-American Activities Committee [hereafter HUAC], "Report of Hearings on Communist Infiltration of Minorities," 428.
27. Robeson, *The Undiscovered Paul Robeson*, 143.
28. Eisenhower quoted in HUAC, "Report of Hearings on Communist Infiltration of Minorities," 425–26.
29. Manning Johnson quoted in HUAC, "Report of Hearings on Communist Infiltration of Minorities," 436. In fact Robeson never joined the American Communist Party. But since many of his closest friends and associates were members and because he advocated many socialist causes such as trade unionism, he was accused of being a Communist Party member. See Duberman, *Paul Robeson*, 249–50.
30. Kahn, *The Era*, 198–200.
31. Balaji, *Professor and the Pupil*, 25, 42–43, 266–69.
32. Robinson and Duckett, *I Never Had It Made*, 95–96.
33. Duberman, *Paul Robeson*, 361–62.
34. Jackie Robinson quoted in HUAC, "Report of Hearings on Communist Infiltration of Minorities," 481–82.
35. Robeson quoted in Foner, *Paul Robeson Speaks*, 219.
36. Bill Mardo, "Robinson-Robeson," in Dorinson and Warmund, *Jackie Robinson*, 103–4.
37. Jackie Robinson quoted in *Daily Worker*, August 29, 1949.
38. Falkner, *Great Time Coming*, 202.
39. Robinson and Duckett, *I Never Had It Made*, 98.
40. Lanctot, *Campy*, 171.
41. Campanella quoted in Lanctot, *Campy*, 172. Lanctot claims that Campanella never spoke those words; rather the confrontation was invented by sportswriters in order to highlight the personality differences between the two black Dodgers stars.
42. Campanella to Tygiel, November 15, 1980, quoted in Lanctot, *Campy*, 173.
43. Erskine and Rocks, *What I Learned from Jackie Robinson*, 107.
44. Newcombe quoted in Aaron and Wheeler, *I Had a Hammer*, 100.
45. Erskine and Rocks, *What I Learned from Jackie Robinson*, 24.
46. Campanella quoted in Dickson, *Baseball's Greatest Quotations*, 71.
47. Erskine and Rocks, *What I Learned from Jackie Robinson*, 24.
48. Newcombe quoted in *At Nightfall: The Roy Campanella Story*.
49. Francis Kinlaw, "Don Newcombe," in Shatzkin, *The Ballplayers*, 801.

50. Snider and Pepe, *Few and Chosen*, 132; Wolff, *The Baseball Encyclopedia*, 2674.

51. "Chandler Warns Robinson to Quit His 'Popping Off,'" *New York Times*, October 10, 1949.

52. Raschi quoted in Halberstam, *Summer of '49*, 258.

53. Robinson and Duckett, *I Never Had It Made*, 98–99.

54. Carter, *Daguerreotypes*, 247.

55. Dan Daniel, "Robinson 'Most Valuable' in N.L.," *New York World-Telegram*, November 18, 1949. The Baseball Writers elected Robinson the National League MVP over Stan Musial of the St. Louis Cardinals by a vote of 264 to 226.

56. Falkner, *Great Time Coming*, 214–15; Robinson and Duckett, *I Never Had It Made*, 99.

57. Lanctot, *Campy*, 207–8; Erskine and Rocks, *What I Learned from Jackie Robinson*, 110.

58. Jackie Robinson quoted in Lanctot, *Campy*, 208.

59. Lester Dworman quoted in Lanctot, *Campy*, 208.

60. Campanella quoted in Klima, *Willie's Boys*, 218–19. Rickey agreed to Campanella's request and sent Wid Matthews, one of the Dodgers' southern scouts, to follow Mays. But Matthews reported back that Mays couldn't hit.

61. Lanctot, *Campy*, 209.

62. Rickey quoted in Campanella, *It's Good to Be Alive*, 152–153.

63. Robinson and Duckett, *I Never Had It Made*, 88.

64. Robinson and Duckett, *I Never Had It Made*, 88–90.

7. Collision Course

1. Franklin and Higginbotham, *From Slavery to Freedom*, 511–13; Kluger, *Simple Justice*, 126–284; D'Emilio, *Lost Prophet*, 161–83.

2. Branch, *Parting the Waters*; Franklin and Higginbotham, *From Slavery to Freedom*, 507–9.

3. Manchester, *The Glory and the Dream*, 580–605; Brinkley, *The Unfinished Nation*, 748.

4. Nichols, *A Matter of Justice*.

5. Interview of Don Zimmer, St. Petersburg FL, November 9, 2010.

6. Don Newcombe quoted in Fussman, *After Jackie*, 63.

7. Newcombe's bitterness toward baseball is reflected in a 2007 interview in which he remarked that he "never loved baseball and never will because of all the [racial discrimination] he had to endure just to play." He added that if he was ever selected to the Hall of Fame he'd "turn it down" and even wrote his decision to reject the honor into his will (Newcombe quoted in Fussman, *After Jackie*, 71).

8. Interview of Carl Erskine, Anderson IN, August 14, 2007.

9. Interview of Monte Irvin, Houston, August 21, 2007.

10. Irvin interview.

11. Campanella quoted in Tom Weiss, "Campy's Leadership Crushed Myths," *USA Today*, June 28, 1993; Campanella, *It's Good to Be Alive*, 271.

12. Broeg, "Campy."

13. Ty Cobb quoted in Robert M. G. Thomas Jr., "Roy Campanella, 71, Dies: Was Dodger Hall of Famer," *New York Times*, June 28, 1993.

14. Erskine interview.

15. Snider and Pepe, *Few and Chosen*, 4–5; Snider quoted in Fimrite, "Triumph of the Spirit," 101.

16. Goodwin, *Wait 'til Next Year*, 93–95.

17. Happy Felton quoted in Broeg, "Campy," 18.

18. Campanella, *It's Good to Be Alive*, 148–49.

19. Roy Campanella quoted in Dickson, *Baseball's Greatest Quotations*, 72. Variations of Campanella's quotation appeared in the *New York Journal-American*, April 11, 1957, and the *San Francisco Examiner & Chronicle*, February 17, 1974.

20. Interview of James A. McGowan, Newtown PA, January 5, 2005.

21. Campanella, *It's Good to Be Alive*, 271.

22. Thorn and Palmer, *Total Baseball*, 1412.

23. Thorn and Palmer, *Total Baseball*, 842, 846, 850, 1005.

24. Broeg, "Campy," 18.

25. Snider, *Duke of Flatbush*, 77; Snider and Pepe, *Few and Chosen*, 4–5.

26. Rachel Robinson quoted in *At Nightfall: The Roy Campanella Story*.

27. Lowenfish, *Branch Rickey*, 488–91.

28. Ward and Burns, *Baseball*, 320.

29. Robinson and Duckett, *I Never Had It Made*, 111–12. According to Duke Snider, spring training was "especially difficult" for Robinson, Campanella, and Newcombe because on long road trips "they'd have to stay on the team bus and eat while the white players ate inside a restaurant." It was so humiliating for Robinson that he stopped riding with the team and had a friend drive him to games instead. See Snider and Pepe, *Few and Chosen*, 39–40.

30. Robinson and Duckett, *I Never Had It Made*, 104–5.

31. Walter O'Malley quoted in *New York Times*, October 11, 1952.

32. Walter O'Malley quoted in Campanella, *It's Good to Be Alive*, 168.

33. Dorinson and Warmund, *Jackie Robinson*, 95.

34. Dick Young, "Robinson Accuses Umps of Ganging Up on Him," *New York Daily News*, April 21, 1951.

35. Dorinson and Warmund, *Jackie Robinson*, 96.

36. Jack Lang quoted in *At Nightfall: The Roy Campanella Story*.

37. Arthur Daley, "End of the Road for Campy?," *New York Times*, January 29, 1958.

38. Broeg, "Campy."

39. Broeg, "Campy."

40. Bryant, *The Last Hero*, 164.

41. Kahn, *Boys of Summer*, 357.

42. Chafets, *Cooperstown Confidential*, 116.

43. "Cancel or Challenge," editorial, *Birmingham World*, October 24, 1953.

44. Red Smith, "Jackie Accused of Bigotry," *New York Herald-Tribune*, October 26, 1953.

45. Robinson-Young conversation quoted in Robinson and Duckett, *I Never Had It Made*, 109–10.

46. Robinson and Duckett, *I Never Had It Made*, 109.

47. Robinson and Duckett, *I Never Had It Made*, 106.

48. Erskine and Rocks, *What I Learned from Jackie Robinson*, 39–40.

49. Irvin interview.

50. Durocher and Linn, *Nice Guys Finish Last*, 208–10; Irvin and Riley, *Nice Guys Finish First*, 146–47.

51. Irvin and Riley, *Nice Guys Finish First*, 141–49.

52. Hirsch, *Willie May*, 234–35. Robinson did not publicly criticize Mays until the 1960s, when he denounced the Giants' outfielder's silence on civil rights (416–17, 469–73).

53. Irvin interview.

54. See "Campy Made Money, Lost Weight on 25-Game Tour," *Sporting News*, November 19, 1952; Aaron and Wheeler, *I Had a Hammer*, 106.

55. Banks and Enright, *Mr. Cub*, 51–52.

56. Ernie Banks quoted in Rogers, *Ernie Banks*, 151.

57. Campanella quoted in Banks, *Mr. Cub*, 91.

58. Interview of Hank Aaron, Atlanta GA, November 2, 2010.

59. Aaron interview.

60. Joe Black quoted in Tom Keegan, "Today's Black Stars Letting Jackie Down," *New York Post*, April 16, 1997.

61. Falkner, *Great Time Coming*, 218–19, 224–25.

62. Joe Black quoted in Keegan, "Today's Black Stars."

63. Erskine interview.

64. Thorn and Palmer, *Total Baseball*, 1600.

65. Lester Rodney, "White Dodgers, Black Dodgers," in Dorinson and Warmund, *Jackie Robinson*, 87; Dave Anderson, "A Flame Grew in Brooklyn," *New York Times*, December 5, 1971; Snider and Pepe, *Few and Chosen*, 42.

66. Jackie Robinson as told to Milton Gross, "Why Can't I Manage in the Majors?," 1957, Jackie Robinson Papers, 1956–57, Manuscript Division, Library of Congress, Washington DC.

67. Pee Wee Reese, "What Robinson Meant to an Old Friend," *New York Times*, July 17, 1977; Reese quoted in *At Nightfall: Roy Campanella Story*.

68. Robinson and Duckett, *I Never Had It Made*, 108–9.

69. Campanella, *It's Good to Be Alive*, 183.

70. Don Newcombe quoted in Fussman, *After Jackie*, 67–68.

71. Don Newcombe quoted in Aaron and Wheeler, *I Had a Hammer*, 90.

72. Irvin interview. Michael Shapiro confirms Irvin's belief that Newcombe was "not close with Robinson" (*Last Good Season*, 272).

73. Thorn and Palmer, *Total Baseball*, 71.

74. Robinson and Duckett, *I Never Had It Made*, 129. Alston's Major League career consisted of one at-bat for the St. Louis Cardinals in 1936. He struck out. See Thorn and Palmer, *Total Baseball*, 933.

75. Walter Alston quoted in Erskine, *Tales from the Dodgers Dugout*, 13.

76. Robinson and Duckett, *I Never Had It Made*, 130.

8. Breakup

1. Among those writers who have promoted the mythology of the Brooklyn Dodgers are Kahn, *Boys of Summer*; Goodwin, *Wait 'til Next Year*; Garvey, *My Bat Boy Days*. The mythology of the team reached a climax in 1997, when Major League Baseball celebrated the fiftieth anniversary of Robinson's historic success at breaking the color line. But the Brooklyn Dodgers' image as "America's Team" continued into 2005, when ESPN released a special two-disc DVD collector's edition titled *The Brooklyn Dodgers: The Original America's Team*.

2. The Brooklyn Dodgers' starting lineup in 1955 was Jim Gilliam, 2B (age 26); Pee Wee Reese, SS (36); Duke Snider, CF (28); Roy Campanella, C (33); Carl Furillo, RF (33); Gil Hodges, 1B (31); Jackie Robinson, 3B (36); and Sandy Amoros, LF (25). See Neyer and Epstein, *Baseball Dynasties*, 202–3.

3. *Boston Globe*, October 1, 1955.

4. Falkner, *Great Time Coming*, 229. Robinson's diabetes had become so bad that his physician admitted he "had never seen a body that was as deteriorated."

5. Thorn and Palmer, *Total Baseball*, 503, 508. Robinson was voted Rookie of the Year in 1947 and MVP in 1949; Campanella was voted National League MVP in 1951 and 1953 and would collect a third MVP in 1955. Newcombe, Black, and Gilliam were voted National League Rookie of the Year in 1949, 1952, and 1953, respectively. And Newcombe would go on to win an MVP in 1956.

6. Lanctot, *Campy*, 320–24.

7. "Big Man from Nicetown," *Time*, August 8, 1955, 54.

8. Shapiro, *The Last Good Season*, 162.

9. Golenbock, *Bums*, 372–73.

10. Golenbock, *Bums*, 385–87.

11. Leavy, *Sandy Koufax*, 85.

12. Leavy, *Sandy Koufax*, 86.

13. Don Newcombe quoted in Leavy, *Sandy Koufax*, 72–73.

14. Allen, *Brooklyn Remembered*.

15. Interview of Hank Aaron, Atlanta GA, November 2, 2010.

16. Neyer and Epstein, *Baseball Dynasties*, 215. Newcombe did win the first Cy Young Award in 1956. He was also an impressive hitter. In 1955 he hit .359 with 9 doubles, 7 home runs, and 23 RBIS in just 117 at-bats.

17. Thorn and Palmer, *Total Baseball*, 1684, 1886, 1789.

18. Thorn and Palmer, *Total Baseball*, 1005.

19. Thorn and Palmer, *Total Baseball*, 1412.

20. Neyer and Epstein, *Baseball Dynasties*, 218–19.

21. Neyer and Epstein, *Baseball Dynasties*, 202–3.

22. Wallace, Hamilton, and Appel, *Baseball*, 111. Elston Howard played in his first game with the New York Yankees on April 14, 1955. The Phillies integrated on April 22, 1957, when infielder John Kennedy took the field. The Detroit Tigers followed a year later, on June 6, 1958, with Ossie Virgil Sr. The Boston Red Sox were the last team to integrate, on July 21, 1959, when Pumpsie Green appeared in a game.

23. Neyer and Epstein, *Baseball Dynasties*, 203.

24. Barra, *Yogi Berra*, 201–4. To this day Berra insists that Robinson was out. Conversely, Robinson insisted to his dying day that he was safe. An obscure film clip of the play shows a reverse angle and reveals that Robinson was in fact safe, as his right foot touched the right side of the plate as Berra's glove hovered over the left or first-base side. See Enders, *100 Years of the World Series*, 136.

25. Campanella, *It's Good to Be Alive*, 181.

26. Interview of Johnny Podres, Queensbury NY, August 20, 2007.

27. Allen, *Brooklyn Remembered*, 181–82.

28. Enders, *100 Years of the World Series*, 138.

29. Podres interview.

30. Allen, *Brooklyn Remembered*, 198–200.

31. Ward and Burns, *Baseball*, 343–44.

32. Campanella, *It's Good to Be Alive*, 182–83.

33. Robinson quoted in Lanctot, *Campy*, 346.

34. Lanctot, *Campy*, 346.

35. Jackie Robinson quoted in Rampersad, *Jackie Robinson*, 291–92.

36. Lanctot, *Campy*, 345. The most popular groupies were two women known as "the hook" and "the nook." See Shapiro, *Last Good Season*, 169.

37. Jackie Robinson quoted in Rampersad, *Jackie Robinson*, 291–92.

38. Branch, *Parting the Waters*, 128–203; Garrow, *Bearing the Cross*, 11–82.

39. Campanella, Robinson, and O'Malley quoted in Rowan and Robinson, *Wait till Next Year*, 261.

40. Bill Keefe quoted in "Southern Scribe Blames Robinson for Race Law," *Los Angeles Times*, August 3, 1956.

41. Interview of Don Zimmer, St. Petersburg FL, November 9, 2010.

42. Shapiro, *Last Good Season*, 169.

43. Interview of Carl Erskine, Anderson IN, August 14, 2007.

44. Michael Gavin, "Burdette Watermelon Taunt Provokes Hodges, Robinson," *New York Journal-American*, August 28, 1956.

45. Robinson and Gross, "Why Can't I Manage in the Majors?"

46. Thorn and Palmer, *Total Baseball*, 166.

47. Shapiro, *Last Good Season*, 314.

48. "Outburst by Jackie Robinson," *New York Times*, November 2, 1956.

49. Robinson and Duckett, *I Never Had It Made*, 133.

50. After dealing him to the New York Giants, Dodgers owner Walter O'Malley wrote Jackie and Rachel Robinson a sympathetic letter, stating that the trade was "a sad day for the Dodgers" but was "best" for both parties. Walter O'Malley to Jackie and Rachel Robinson, Brooklyn, December 14, 1956, Jackie Robinson Papers, Manuscript Division, Library of Congress.

51. Robinson and Duckett, *I Never Had It Made*, 134.

52. Rampersad, *Jackie Robinson*, 306.

53. *Newsday*, December 14, 1956.

54. Hirsch, *Willie Mays*, 234–35.

55. Hirsch, *Willie Mays*, 234–35.

56. Red Smith, "The Quality of Candor," *New York Herald Tribune*, January 7, 1957.

57. Gordon S. White Jr., "Robinson Ends Wavering and Confirms Quitting," *New York Times*, January 7, 1957.

58. "Robinson Says He Is Too Old to Help Giants," *New York Times*, January 8, 1957.

59. Rachel Robinson quoted in *Jackie Robinson: Breaking Barriers*.

60. Robinson and Duckett, *I Never Had It Made*, 134.

61. Dick Young, "Campy Ridicules Robinson: 'I'll Catch 5 More Years,'" *New York Daily News*, January 20, 1957; Chafets, *Cooperstown Confidential*, 116.

62. Jackie Robinson quoted in "'Campy Envied Me,' Busy Robby Hastens to Explain," *New York Daily News*, January 22, 1957.

63. Campanella quoted in "Campy: 'Robinson Can't Hurt Me,'" *New York Daily News*, January 26, 1957.

Epilogue

1. Falkner, *Great Time Coming*, 288–93.

2. Franklin and Higginbotham, *From Slavery to Freedom*, 548–61.

3. Jackie Robinson quoted in "Harlem Pickets Switch Tactics: Threaten a Demonstration against Jackie Robinson," *New York Times*, July 14, 1962.

4. Jackie Robinson quoted in Woody Klein, "Jackie Robinson . . . on Sports, Blacks, Politics, Dope and Children," *Baltimore Sun*, October 12, 1969. Robinson's reference to a "talented tenth" of the black population recalled a term first coined by Du Bois in 1903. See Du Bois, "The Talented Tenth," in Washington, *The Negro Problem*, 31–32.

5. Falkner, *Great Time Coming*, 293.

6. "Robinson Backs Defense of Black Group," *Pan African Press*, October 24, 1968.

7. "Jackie Robinson Criticized Police in Panther Inquiry," *New York Times*, April 11, 1969; U.S. Department of Justice, "Memorandum: Jackie Robinson and Black Panthers," J. Edgar Hoover to John D. Ehrlichman, July 24, 1969, FBI Document No. 100-428850-A, declassified on March 13, 1984.

8. "Jackie Robinson Says Son's Plight Now 'A Family Problem,'" *St. Petersburg Times*, March 6, 1968; William Borders, "Jack Robinson, Jr. Is Arrested on Heroin Charges in Stamford," *New York Times*, May 15, 1968; Robinson and Duckett, *I Never Had It Made*, 165–72, 229–46.

9. Rachel Robinson, *Jackie Robinson*, 193–207.

10. Robinson was elected to the Hall of Fame in 1962, his first year of eligibility. He received 77.5 percent of the baseball writers' votes, just 2.5 percent over the required 75 percent for induction. Of the ten players elected during the decade of the 1960s, only Lou Boudreau, Cleveland's manager-shortstop, received fewer votes. Nor did Robinson's original plaque make any mention of his breaking the color barrier; this was added more than half a century after his historic quest. See Bryant, *The Last Hero*, 166; Chafets, *Cooperstown Confidential*, 116.

11. Jackie Robinson, "Speech at Pregame Ceremony," World Series, Game Two, Cincinnati, Ohio, October 15, 1972, Jackie Robinson File, National Baseball Library, Cooperstown NY. During the last year of his life, Robinson constantly promoted the hiring of a black manager in baseball. See Anderson, "A Flame Grew in Brooklyn"; Eric Lincoln, "Robinson Sees Little Progress after 25 Years," *New York Mirror*, December 8, 1971; "Rap with Jackie Robinson on Racism in Sports, 'Progress' and the Black Athlete," *Black Sports Magazine*, March 1972, 19–22, 51–54.

12. Roy R. Silver, "Campanella Fractures His Neck in Crash: Recovery Is Expected," *New York Times*, January 29, 1958; Tommy Holmes, "Campy's Crash Ends Brilliant Career," *New York Herald Tribune*, January 29, 1958; Lanctot, *Campy*, 368–86.

13. Newton H. Fulbright, "Campanella's 'Heartsick' over His Son's Plight," *New York Herald Tribune*, February 16, 1959; "Campy's Heart Is Hurt," *New York World Telegram*, February 25, 1959; Harold A. Rusk, "Campy's Unforgettable Courage," *Reader's Digest*, October 1978, 153–56.

14. Henry Machinella and Loren Craft, "Campy Suing for a Separation, Says Wife Broke Training Rules," *New York Daily News*, August 12, 1960; Fimrite, "Triumph of the Spirit," 100.

15. Lanctot, *Campy*, 398–402.

16. Fimrite, "Triumph of the Spirit," 100; "Roy Campanella, 71, Dies," *New York Times*, June 28, 1993.

17. Campanella quoted in Robinson, *Baseball Has Done It*, 81, 85–86.

18. Campanella quoted in *Pittsburgh Courier*, February 25, 1961.

19. Lee Marguillies, "Campanella Jr. Focuses In on Blacks in Films," *Los Angeles Times*, May 13, 1986; Dan Chu, "Roy Campanella Jr. Begins a Hit Streak of His Own as a Director of TV Films," *People*, May 19, 1986, 22–23.

20. *New York Amsterdam News*, May 16, 1964.

21. Maury Allen, "Campy: Time for a Black Pilot Is Now," *New York Post*, February 9, 1972. In 1974 Buzzie Bavasi, then president of the San Diego Padres, gave serious consideration to naming Campanella manager of the team. But Campy's physical condition as a quadriplegic who struggled with diabetes ruled out his candidacy. Instead the honor of becoming baseball's first African American pilot went to Frank Robinson in 1975, when the Cleveland Indians signed him as a player-manager. See Associated Press, "Campanella Ready to Manage Padres," *San Francisco Chronicle*, June 29, 1974; Lanctot, *Campy*, 407–8.

22. Red Smith, "From Jim Crow to Cooperstown," *New York Times*, February 14, 1978.

23. Lanctot, *Campy*, 422–24.

24. Campanella quoted in Anderson, "In Roy Campanella, the Heart of a Hero."

25. Robert M. G. Thomas Jr., "Roy Campanella, 71, Dies. Was Dodger Hall of Famer," *New York Times*, June 28, 1993.

26. Red Smith, "Man behind the Plate," *Time*, February 10, 1958, 13.

Bibliography

Archival Sources

Jackie Robinson Papers. Manuscript Division, Library of Congress, Washington DC.

National Baseball Hall of Fame and Library. Cooperstown NY.

U.S. Department of Justice. FBI Freedom of Information Act Unit, Office of Public and Congressional Affairs, Federal Bureau of Investigation, Washington DC.

Published Sources

Aaron, Hank, with Lonnie Wheeler. *I Had a Hammer: The Hank Aaron Story*. New York: Harper Collins, 1991.

Adomites, Paul et al. *Cooperstown: Hall of Fame Players*. Lincolnwood IL: Publications International, 2007.

Allen, Maury. *Brooklyn Remembered: The 1955 Days of the Dodgers*. Champaign IL: Sports Publishing, 2005.

Ambrose, Stephen. *Eisenhower: Soldier and President*. New York: Simon & Schuster, 1990.

Angell, Roger. *Five Seasons*. New York: Simon & Schuster, 1997.

At Nightfall: The Roy Campanella Story. Video. Produced by ESPN, 1996.

Balaji, Murali. *Professor and the Pupil: The Politics and Friendship of W. E. B. Dubois and Paul Robeson*. New York: Nation Books, 2007.

Bankes, James. *The Pittsburgh Crawfords*. Dubuque IA: William C. Brown, 1991.

Banks, Ernie, and Jim Enright. *Mr. Cub*. New York: Rutledge Books, 1971.

Barra, Allen. *Yogi Berra: Eternal Yankee*. New York: Norton, 2010.

Before You Can Say Jackie Robinson: Black Baseball in America in the Era of the Color Line. Video. Produced by Lawrence D. Hogan, n.d.

Black Diamonds, Blues City: Stories of the Memphis Red Sox. Video. Produced by University of Memphis, 1996.

Branch, Taylor. *Parting the Waters: America in the King Years, 1954–63*. New York: Simon & Schuster, 1989.

Braxton, Joanne M., ed. *The Collected Poetry of Paul Laurence Dunbar*. Charlottesville: University Press of Virginia, 1993.

Brinkley, Alan. *The Unfinished Nation: A Concise History of the American People*. 6th ed. New York: McGraw-Hill, 1993.

Brooklyn Dodgers: The Original America's Team. Video. Produced by ESPN, 2005.

Bryant, Howard. *The Last Hero: A Life of Henry Aaron*. New York: Pantheon, 2010.

Campanella, Roy. *It's Good to Be Alive*. 1959. Reprint, New York: New American Library, 1974.

Campanella, Roy, and Dick Young. *The Roy Campanella Story*. New York: A. S. Barnes, 1954.

Carter, Craig, ed. *Daguerreotypes: The Complete Major and Minor League Records of Baseball's Greats*. 8th ed. St. Louis: Sporting News, 1990.

Chadwick, Bruce. *When the Game Was Black and White: The Illustrated History of Baseball's Negro Leagues*. New York: Abbeville, 1992.

Chafets, Zev. *Cooperstown Confidential: Heroes, Rogues and the Inside Story of the Baseball Hall of Fame*. New York: Bloomsbury, 2009.

Chambers, Whittaker. *Witness*. New York: Random House, 1952.

Clark, Dick, and Larry Lester, eds. *The Negro Leagues Book*. Cleveland: Society for American Baseball Research, 1994.

Cottrell, Robert C. *Two Pioneers: How Hank Greenberg and Jackie Robinson Transformed Baseball—and America*. Dulles VA: Potomac Books, 2012.

Davis, F. James. *Who Is Black? One Nation's Definition*. University Park PA: Penn State University Press, 1991.

D'Emilio, John. *Lost Prophet: The Life and Times of Bayard Rustin*. New York: Free Press, 2003.

Dickson, Paul. *Baseball's Greatest Quotations*. New York: Harper Collins, 1991.

——— . *The Unwritten Rules of Baseball*. New York: Harper Collins, 2009.

Donovan, Robert J. *Conflict and Crisis: The Presidency of Harry S. Truman, 1945–1948*. New York: Norton, 1977.

Dorinson, Joseph, and Joram Warmund, eds. *Jackie Robinson: Race, Sports and the American Dream*. Armonk NY: M. E. Sharpe, 1998.

Dray, Philip. *At the Hands of Persons Unknown: The Lynching of Black America*. New York: Random House, 2002.

Duberman, Martin B. *Paul Robeson*. New York: Alfred A. Knopf, 1988.

Du Bois, W. E. B. *The Philadelphia Negro: A Social Study*. 1899. Reprint, Philadelphia: University of Pennsylvania, 1996.

——— . *The Souls of Black Folk*. 1903. Reprint, New York: New American Library, 1969.

Durocher, Leo, with Ed Linn. *Nice Guys Finish Last*. New York: Simon & Schuster, 1975.

Enders, Eric. *100 Years of the World Series*. London: Barnes & Noble, 2003.

Erskine, Carl. *Tales from the Dodgers Dugout*. Champaign IL: Sports Publishing, 2004.

Erskine, Carl, with Burton Rocks. *What I Learned from Jackie Robinson: A Teammate's Reflections on and off the Field*. New York: McGraw-Hill, 2005.

Falkner, David. *Great Time Coming: The Life of Jackie Robinson from Baseball to Birmingham*. New York: Simon & Schuster, 1996.

Foner, Philip S., ed. *Paul Robeson Speaks*. New York: Brunner/Mazel, 1978.

Franklin, John Hope, and Evelyn Brooks Higginbotham. *From Slavery to Freedom: A History of African Americans*. 9th ed. New York: McGraw-Hill, 2011.

Frommer, Harvey. *Rickey and Robinson: The Men Who Broke Baseball's Color Barrier*. New York: Macmillan, 1982.

Fussman, Carl. *After Jackie: Pride, Prejudice, and Baseball's Forgotten Heroes; An Oral History*. New York: ESPN Books, 2007.

Garrow, David J. *Bearing the Cross: Martin Luther King, Jr. and the Southern Christian Leadership Conference*. New York: William Morrow, 1986.

Garvey, Steve. *My Bat Boy Days: Lessons I Learned from the Boys of Summer, 1956–1961*. New York: Scribner, 2008.

Golenbock, Peter. *Bums: Oral History of the Brooklyn Dodgers*. New York: G. P. Putnam, 1984.

Goodwin, Doris Kearns. *Wait 'til Next Year: A Memoir*. New York: Simon & Schuster, 1997.

Greenberg, Hank, with Ira Berkow. *Hank Greenberg: The Story of My Life*. New York: New York Times, 1989.

Halberstam, David. *Summer of '49*. New York: William Morrow, 1989.

Hamby, Alonzo L. *Beyond the New Deal: Harry S. Truman and American Liberalism*. New York: Columbia University Press, 1973.

Higbe, Kirby. *The High Hard One*. Lincoln: University of Nebraska Press, 1998.

Hirsch, James S. *Willie Mays: The Life, the Legend*. New York: Scribner's, 2010.

Hogan, Lawrence D. "Before You Can Say Jackie Robinson: Black Baseball in America in the Era of the Color Line." In *Shades of Glory: The Negro Leagues and the Story of African-American Baseball*. Washington DC: National Geographic, 2006.

——. *Shades of Glory: The Negro Leagues and the Story of African-American Baseball*. Washington DC: National Geographic, 2006.

Holway, John B. *Josh and Satch: The Life and Times of Josh Gibson and Satchel Paige*. New York: Carrol & Graf, 1991.

Irvin, Monte, with James A. Riley. *Nice Guys Finish First: The Autobiography of Monte Irvin*. New York: Carroll & Graf, 1996.

Jackie Robinson: Breaking Barriers. Video. Produced by Major League Baseball, 1997.

Jackie Robinson Story. Video. Originally produced by 20th Century Fox, 1950. Re-released by MGM Home Entertainment, 2005.

Jackson, Kenneth T. *The Encyclopedia of New York City*. New Haven CT: Yale University Press and New York Historical Society, 1995.

Jordan, David M., Larry R. Gerlach, and John P. Rossi. "Bill Veeck and the 1943 Sale of the Phillies: A Baseball Myth Exploded." *National Pastime: A Review of Baseball History* 6 (1995): 3–13.

Kahn, Roger. *The Boys of Summer*. New York: Harper & Row, 1987.

——. *The Era*. New York: Ticknor & Fields, 1993.

Kavanaugh, Jack, and Norman Macht. *Uncle Robbie*. Lincoln: University of Nebraska Press and Society for American Baseball Research, 1999.

Kings on the Hill: Baseball's Forgotten Men. Video. Produced by San Pedro Productions, 1994.

Klimer, John. *Willie's Boys: The 1948 Birmingham Black Barons, the Last Negro League World Series and the Making of a Baseball Legend*. Hoboken NJ: Wiley, 2009.

Kluger, Richard. *Simple Justice: The History of* Brown v. Board of Education *and Black America's Struggle for Equality*. New York: Vintage, 1977.

Kuklick, Bruce. *To Every Thing a Season: Shibe Park and Urban Philadelphia, 1909–1976*. Princeton NJ: Princeton University Press, 1991.

Lamb, Chris. *Blackout: The Untold Story of Jackie Robinson's First Spring Training*. Lincoln: University of Nebraska Press, 2006.

Lanctot, Neil. *Campy: The Two Lives of Roy Campanella*. New York: Simon & Schuster, 2011.

——. *Negro League Baseball: The Rise and Ruin of a Black Institution*. Philadelphia: University of Pennsylvania Press, 2004.

Leavy, Jane. *Sandy Koufax: A Lefty's Legacy*. New York: Harper Collins, 2002.

Lewis, David Levering. *W. E. B. Du Bois: Biography of a Race, 1868–1919*. New York: Henry Holt, 1994.

——. *W. E. B. Du Bois: The Fight for Equality and the American Century, 1919–1963*. New York: Henry Holt, 2000.

Lowenfish, Lee. *Branch Rickey: Baseball's Ferocious Gentleman*. Lincoln: University of Nebraska, 2007.

Manchester, William. *The Glory and the Dream: A Narrative History of America, 1932–1972*. New York: Bantam, 1975.

Mann, Arthur. *Branch Rickey: American in Action*. Boston: Houghton Mifflin, 1957.

——. *The Jackie Robinson Story*. New York: Grosset & Dunlap, 1950.

Marshall, William. *Baseball's Pivotal Era, 1945–1951*. Lexington: University Press of Kentucky, 1999.

Marzano, Rudy. *The Brooklyn Dodgers in the 1940s*. Jefferson NC: McFarland, 2005.

Mayer, Robert. *Notes of a Baseball Dreamer*. Boston: Houghton Mifflin, 2003.

McCullough, David W. *Brooklyn . . . and How It Got to Be That Way*. New York: Dial Press, 1983.

McGee, Bob. *Greatest Ballpark Ever*. New Brunswick NJ: Rutgers, 2006.

Monteleone, John J., ed. *Branch Rickey's Little Blue Book*. New York: Macmillan, 1995.

Moore, Joseph T. *Pride against Prejudice: The Biography of Larry Doby*. New York: Greenwood Press, 1988.

Morris, Peter. *Catcher: How the Man behind the Plate Became an American Folk Hero*. Chicago: Ivan R. Dee, 2010.

Naison, Mark. *Communists in Harlem during the Depression*. Champaign: University of Illinois Press, 2005.

Neyer, Rob, and Eddie Epstein. *Baseball Dynasties*. New York: Norton, 2000.

Nichols, David A. *A Matter of Justice: Eisenhower and the Beginning of the Civil Rights Revolution*. New York: Simon & Schuster, 2007.

Oates, Stephen B. *Let the Trumpet Sound: The Life of Martin Luther King, Jr.* New York: Harper & Row, 1982.

Only the Ball Was White: The Forgotten Athletes of Baseball's Negro Leagues. Video. Produced by MPI Home Video, 2007.

Parrott, Harold. *The Lords of Baseball*. New York: Praeger, 1976.

Peterson, Robert. *Only the Ball Was White: A History of Legendary Black Players and All-Black Professional Teams*. New York: Oxford University Press, 1992.

Plaschke, Bill, with Tommy LaSorda. *I Live for This! Baseball's Last True Believer*. Boston: Houghton Mifflin, 2007.

Polner, Murray. *Branch Rickey: A Biography*. New York: Atheneum, 1982.

President's Committee on Civil Rights. *To Secure These Rights*. Washington DC: Government Printing Office, 1947.

Pritchet, Wendell. *Brownsville, Brooklyn: Blacks, Jews, and the Changing Face of the Ghetto*. Chicago: University of Chicago Press, 2002.

Rampersad, Arnold. *Jackie Robinson: A Biography*. New York: Knopf, 1997.

Reeves, Thomas C. *The Life and Times of Joe McCarthy*. New York: Stein & Day, 1982.

Rice, Damon. *Seasons Past*. New York: Praeger, 1976.

Ritter, Lawrence S. *Lost Ballparks*. New York: Penguin Books, 1996.

Robbins, Michael W., and Wendy Palitz. *Brooklyn: A State of Mind*. New York: Workman, 2001.

Roberts, Gene, and Hank Klibanoff. *The Race Beat: The Press, the Civil Rights Struggle, and the Awakening of a Nation*. New York: Vintage, 2006.

Robeson, Paul, Jr. *The Undiscovered Paul Robeson: Quest for Freedom, 1940–1976*. New York: Wiley, 2011.

Robinson, Jackie. *Baseball Has Done It*. New York: 1964.

Robinson, Jackie, as told to Alfred Duckett. *I Never Had It Made*. New York: G. P. Putnam's Sons, 1972.

Robinson, Rachel. *Jackie Robinson: An Intimate Portrait*. New York: Harry N. Abrams, 1996.

Rogers, Phil. *Ernie Banks: Mr. Cub and the Summer of '69*. Chicago: Triumph Books, 2011.

Rowan, Carl T., with Jackie Robinson. *Wait till Next Year*. New York: Random House, 1960.

Shapiro, Michael. *The Last Good Season: Brooklyn, the Dodgers and Their Final Pennant Race Together*. New York: Broadway Books, 2003.

Shatzkin, Mike, ed. *The Ballplayers: Baseball's Ultimate Biographical Reference*. New York: William Morrow, 1990.

Simon, Scott. *Jackie Robinson and Integration of Baseball*. Hoboken NJ: Wiley, 2007.

Snider, Duke. *The Duke of Flatbush*. New York: Kensington, 1998.

Snider, Duke, with Phil Pepe. *Few and Chosen: Defining Dodgers Greatness across the Eras*. Chicago: Triumph, 2006.

Snyder-Grenier, Ellen M. *Brooklyn: An Illustrated History*. Philadelphia: Temple University Press, 1996.

There Was Always Sun Shining Someplace: Life in the Negro Leagues. Video. Produced by Refocus Productions, 1989.

Thorn, John, and Pete Palmer, eds. *Total Baseball*. New York: Warner Books, 1989.

Trouppe, Quincy. *20 Years Too Soon*. Los Angeles: Sands Enterprises, 1977.

Trucks, Rob. *The Catcher: Baseball behind the Seams*. Cincinnati: Emmis Books, 2005.

Tye, Larry. *Satchel: The Life and Times of an American Legend*. New York: Random House, 2009.

Tygiel, Jules. *Baseball's Great Experiment: Jackie Robinson and His Legacy*. New York: Oxford University Press, 1983.

Uhlberg, Myron. *Hands of My Father: A Hearing Boy, His Deaf Parents and the Language of Love*. New York: Bantam Books, 2009.

U.S. Bureau of the Census. *Negroes in the United States, 1920–32*. Washington DC: Government Printing Office, 1935.

U.S. House of Representatives, Un-American Activities Committee. "Report of Hearings on Communist Infiltration of Minorities." Washington DC: U.S. Government Printing Office, 1949.

U.S. Senate, Armed Services Committee. "Report of Hearings on Universal Military Training." Washington DC: U.S. Government Printing Office, 1948.

Veeck, Bill, with Ed Linn. *Veeck as in Wreck: The Autobiography of Bill Veeck*. New York: G. P. Putnam, 1962.

Voigt, David Q. *American Baseball: From the Gentleman's Sport to the Commissioner System*. University Park PA: Penn State University Press, 1983.

Wallace, Joseph, Neil Hamilton, and Marty Appel. *Baseball: 100 Classic Moments in the History of the Game.* New York: Dorling Kindersley, National Baseball Hall of Fame, 2000.

Ward, Geoffrey C., and Ken Burns. *Baseball: An Illustrated History.* New York: Knopf, 1994.

Warner, Sam Bass. *The Private City: Philadelphia in Three Periods of Growth.* Philadelphia: University of Pennsylvania Press, 1987.

Washington, Booker T., ed. *The Negro Problem.* New York: James Potts, 1903.

——. *Up from Slavery: An Autobiography.* Garden City NY: Doubleday, 1900.

Weigley, Russell F., ed. *Philadelphia: A 300-Year History.* New York: Norton, 1982.

Westcott, Rich, and Frank Bilovsky. *Phillies Encyclopedia.* Philadelphia: Temple University Press, 2004.

Wexler, Laura. *Fire in a Canebrake: The Last Mass Lynching in America.* New York: Scribner, 2003.

White, Sol. *History of Colored Baseball.* 1907. Reprint, Lincoln: University of Nebraska Press, 1995.

Wilder, Craig S. *A Covenant with Color: Race and Social Power in Brooklyn.* New York: Columbia University Press, 2000.

Willensky, Elliot. *When Brooklyn Was the World, 1920–1957.* New York: Harmony Books, 1986.

Wolf, Edward. *Philadelphia: Portrait of an American City.* Philadelphia: Camino Books, 1990.

Wolff, Rick, ed. *The Baseball Encyclopedia.* New York: Macmillan, 1990.

Index

Lynn Red Sox, 87, 89

Mack, Connie, 67
Mackey, "Biz," 35, 70, 72
MacPhail, Larry, 27–30, 47
Maglie, Sal, 174–75
Malcolm X, 182, 185
Maltin, Sam, 85
Manley, Abe, 107–8
Manley, Effa, 42, 75–76, 107–8
Mantle, Mickey, 175
Marquard, "Rube," 21
Matthews, Wid, 36, 48–49
Mauch, Gene, 93, 110
Mayer, Robert, 104–5
Mays, Willie, 133, 139, 151–52, 174, 176
McAlpin Hotel, 103
McCarthy, Joseph, 91
McDougald, Gil, 170
McDuffie, Terris, 48
McGowan, Jim, 26, 142
McKeever, Edward, 14–15
McKeever, Jennie, 15–16
McKeever, Stephen, 14
McLaughlin, George V., 27, 35
McLish, Cal, 93
Memphis Red Sox, 106
Mercer, Sid, 27
Mexican League, 74
Meyer, Russ, 120, 162
Milwaukee Braves, 153, 165, 174
Minneapolis Millers, 109
Monterrey Sultans, 74
Montreal Royals, 81–85
Moulton, Jane, 34
Muckerman, Richard, 106–8
Mullin, Willard, 27
Murder, Inc. mob, 24
Murray, Arch, 119
Musial, Stan, 111, 132

Nashua NH, 11, 85
National Association of Colored People

(NAACP), 8, 40, 46, 89, 126, 137, 156, 172, 179, 181–82
National Baseball Hall of Fame, 3, 183–86
National Labor Relations Board, 46
National League, 18, 20–21, 101, 104, 136, 167
National Negro Congress, 46
Negro Leagues, 10, 22–23, 35–40, 47, 64–65, 68–80, 103–4; 1945 Negro League American All Star team, 77–80; American League, 35; Eastern Colored League, 22; East-West All Star Game, 56, 73; National League, 35, 72, 73; reputation of, 48, 62, 103–4; United States League, 48
Newark Eagles, 22–23, 35, 41–42, 48, 70, 72, 74, 75, 85, 106
Newcombe, Don, 2, 124, 125, 151, 152, 162, 163, 167; and Campanella, 85–89, 129–30, 132–33, 138, 186; in military, 155; integrating Chase Hotel, 157–58; personality of, 87; pitching statistics of, 165–66; and Robinson, 129–30, 132–33, 157–58
New Orleans Times-Picayune, 173
Newsday, 176
Newsome, Lamar "Skeeter," 98
Newton, Huey P., 182
New York City, 18–19
New York Cubans, 35–36, 48
New York Daily Mirror, 27–28, 110
New York Daily News, 119, 148–50, 163–64, 170, 178, 179
New York Daily Worker, 34–35, 47–48, 91
New York Giants, 46, 115, 159, 163; black players on, 139, 150–52; and rivalry with Dodgers, 9, 18, 20, 114, 150–52, 173–74; Robinson traded to, 175–77
New York Herald Tribune, 104, 148, 176
New York Highlanders, 34

Riverfront Stadium, 183–84

Roberts, Rick, 41

Roberts, Robin, 111–12, 166

Robeson, Paul, 46, 125–28

Robinson, Jackie, Jr. (son), 103, 183

Robinson, Jack Roosevelt: as advisor to Martin Luther King, Jr., 181–82; and Alston, 156, 159, 163–64; approachability of, 59, 173; and approach to civil rights, 1–3, 57, 123, 134–35, 158–59, 172–73; barnstorming, 132–34, 148–149, 152–53; bench jockeying and umpire baiting, 115–16, 120, 122, 129, 131, 146–47, 150–51, 156; on black managers, 183–84; books written by, 3, 184–86; breaking color line, 81–85, 91–105; as candidate to break color line, 44–46, 48–55; childhood of, 58–59; as civil rights pioneer, 1–2, 17, 56–58, 81–85, 91–105, 123, 156–59; and collegiate athletic career, 59–61; compared to Campanella, 187; and competitiveness, 59, 112, 129; and conflict with Campanella, 11–12, 132–34, 136, 141, 156–59, 163–64; criticizing Campanella, 171, 172–73 178–79; and court-martial, 62–63; criticizing Negro Leagues, 205n25; death of, 184; and different approach to civil rights than Campanella's, 2–4, 57, 128–29, 142–43; discrimination against, 3, 58, 60–61, 62, 64, 84–85, 95–101, 102–3, 111–12, 123–25, 154, 209n29; and Dressen, 155, 164; and Durocher, 92–93, 109–13, 150–51; and fans, 121–22, 125, 175–76; and friendship with Campanella, 10–11, 56, 117, 119, 121; Hall of Fame induction of, 183, 214n10; health of, 162–64, 183; in high school, 59; home and family of, 58, 103, 103, 117, 183; and Hopper, 82–83; and jealousy, 3–4, 113–14, 142, 171;

kindness of, 103, 123; loyalty of, 52, 113; Major League statistics of, 3, 105, 115, 132, 142, 166, 175; and mentoring Aaron, 153–54; and mentoring Banks, 152–53; and mentoring Black, 154–55; and mentoring Gilliam, 157–58; and mentoring Mays, 151–52; and mentoring Newcombe, 120, 129–30, 132–34; military career of, 62–63; Minor League statistics of, 84–85; as MVP (International League), 85; as MVP (National League), 132, 134, 142; Negro League career of, 49, 62, 64–65; on "no fighting back" ban, 119–20; and O'Malley, 136, 144–45, 173, 175–76; post-baseball life of, 181–84; and pride, 44, 52, 61, 81, 94, 118, 173, 176; and reconciliation with Campanella, 184–86; retirement from baseball, 12, 175–79; and Rickey, 49–55, 81–83, 92–98, 118, 145; as Rookie of the Year, 3, 105; and sportswriters, 148–50, 179; and teammates, 119–23, 129–32, 148–49, 155–58, 164–65, 173–74; temper of, 3, 44, 49, 57, 95–96, 105, 110–11, 120, 129, 146, 146–47; testifing before HUAC, 125–28; traded to Giants, 175–77, 213n50

Robinson, Jerry (father), 58

Robinson, Mallie (mother), 58

Robinson, Rachel Isum (wife), 50, 61, 85, 103, 117, 118, 123, 126, 143, 144–45, 177–78

Robinson, Wilbert "Uncle Robbie," 21, 27

Rockefeller, John D., 6

Rockefeller, Nelson, 181

Rodney, Lester, 34–35, 47

Roe, Elwin Charles "Preacher," 114–15, 155–56

Roosevelt, Franklin D., 40, 45, 89–90

Roosevelt, Theodore, 6